Thoth,

Architect of the Universe

Thoth,

Architect of the Universe

Controversial and revolutionary answers to the design and function of
the great henges and pyramids

Ralph Ellis

Edfu Books

Adventures Unlimited

Thoth,
Architect of the Universe
First published in 1997 by Edfu Books

Published in the U.K. by:
Edfu Books
PO Box 165
Cheshire
CW8 4WF
info@edfu-books.com
U.K.

Published in the U.S.A. by:
Adventures Unlimited
PO Box 74
Kempton, Illinois
60946
auphq@frontier.net
U.S.A.

First Edition Nov 1997
revised & updated
Second Edition Oct 1998
revised
Third Edition Aug 2001

U.K. paperback edition
ISBN 0 9531913 54

U.S.A. paperback edition
ISBN ISBN 0 932813 186

Printed in the United Kingdom by T. J. International, Padstow

Acknowledgements

For much of the time, I was working on this book in complete isolation but, every now and then, just when I required some moral support, someone would call with encouragement. In chronological order as the manuscript evolved, I would like to thank Henry Lincoln, Sir Laurence Gardner and Graham Hancock. They all saw my work at an early stage, when it was really quite unreadable, yet they each saw a worthy core to it and gave much needed advice. Thank you also to Chris Ogilvie-Herald, who was the first to publish articles based on *Thoth* in *Quest* magazine.

Then there came some dark days, when I thought I had lost the manuscript for *Thoth* to a plagiarist. But in the midst of this despair came Chris Knight and Robert Lomas, to lend support. They were closely followed by Colin Wilson, Alan Alford, Andrew Collins, Mike Hayes and Graham Hancock. All gave much needed assistance in a difficult situation and their moral support when I needed it most.

Thanks also go to my solicitor, Nigel Brain of Pye-Smiths, Salisbury. It took a move out of London, to a provincial solicitor, to really get to grips with the legal problems that have dogged this book, and a fine job he did too. Linda Doeser not only edited the final manuscript, but checked all the historical content as well and I am most grateful for her professionalism. Jane Tatam of Amolibros packaged the new edition of the book into a professional format and generally made sure that production ran according to plan. She also arranged for the UK distribution, an aspect of the business that was conspicuously lacking on the first edition.

I would also like to express my thanks to all readers, especially those who wrote encouraging and approving letters. I hope this new and much revised edition is acceptable to you all.

Ralph Ellis
1999 Dorset.

www.edfu-books.com

Muse

And lately by the Tavern Door agape,
Came stealing through the Dusk an Angel Shape,
Bearing a Vessel on his Shoulder; and
He bid me taste of it; and 'twas – the Grape!

From the Rubaiyat
Omar Khayyam.

Dedication

With thanks to my wife for her great patience and midnight offerings of coffee and biscuits.

Contents

Prologue

First Letter

I had been poring over diagrams of the pyramids for years, seeing the technical complexity of their construction and playing with concept after concept, with no particular success at deriving a satisfactory solution. Suddenly, however, there was a minor triumph. Having studied the pyramid dimensions exclusively in cubits, I noticed that the Great Pyramid's perimeter length was 1,760 cubits and the Imperial mile length was 1,760 yards. From this small gem evolved a theory that encompassed all of the peculiarities of the Imperial Measurement System, and indicated very ancient roots for British measurement system. This at last seemed to be something fresh and new; a novel concept that was not to be found anywhere in the popular press and was worth putting onto paper in the form of a short manuscript. Although it was an interesting theory, however, it would be a brave individual who would contemplate writing solely about a set of measurements and manage to make the subject interesting to the reader. Something more was required to make a worthwhile book; something a little more dramatic.

That something was not long in coming. An acquaintance had advised me that the pyramids were too complicated, too many people had been poring over them for centuries and finding nothing, so why should my research be any different? Go down to Stonehenge, was the advice, it is much simpler than the pyramids and, if there are any secrets in Egypt, they will be mirrored at Stonehenge and they will be easier to find there. The last part of the advice did not even register, for what would make anyone so sure that Stonehenge mirrored Giza? In any case, that was not the major concern; the biggest doubt about the whole enterprise was that I had been to Stonehenge on numerous occasions and seen absolutely nothing of special interest. In fact, a long time ago, my father had spent many a weekend there on some of the archaeological digs in the West Kennet area. The subject was more than well known; it was a part of the family's history and, since nothing had changed at Stonehenge, why should I bother looking again?

With some reluctance, I nevertheless made the trip once more and, surprisingly, the mission was not without its rewards, for there *had* been a big change. The layout of the stones had not changed, of course, but my perceptions and perspectives *had,* and this made the difference. The previous two years of study had revolved exclusively around a search for the ancient usage of the mathematical constant Pi, for this number was intimately involved in the solution that I had derived for the Imperial Measurement System. In addition, my perspective of the Stonehenge site had been elevated, literally, for I was circling above it in an aircraft. Only then, with a little prompt from my mother-in-law, did I see the evidence and the breakthrough that I had been seeking for so long. Standing there, on the plains of Salisbury, was the letter Pi (Π), in all its graphic detail; it had been there for thousands of years and yet it should not really be there at all.

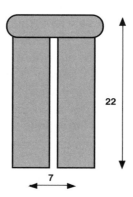

Fig 0.   The Stonehenge Pi Trilithons

Of course, it is very easy to see something in a picture because the human mind is quite adept at picking out the shapes that it wants to see. Was this a mirage of the eye or imagination, or was it something more tangible? All it took was a quick look at the measurements involved in the construction of Stonehenge to displace any doubts, because they not only matched the new theory on ancient measurements that was evolving in my parallel research, but they also resolved themselves into the number 3.14286, or Pi. It was apparent that Pi was not only being depicted physically at Stonehenge, but mathematically as well. But how could this be explained? How did ancient man understand the concept of this fundamental mathematical constant? Why was it so important to them? How did this constant find its way into common usage in the modern world?

There were innumerable questions that flowed from this one simple observation; questions that were answered in such quick succession that this just had to be a real and planned physical representation of Pi. If I had been trying to force a theory to fit the facts, the process would have been slow and tedious, as the ill-fitting theory was artificially bent and cajoled into agreeing with the data. Here, however, the process was just the reverse; a veritable torrent of new theories and new perspectives flowed from this one small observation. These theories fitted not just the Stonehenge site, but also Avebury and, eventually, the Giza plateau as well. It was a fantastic roller-coaster ride of ideas that lasted just over a year. This book is the result, although the book itself took much longer to incubate than the theory. The final outcome of these investigations was nothing less than a completely new history of mankind, for there is more evidence and much more information to be gleaned from these ancient monuments. It is only a matter of looking.

Chapter I

Stirlings to Stonehenge

The young airman in the photo stood in front of the crashed Stirling bomber, legs astride in the confident manner of many a victorious soldier. He wore the cheeky grin of youth, a typical Royal Air Force (RAF) 'chip-bag' hat was perched jauntily on his head and a rebellious quiff of hair flowed across his forehead. The mighty flying machine behind him sat drunkenly on the grass; its starboard gear collapsed, the massive propellers bent backwards under the engines, its destructive powers temporarily faded into a distant memory. It was a minor event in a much larger conflict that had ebbed and flowed across North Africa and the wider world, and the eventual fate of the unlucky bomber 'Delta Charlie', at Lydda airport in Palestine, would soon be lost in the mists of time. All those important documents and records of the construction, maintenance and operation of this complex fighting machine would be cherished and kept for just a brief two or three years and then they would be gone, lost to history like so many millions of documents from this region before them. Even in this information-rich age, the written word remains as ephemeral as ever. Is it any wonder that we know so little of our past?

It was October 1942 and, like so many army commanders before him, Rommel had stormed across these deserts in search of new pastures for the empire. He came firstly for oil and minerals but, most importantly, he wanted to claim the main artery connecting the Middle East to the wider world: the Suez Canal. He came like a whirlwind out of the western desert. The battle had raged over thousands of kilometers of open wastelands; more like a flowing naval engagement than the normal entrenched battle between armies. Tobruk had finally fallen, the British had fallen back to a small town called El Alamein, and Cairo was in turmoil: all non-essential

1. Stirlings to Stonehenge

personnel were being evacuated. Men were preparing once more for a siege on these historic sands, and the task for the young airman – my father – was to keep the engines turning on these new monsters of war. The goals of war had not changed here for thousands of years; the strategy of Moses's campaign against the Ethiopians was much the same as Rommel's, it was only the technology that had moved on.[1] However, history turned at this particular point in our more recent past; Monty made his stand, El Alamein held the line, Rommel retreated, and poor 'Delta Charlie' finally got back into fighting condition to play its small part in this international game of chess. A relative calm descended on Cairo once more and my father was able to have some well-deserved leave.

The album, from which the photo was taken, was a heavy leather-bound affair – a historical document in its own right – filled with evocative images in shades of grey and sepia. As I turned those pages in my youth, little did I realize that I would follow in my father's footsteps; not only in an aviation career, but also to Egypt. The front of the album was heavily embossed with the outline of a camel and the pyramids of Giza, and the aroma that it still exuded was pure distilled Egypt. It was one of those smells that created instant pictures in the mind – pictures of an ancient civilization and perhaps of more peaceful times.

Indeed, although some of the pictures brought with them images of death and destruction, of a population fleeing in terror from the horrors of modern warfare, most of the album told a different story. Here was a tour of the impregnable fortress of Aleppo; further on was the tomb of Tutankhamen, the colossi of Memnon, the Armistice Day parade in Cairo in 1942. Finally, there was a character who was just known as 'Curly', standing on top of the Great Pyramid of Giza, now more commonly known as the Great Pyramid. The album was a joyous assortment of evocative images for an impressionable boy. It was a history of an army of young teenagers that had passed through this region briefly, in the dying years of the second millennium AD. They had stood under the pyramids and marvelled at their size and perfection. They had crawled inside and seen the majestic galleries, and the enigmatic and empty chambers. They had dreamed of the ancient past and passed this on to their sons and daughters, as soldiers had done throughout history.

The Persians had conquered Egypt in the sixth century BC, and they were closely followed in the fourth century by Alexander the Great, as the great empires of the ancient world ebbed and flowed across the continents. If cameras had been available at the time, the scene would have been remarkably familiar. The young soldiers of Alexander, battle-weary from their struggles in modern Turkey and Israel, would have come to Giza for

1. *Stirlings to Stonehenge*

rest and relaxation. They would have sat on the same stones and walked the same pavements as my father. By 1942, history had moved on, but both mankind and Giza remained strangely unchanged, locked in a time warp of myth, mystery and conflict.

The images in that dusty old book remained and they were rekindled many years later by a torrent of new information that suddenly burst upon the scene, that had either been lost or deliberately suppressed for generations. It was fascinating and thought-provoking to see some of the more intriguing possibilities for the true history of mankind. Had there been an ancient technical civilization? Was ancient man in command of much more complex knowledge and technology than we had given him credit for? It was a very interesting subject, but not one that pertained to my current situation. I was sitting in an apartment in Otradnye, north Moscow; it was - 25 °C outside and snowing gently. The bottom had dropped out of the aviation industry in Britain and so the company for which I worked had arranged for the pilots to have six months of unpaid leave each winter. But life goes on and the bills need to be paid. So, the mission in Moscow had been the setting up of an importation business, looking at the myriad possibilities that existed when the Berlin Wall came down and the USSR became another of the many empires to have waxed and waned throughout history.

The apartment was a one-room affair, but in Russian parlance this was not one bedroom but just one room plus a small kitchen and bathroom. It was comfortable but, like so many Russian flats, it had been poorly finished. It was the little things that differentiated this from any other apartment in the world: there was only one tap to share between the sink and the bath, the toilet seat was hand-cut from a plank of wood, and the central heating system could only be controlled by opening or shutting the windows. Each item in itself was insignificant, but multiplied a hundred-fold it made the environment seem quite alien. Some alternative Egypt books were essential reading during a slack period in the schedule, but they were enough to provoke a concentrated bout of study using every relevant English text that I could lay my hands on.

Take that picture of 'Curly' in the album, for instance, proudly standing on the top of the Great Pyramid in his RAF number 1 uniform. We are told the same now as they were then; that we somehow have a full understanding of these pyramids, including their design and function. This information comes directly to us, complete with the names of the pharaohs to whom they were dedicated and the precise year of their construction. But here on the outskirts of Moscow, a more radical book was showing compelling new information that formed an alternative chronology and entirely new reasons for the construction of the pyramids. Yet this new information, that has helped to shake the foundations of orthodoxy, was in itself incomplete: the new chronology and motivation for the construction of the pyramids had as many areas of uncertainty as the orthodox creed. Despite this, many people, including myself, had the distinct feeling that there was a kernel of truth in these new hypotheses. The old orthodoxy never did explain why the most ancient architects built the finest and most massive constructions in the world to this day; why the pyramid-building empires stretched across the entire globe; or why the pharaohs did not inscribe their names on so many of these marvellous monuments. Nature abhors a vacuum, so quite naturally a flood of new ideas has been proposed to fill these gaps. But the story was still missing something important.

One of the questions that is probably most central to this enigma must be the purpose of these great monuments. The normal explanation – that the pyramids of Egypt were tombs – was looking increasingly untenable, yet there did not appear to be a reasonable theory with which we could replace this concept. But this is wrong: there has always been an alternative explanation, one that is provided by the legends of Egypt herself. The myths and legends that have filtered down to us from the distant past can tell us a different tale, and the myth that could be thought of as being central to this quest is that of Thoth (known as Djeheuti in Egyptian).

The legends of the god, Thoth, indicate that – apart from educating mankind in maths, physics and astronomy – he left some repositories of knowledge around the world so that his knowledge would be preserved. These repositories were supposedly hidden in such a fashion that only the dedicated or initiated could find them. Since many people have assumed that the Great Pyramid was one of those repositories, a veritable army of explorers have attempted, over the years, to drill and excavate every crevice at this site. It does not even matter too much at this stage if these myths are based on ancient facts or not. What seems to be apparent is that the pyramid builders themselves thought it was true and put considerable efforts into passing this information on.

However, the repositories were supposed to be found by the most dedicated of seekers, so it is unlikely that such a quest would be so easy as simply finding treasure buried under the pyramids. But if the pyramids are not going to be the repositories themselves, perhaps instead they were designed as indelible messages; devised so that the location of these repositories of knowledge were not lost. At the same time, one might also speculate that the great henges of southern Britain – Avebury and

1. Stirlings to Stonehenge

Stonehenge – were designed with the same intention. This may seem like a leap of faith at this stage, but we shall uncover great parallels between the henges and the pyramids later in the book.

Monuments

There are two main sites of interest in this book: the Avebury and Stonehenge complexes in Britain, and the mighty Giza site itself. I shall attempt to show that both of these sites are more than simple tombs or temples for religious worship: instead, they appear to be, among other things, mathematical conundrums. It is beyond doubt that maths was central to their construction and we shall see a few snippets of this later, but why should this be so? Religious monuments have no need of maths, so why encode maths into their construction? The purpose for the maths becomes much clearer, however, if we divorce ourselves from the tomb concept. The maths then becomes, instead, a direct invitation to look further into the secrets that the monuments hold; and that is what we must do.

We shall especially investigate, in some detail, the link between all of these great monuments and the British Imperial Measurement System; and see why it is regarded by some as a sacred measurement system, handed down to us by the gods. We shall also see why this measurement system is derived from the very system of measurements that Sir Isaac Newton was searching for in his missive, called *A Dissertation upon the Sacred Cubit of the Jews*. After chapter IV, one can begin to understand why so many eminent people have clung on so tenaciously to the British Imperial measures. The Imperial Measurement System may be difficult to understand and work with, but it was supposed to be 'sacred' in some fashion and it will transpire that it was none other than an amalgam of the units used to design Avebury in Britain, and the Great Pyramid at Giza. In short, then, this book will be a bold attempt at explaining the entire history of Giza, Avebury and Stonehenge, and how the pyramid-building empire of Egypt and the henge-building civilization of Britain managed their great feats.

Were these great monuments messages for the future? This book will attempt to address that issue, perhaps to the dismay of classical archaeologists. There is, nevertheless, a convincing argument to be made that the ancients were indeed making statements in stone, designed to be discovered in the far future; and shortly, we will be able to uncover and read those ancient messages. For if there were any ancient statements encoded into the design of these monuments, those messages should not be too difficult for us to decipher. If they were that challenging, it would defeat the whole purpose for these great monuments. In fact, we shall find that is just the case and, quite possibly, it is easier for a child to see the answer than an adult.

These megalithic messages are positively simple in concept; all we need is some lateral thinking, a healthy disregard for the established dogma, and a child's view of the world. One cannot, however, promise to uncover all the mysteries or to explain the reasoning behind all these ancient efforts, but hopefully this book will take the reader further than any has taken them before. But for every question it answers, inevitably another question will be posed, and there are likely to be many questions indeed.

Forbidden mystery

In essence, the starting point for this whole idea of a lost technical civilization was, for many people, the connection discovered long ago that the height of the Great Pyramid – the largest pyramid on the Giza site – is linked to its circumference by a factor of Pi. For a long time this was hotly disputed, but, the more carefully people have measured this pyramid, the more accurate this ratio has become and Mark Lehner, in his absorbing work *The Complete Pyramids,* gives the Pi slope angle for the Great Pyramid to the nearest six seconds of arc. Such accuracy in stonework is unparalleled, even in modern architecture. Surprisingly, instead of rejoicing at this marvel, the Egyptologists seem to be driven to despair; for it is difficult to equate these high levels of knowledge with a Bronze Age culture. Accordingly, even though this fact is now grudgingly accepted for the Great Pyramid, it is instantly dismissed with brush-off exclamations of 'accident' or 'coincidence'.

In a similar way, we are not really taught that no pyramid has ever been found to contain a mummy and that the Giza pyramids have no verifiable inscriptions or hieroglyphs anywhere on the whole plateau. Even seasoned and respected authors talk of the Giza pyramids and then discuss the wealth of hieroglyphic texts in the pyramids in almost the same breath. What they have done, of course, is to jump on to describing what is known under the traditional chronology as being the fifth and sixth dynasty pyramids, but the reader is still left with images of the Great Pyramid of Giza, and perhaps draws the wrong conclusions.

This can be likened to the way in which religions are taught. After more than 1,500 years of Christian teaching in the Western world, the vast majority of people do not know that Jesus had brothers and sisters.[2]

1. Stirlings to Stonehenge

People are taught a standard doctrine and they tend to pass it on without question. It is easier for them: it stops the boat from rocking, especially when careers and vast social empires have been built upon those doctrines. It suits the Christian teachers very nicely not to worry the proletariat about mere brothers and sisters; it suits the Egyptologists not to worry the proletariat about Pi ratios and the lack of any verifiable inscriptions in the Giza pyramids. Our teachers have secrets and we are kept very much in the dark.

Esoteric ideas

The next major revelation was the possibility that this Great Pyramid at Giza had a perimeter length that was directly linked to the circumference of the Earth, through a scale ratio of 43,200:1.[3] The ratio fits very nicely, of course: the Earth is just about 43,200 times larger than the 'Khufu' or Great Pyramid, to within 0.5%. Whatever the accuracy of these results, though, they should be taken with a great deal of caution, as anyone can find a ratio to fit any solution. If the ratio is a true ratio, then the proof or coincidence has to be overwhelming. In other words, the ratio has to have some other meaning; it cannot be just a figure plucked from the air. It must have some crosscheck for verification and a rationale for its existence. This, then, is one of the central items I was searching for in the early years: can we find real meanings for these proposed monument-to-Earth ratios? Are they real or just a coincidence?

The solution to this was quick in coming. The Great Pyramid had been cleared of the debris that had accumulated around its base many years ago and Flinders Petrie, the grandfather of alternative Egyptology, was then able to derive a circumference for the base of the pyramid of 921.45 meters, in his 1883 survey of the site. This was confirmed by J. H. Cole in his survey, entitled *Exact Size of the Great Pyramid*, in which he gave a figure of 921.47 m.[4] These figures are still valid today and Mark Lehner, for comparison, gives a figure of 921.32 m, but it has to be pointed out that this figure is based on an Imperial measurement that has been rounded down to the nearest foot.

But perhaps the prime question in regard to the geometry of these structures is why did the architect choose such difficult working angles for the sides of the Great and Second Pyramids? Why not choose something shallower and easier to build? The answer to this is relatively straightforward and has been stated many times before. The Giza pyramids are more mathematical in their construction than sepulchral, and so the slope angles for each pyramid have been chosen, simply because they embody some fundamental maths. Although the slope angles of the Great and Second Pyramids are more difficult to construct than, say, the Red Pyramid at Dahshur, the maths that they embody is more fundamental than the maths of the Red Pyramid.

The Great Pyramid, for example, is designed around the '2 x Pi x radius' formula of a circle. The perimeter length around the base of the pyramid is the equivalent of the perimeter of a circle, and the height of the pyramid represents the radius of the same circle. The angles of elevation that can be obtained from such a design are as follows:

Exact Pi circle formula angle	51° 51.2′
Fractional circle formula angle	51° 50.5′
Great Pyramid angle of elevation	51° 51′ [5]

The first thought that comes to mind is that the value of Pi was deemed to be an important discovery by the ancients and that is why they chose this particular angle. The orthodox camp would disagree with this and claim that the ancients were simply building seven units of measure upwards, for every five-and-a-half units horizontally. In other words, this was just a convenient method of measuring, and the connection with Pi is simply coincidence. This proposal might have been given some credence were it not for the fact that the Second Pyramid, which is just next door, contains another mathematical formula.

The Second Pyramid has a slightly steeper angle to flanks, and this is not just the result of imperfect surveying on the part of the designer – far from it. The Second Pyramid has simply been made to a different mathematical design from its neighbour; it has an angle of elevation that is based around the Pythagorean 3-4-5 triangle principle, with the unit of '4' representing the vertical height of the pyramid. The angles that would result from such a pyramid would be as follows:

3-4-5 triangle angle of elevation	53° 7.8′
Second Pyramid angle of elevation	53° 5′ [6]
or	53° 10′ [7]

It is quite apparent that the design principle of both these pyramids revolves around fundamental mathematical formulae. One simple building technique that accidentally derives a mathematical function is plausible; two neighbouring monuments that derive two different formulae is beyond coincidence. Besides, there are other pyramids at Dahshur that will also result in mathematical functions, so there is absolutely no chance that these fundamental numbers have appeared by sheer coincidence: they have to be designed in. This inclusion of mathematical formulae within the structure of the pyramids just has to be a direct invitation for us to look further into their designs, to find out what else they contain within their fabric.

The task was fast becoming a mathematical puzzle; something that I became proficient at in my days as a computer professional. Computer programming is simply a very long and complicated series of simple tasks that are given to a computer, and which eventually gives the results that a customer is looking for. It may be a simple stock-control program or a complicated system for predicting the weather; whatever it is designed to do, it can be resolved into a long series of simple tasks for the computer. The computer is told to add this to that, divide by this and place the result of this calculation here. It is very simple in concept, but often mind-numbingly complex in execution. A common device to simplify the task is to draw vast flow charts of what the program is trying to do, so the designer can follow the path of the computations, section by section. There is another method though. After staring at a particular program for days on end, it seemed as if the program's layout was mimicked in the synapses of the brain. If there was a problem with the execution of the program, the brain just knew where to go to; it was as simple as that.

The problem of the numerology of Egypt and Britain was the same sort of problem: stare long enough at the designs, immerse yourself in the problem for a few months, and suddenly it is very easy to see what the designer was trying to do at these sites. However, to make any sort of headway in this task, it is necessary to use the right units; otherwise, we will only confuse the issue. When I read the standard texts on ancient history, I could not believe that the author was fixed to the traditional feet and inches. While the Imperial System of measures has a long history, it is unnecessarily complex for technical usage and it positively falls down when faced with fractional calculations. Occasionally, a text book may translate the measurements into the metric system, which is an improvement, but even this cannot solve the problems of the pyramid designs. It is axiomatic that the Egyptians used cubits for the construction of their buildings, not feet and inches, or even meters. This small change can actually make a huge difference to the resolution of these issues, as I shall explain.

The unit of 52.4 cm for the Royal cubit was derived from John Greaves's and Sir Flinders Petrie's measurements of the King's Chamber in the Great Pyramid. The King's Chamber, however, has been distorted slightly and some of the granite slabs have been moved apart slightly by seismic activity, so that any calculation within this chamber is somewhat subjective when calculating the last decimal points of the cubit's length. But when looking at the exterior of the Great Pyramid, the first thing that one notices is that it would seem that a more accurate figure for the cubit can be obtained. The Royal cubit was not quite 52.4 cm, but was closer to 52.35 cm, and this is the cubit length that I shall use throughout this book. I shall call this unit of length the Thoth cubit (tc) in honour of Djeheuti, the ancient Egyptian god of mathematics. But what of this insignificant change? What possible difference can 0.05 cm make to the measurements of a pyramid? Quite a lot, as it happens.

When we are dealing with large buildings the size of the Great Pyramid, it is easy to lose the whole-number size of the building that the builder intended, even when dealing with such small errors. But if the magic integers are lost, then we can also lose the architect's train of thought and therefore, the entire reason for the building's existence. Feet (ft) or meters (m) mean absolutely nothing in terms of Egyptian architecture; it is not possible to see the coincidence in numbers if we are not using the right scales. Of course, the proportions of the structure remain the same whatever the unit of measure, but without the right measurement unit the magical lengths, or multiples of lengths, that form the structure disappear in a fog of decimal points and fractions. But if we calculate using the designer's cubits, we start to enter into the way he was thinking.

For example, the maximum front and rear underfloor cargo loading weights on a particular small jet aircraft are 1,818 kg and 2,727 kg respectively. An aviation historian in the distant future may be led to infer from this that, not only do the weights need to be very precise for this critical area in the design, but there is also some numeric symmetry to be associated with the maximum loading weights. However, when a colleague comes up with a conversion of 2.2 to the historic 'pound' (lb.), the picture suddenly changes and the answer becomes whole numbers of 4,000 lb and 6,000 lb. It transpires that the aircraft designer was just choosing round numbers, and suddenly the whole conception of the problem changes completely and becomes both clearer and simpler.

Exactly the same happens if we look at these ancient monuments and by switching into using cubits for our measuring system, we find numerous benefits. Most importantly, it provides a mathematical simplicity that can make numbers leap off the page; a method of picking at the architect's ancient, but very real, thoughts. It is by this method that we shall see some rather clever and technical whole-number cubit symmetries within the internal galleries and chambers of the Great Pyramid in chapter II. But if the Thoth cubit (tc) is actually 52.35 cm, then what impact will this have on the external size of the Great Pyramid? Take the base of this pyramid, which is 230.36 m in length, divide this by 0.5235 and the result is 440.04 tc, which is fairly close to the whole-number of 440. In the same manner, the pyramid's height of 146.59 m, when divided by 0.5235, becomes 280.02 tc which is again quite close to a whole-number value of 280. In the following table are some more of these whole-number measurements to be found within the Great Pyramid (GP).

Measurement	Length (m)	Length (tc)	Whole number
GP base length	230.36	440.04	440
GP circumference	921.45	1760.15	1760
Grand Gallery	46.08	88.02	88
Ascending passage	39.27	75.01	75
Desc. passage to asc.	28.30	53.93	54
Descending passage	104.90	200.50	200
King's Chamber	10.48	20.02	20
by	5.24	10.01	10
Queen's Chamber	5.76	11.01	11
by	5.24	10.01	10

The list will continue as this story unfolds, but it demonstrates a high level of accuracy to round figures in using the cubit length of 0.5235 m. This is a real unit of measure, as used by the original architect, and therefore *this* is the unit that should be used when studying these designs. For instance, the list above highlights the perimeter length measurement of 1,760 for the Great Pyramid, as opposed to the 1,758 that the usual conversion into cubits gives, and this is why I have so confidently used this particular length for the Thoth cubit. This number of 1,760 was central to discovering one of the core mysteries of the pyramids, although few people in Britain will recognize it today, as it is in fact a well established unit of measure. This topic will be discussed more extensively in a chapters III and IV.

It was at this point that I needed some more background information, but since much of this has been published previously by other authors, it will be kept brief and to the point, and I shall only dwell on concepts that have not been aired previously.

Pyramid histories

Pyramid building first began, according to standard texts, with the building of mastabas, like the mastaba at Meidum. These were vast, low-lying structures made of brick and small stones, not unlike the long barrows of southern England. These mastabas were invariably tombs, often internally decorated with hieroglyphs and artwork. They are often aligned with the cardinal compass points, as most pyramids were and Christian churches are to this day. Mastabas are dated classically from the first and second dynasties (3000-2650 BC), but were also built before, during and after the classical pyramid-building era. There are over 200 mastabas on the Giza site alone and they are mostly thought to be the tombs of lower dignitaries and princes. This dating system for the early mastabas and pyramids, however, has many critics. The current system of dating the dynasties comes from a series of king lists – the Karnak tablet, the Abydos tablet, the Saqqara tablet and the list of Manetho – with the latter being the system that is the basis of the sequence of dynasties that are still used in modern texts. Needless to say, these different king lists in no way agree with each other, so, while a history of Egypt can be traced with reasonable confidence back to the New Kingdom (1400s BC), it is clear that, even in these times, the history of the Old Kingdom (2500s BC) was confused.

The king lists of Manetho have been lost to history and they reach us by way of Julius Africanus and Eusebius.[8] Again, even these two versions of the same history differ, with the historian, Budge, giving Africanus's version about 560 kings and 5,520 years, and Eusebius's 360 kings and 4,480 years (including pre-dynastic kings). In fact, the king 'Khufu' does not even appear in these lists; his position being replaced by 'Souphis'. This has led some commentators to say that 'Khufu' is a generic term for a god rather than a pharaoh. Because of this confusion, and because of the rather cavalier assumption that pharaohs without a definite reign length reigned for 25 years, the estimated dates for the start of the first dynasty among nineteenth-century Egyptologists ranged from 2300 to 5000 BC. Today, there is greater consensus of opinion, but since there has been little new significant information found to alter the picture, early dynasty dates are highly uncertain and based on convention rather than fact.

The next step in the conventional history of Egypt was the construction of step-pyramids, which could be considered as a series of mastabas on top of each other, although the construction technology is different and slightly more advanced. The concept of the pyramid is generally thought to have come from the idea of a stairway of sunbeams that could be climbed up to heaven, like the pyramidal array of the Sun's rays streaming through a gap in some distant clouds. This idea is not necessarily correct: the idea of a stairway of sunbeams may be valid, but it is quite apparent from the furniture in the tomb of Tutankhamen, that in the eighteenth dynasty, it was thought that the sunbeams forming the pyramid originated on the Earth and were beamed upwards. Two beams were used and these formed a pyramid, just like two searchlights pointing up and crossing in the sky. This can be seen quite clearly on the aprons of the tomb guardians. The aprons themselves have been shown to be based on the pyramid geometry of Giza, with the apron angles being similar to the angles used on many of the pyramids.

Initially, under the classical dating of the pyramids, the proto-pyramids in Egypt were built within a large compound. Djoser's step-pyramid at Saqqara (*circa* 2500 BC) is perhaps the most well known and best preserved of these enclosed compounds. The site dates from the third dynasty and its construction is credited to the master mason, Imhotep. What is not so generally known is that this pyramid probably represents many generations of work and, in addition, it is not the first step-pyramid in Egypt. Djoser's Pyramid is the first 'large' step-pyramid, but there were at least ten smaller step-pyramids of only 20–25 meters' base length that were built before this time. [9]

The order of construction at the Saqqara site is probably as follows: firstly, a large mastaba enclosure was made, which was extended on three occasions. To this was added a shaft-tomb and small step-pyramid above it; and, at some later time, this step-pyramid was enlarged on two further occasions into the present six-tier structure. So is this really the tomb of the pharaoh Djoser? Egyptologists seem confident, but the contemporary name for the pharaoh concerned is likely to have been Tosorthros, sometimes known as Netjerikhet (meaning 'godlike body'). Djoser simply means 'holy one', so the complex could have been dedicated to the gods, not Tosorthros. Over 35,000 shards of pottery were found under Djoser's Pyramid, which places it with some confidence into the historical record, but these *ostra* simply create further problems for the pharaonic chronology:

> It is an interesting question why so many of these vases were incised with the names of Zozer's (Djoser's) predecessors. On the various kinds of stone ... are the names of pharaohs of archaic Egypt including Narmer, Djer, Djet, Den and Khasekhemwy. Were they heirlooms ... or were they the pious re-burial of vessels disturbed by looting? [10]

The answer to this problem is simple: stop calling the pyramids tombs and call them, instead, cathedrals or religious monuments. In that way the problems of multiple associations with successive pharaohs; multiple extensions of the structures; and incredibly tight building schedules; simply disappear. We are quite comfortable with the idea of the great henges of

1. Stirlings to Stonehenge

Britain being religious sites, not tombs; so why cannot the pyramids be the same? Besides, it is not only an established fact that no original burial has ever been found in any pyramid, but that at two completely undisturbed sites – the tomb of Hetepheres and the pyramid of Sekhemket – sealed sarcophagi were found. On being opened, both were discovered to be empty.

While we cannot say for certain why this was done, it is likely that these sarcophagi were buried for ceremonial purposes, and the evidence for this is reinforced by modern Masonic rituals. Masonry claims a fundamentally Egyptian heritage and one of its basic rites involves a ritual death and burial, followed by a resurrection. This ritual is likely to predate the symbolic resurrections of Jesus and Lazarus in the Bible, and it is more likely to be a ritual that was based on the death and resurrection of Osiris. It is clear that death and rebirth were important aspects of Egyptian theology and the presence of deep, cathedral-like chambers under the pyramids, complete with empty sarcophagi, provide all the ritual elements required for a third-degree initiation.

The finished structure of Djoser's Pyramid – while often being accredited under the classical chronology as being the first such structure made by man – was not unique by any means. In Britain, a civilization in exactly the same era, again according to classical ideas, was designing and building a similar project; the 'step-pyramid' of King Zil, the structure known as Silbury Hill. The legends say that the mythical King Zil was buried under the 'pyramid', complete with his horse and a set of golden armour, but, just as in the pyramids of Egypt, no actual burial was discovered during excavations. While the identity of the builders of Silbury lie in the prehistoric era of Britain, and the mythical King Zil is probably a later invention, I shall use this name as a convenient tag with which to identify the architect and society that commissioned this 'pyramid'.

Looking at the similarity in the two structures, one wonders what the common urge for this type of construction was. The prevailing ideas of history would deny any links between northern Europe and Egypt in the Neolithic/Bronze Age era, and yet we cannot deny the similarity of these monuments, both in shape and size. Djoser's Pyramid at Saqqara measured 125 m x 60 m while the Silbury 'pyramid', being of a slightly simpler design, is a somewhat flatter 160 m x 40 m; but Silbury is nevertheless a substantial construction, utilizing about the same volume of material.

It may seem inappropriate to compare directly the Silbury 'pyramid' with Djoser's Pyramid, but Silbury is more similar in its design than it initially appears. Just like Djoser's Pyramid, Silbury has had at least three enlargements to the structure and the final edifice comprises a step-pyramid, containing six steps. Like many of the Egyptian step-pyramids, each step at Silbury has large facing blocks – although here made of chalk – and a rubble interior. The steps were further subdivided into cells, or segments, with the cell walls helping to stabilize the structure. At this stage in the construction, Silbury would have strongly resembled the step-pyramid of Djoser, except in having a circular perimeter and being faced with gleaming white chalk.

One can only presume that the finished structure at Silbury was subsequently covered by earth, in order to protect the relatively fragile chalk blocks that were used in the exterior cladding. There is a further mystery in this respect, because this same construction technique was also used in the Mexican pyramids at Teotihuacan. In a very similar fashion, these pyramids were also constructed of clay cores, which were then faced with stone blocks. The Teotihuacan pyramids were then subsequently buried, just as at Silbury.

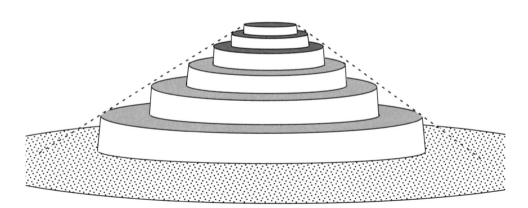

Fig 1.   Silbury 'pyramid'

Avalanche

Under the classical dating system, at the beginning of the fourth dynasty there was another change in the styles of pyramid building. The large mastabas were reduced in size, as was the perimeter wall, and the balance of the building effort was placed on the pyramid. Also, the step-pyramid was now being covered with a stone cladding to give it a true pyramidal shape. The first of these new constructions, at Meidum, was a steep-sided step-pyramid, to which pyramidal cladding was added. This pyramid had apparently been in existence as a step-pyramid for some time, and then extended on more than one occasion before the final cladding was being added. This is known because, just as at Djoser's Pyramid at Saqqara, the steps themselves had been formed in several places from smooth, dressed stones, indicating a finished structure. Despite this evidence, modern Egyptologists still try to ascribe this and all other pyramids to just one pharaoh, when this is patently not so. This was not always the case, as Sir Flinders Petrie says of Meidum, for instance:

> From the successive coats of the mastaba-pyramids of Meidum, and Saqqara ... it shows that the buildings quoted were completely finished and cased many times over, probably by successive kings.[11]

Pyramids were not always ascribed to a single pharaoh because it was noticed and understood that they were rebuilt in different eras. In the case of Meidum, we can clearly see these different eras in the sequence of construction of the entrance passageway, which has three distinct styles. The sequence of construction is roughly as follows:

a.   A small tumulus was made at ground level. The interior construction of the overlapping stones in this chamber is quite rough; the entrance passageway is in the floor of the chamber and it tunnels through the bare earth. The standard of workmanship in the tumulus and in the passageway is not unlike the technology used in a long barrow in ancient Britain.

b.   Perhaps during the construction of the step-pyramid above, the entrance to the tumulus was reworked. The new entrance was formed by placing huge monolithic blocks around the small chamber, with each massive block of white Tura limestone being jointed together with extreme care. (These blocks may even underlie the small chamber.) The workmanship here is comparable to anything at Giza and it is claimed that the mastaba chamber next door is carved within one single block of limestone; a massive block indeed. The passageway to the pyramid chamber was then formed by tunnelling bodily and very roughly through these finely jointed blocks; which is a curious method given the care employed on the blocks themselves.

c.   After the construction of the step-pyramid, when the pyramidal cladding was being added at a later date, the form of the passageway alters into the more usual method of construction. Separate stone blocks now form the smooth sides of the tunnel.

Another clue to the true age of this pyramid can be derived from the missing upper pyramidal cladding stones: what happened to them? Many commentators have said that these stones – the remaining lower portions of which are still apparent under the piles of rubble around the pyramid – have either been stolen in subsequent eras or they have collapsed in a kind of pyramidal avalanche. But this was not the case. From a later excavation of the rubble surrounding the pyramid in the early 1990s, it was quite apparent that the pyramid had simply been eroded away by the weather, like so many of the less well made pyramids in the area.

Unfortunately for the builders, while the central core of the pyramid was made of a fairly durable limestone, the attempt to turn the edifice into a true pyramid used a very weak and friable stone. This stone has proved about as durable as mud-brick and, although initially quite solid-looking, the blocks that have been exposed to the elements are extremely fragile.

The fact that the pyramid has eroded and not collapsed, can be clearly seen in the rubble around the pyramid, which consists of layer upon layer of sand and small stones. These stones form the type of strata that are always associated with eroded and deposited materials. It can also be seen that where the rubble falling down from above has protected the base of the pyramid, the cladding stones there survive intact. But higher courses, which were exposed to the elements for a longer period, have been successively eroded more and more until, at about six meters up, there is complete erosion.

Clearly this is due to exposure to the elements, with the lower cladding stones that were first covered with rubble being preserved the most. Yet one still wonders how long it takes to erode a complete pyramid, even if the stone was a little friable for, in places, some ten meters of stone have eroded away at Meidum. The current shape of the pyramid results from the fact that the upper flat section at the top of the rubble marks the start of another step of harder limestone just under the surface; the present layout is therefore quite stable and may not have changed for some considerable time. Is it really possible that ten meters of solid stone can be eroded in just under 5,000 years?

Dahshur

There are two notable pyramids at Dahshur: the Red Pyramid and the Bent

1. Stirlings to Stonehenge

Pyramid. These are not the best of appellations but, as is often the case, there is some confusion as to who was supposed to have built these pyramids, with both being traditionally ascribed to the pharaoh, Snorferu. This is an obvious clue that these pyramids are not tombs, for why would Snorferu want to have two pyramids at Dahshur, plus the one further south at Meidum?

Again, it has to be asked, how do we know who built these pyramids? At the Red Pyramid, the designation is due to carved reliefs of Snorferu. But these reliefs were found outside the pyramid, in the mortuary complex. The interior of this pyramid, as in all the pyramids we shall be looking at, is entirely devoid of inscriptions. If these incised blocks are to be used as evidence, however, it should be noted that a number of pharaohs have had the habit of inscribing their name on every available monument: Ramesses II, for instance, has often been called the 'great chiseller'. All this intrusive inscribing was done for a good reason: the name of the pharaoh was very important in Egyptian theology, as we shall see later. Further 'evidence' in favour of Snorferu constructing the Dahshur pyramids comes from some eighteenth dynasty graffiti, penned by an ancient tourist. This was the scribe Aakheperkare-senb, who writes:

> May heaven rain with fresh myrrh, may it drip with incense upon the roof of the temple of King Snorferu. [12]

Not only is this source unreliable – it was written at least 1,000 years after the conventional date given for the reign of Snorferu – but we also end up with a situation where the early parts of the fourth dynasty seem to have more pyramids than pharaohs, with what Sir Alan Gardiner calls:

> The unpalatable conclusion that Snorferu did possess three pyramids.

The northern pyramid on the Dahshur site is known for the colour of the sandstone used in its construction. The 'Red' Pyramid, as it is known, has exterior elevations of the more stable angle of 43° 36' [13], and once more it does not exhibit any indication of having ever been used as a tomb. The quality of the construction of the Red Pyramid is far superior to those of Meidum or Saqqara, with the quality of the stonework in the chambers, for example, being particularly fine. The Red Pyramid would still have been a very imposing monument, were it not for the stone robbers who have stripped the casing off.

Next, we visit the southern pyramid at Dahshur. The name given to this mighty monument results from the fact that the upper courses of this pyramid have had their angle changed to a more stable 43.5°, giving a noticeable bend in the line of the casing. This change in angle of the Bent Pyramid is traditionally ascribed to some cracking of the structure, which may have been sufficient to warrant the designer to change his plans, but there is another explanation for the design in later chapters and this idea is more fully explained in the sequel *K2, Quest of the Gods.* One of the intentions of the architect was to make the Dahshur pyramids appear unique in their appearance, not only from each other, but also from the pyramids at Giza.

Like the Red Pyramid, Bent is of much superior construction to those at Saqqara and Meidum, as is witnessed by its near complete survival. Nearly all the casing stones have survived intact, which gives us a good example of what the pyramids of Giza must have looked like in the past. Only the colour has changed over the years, from the original brilliant white to the sandy buff hue that we see today.

It is my assertion that these pyramids were actually designed and built many millennia ago, perhaps as many as twelve millennia. The evidence for this may appear to be circumstantial at present, but the evidence will become much more convincing shortly. In the sequel, *K2, Quest of the Gods,* I will show further hard, physical evidence that this is so. The evidence in the sequel is derived from the erosion patterns on the face of the Dahshur pyramids and it is quite compelling. However, there is other erosion evidence to be found, both at this site and on the Giza plateau, and I stumbled across this evidence whilst wandering around the pyramids with my wife, one scorching afternoon.

Lines

My wife asked, 'Why is there a line running down this pavement?' The initial answer to this was easy for, when fully finished, the casing blocks of each of the pyramids invariably stopped short of the pavement edge, such that one particular pavement slab was partly covered by the casing and also partly exposed to the elements. The exposed portion of this slab was therefore beginning to erode over the years, slowly but surely as the years went by; as exposure to weather and the feet of millions of pilgrims took its toll. But the stone masons were normally wise in their choice of stone and the amount of weathering is minimal in comparison with what we find at Meidum. As we can see from the remaining cladding stones that still cover the Bent Pyramid and the upper portions of the Second Pyramid, in the desert climate, good quality stone usually weathers very slowly.

1. Stirlings to Stonehenge

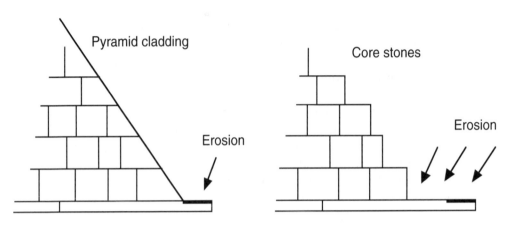

Pavement covered

Pavement exposed

Fig 2.

Then, after many millennia, someone came along and started pilfering the cladding stones from the pyramids; something that is usually ascribed to the eighth or ninth century AD. From this time onwards, the whole of the paving slab was now exposed to the elements and started to weather, hence a line was formed in the paving stones between the two periods of weathering.

But there was a curious anomaly here that made me sit and think for a while. When looking at both the Dahshur and the Giza pyramids, there would appear to be a large differential between the surface of the pavement that has been covered for much of its life, and the portion that has always been exposed. This is true even within one single slab of stone, so it is not a case of dissimilar stone strengths. Then there was a little pause in the discussion, for it was obvious that this little line in the pavement could now be used to date the pyramids, but what would it tell us?

With ruler in hand, I tried to estimate the extent of the erosion, using the base of the remaining facing blocks as a guide to the original surface of the pavement. It was not the most precise of experiments, given the tools at my disposal, but luckily the amount of erosion was easily visible. At Dahshur, the amount of erosion on the covered half of the slab was approximately 5 mm, the sort of erosion one might expect in such a climate over 1,000 years of weathering; yet, on the exposed portion of the stone, there was about 50 mm of erosion. At Giza, the differential was even greater. The amount of erosion on the covered portion of the stone was again about 5 mm, and the exposed section had between 50 mm and a massive 200 mm of erosion.

In general, it would appear that there was a minimum of ten times as much erosion on the exposed section of each block as on the portion that had been covered with the cladding stones, and this ratio would in turn give us a direct indication of the true age of these pyramids. If a constant erosion rate is presumed, and if the time elapsed since the cladding was stolen is about 1,000 years, then the time required for the erosion of the exposed sections of each slab would equate to about 10,000 years, and quite possibly, much much longer.

Remember that this is true for a single slab of stone, so it is not a case of dissimilar stone strengths. Indeed, some of the softer slabs in the pavement have been eroded more than usual on both the covered *and* the exposed sections, and this weathering is in direct proportion to the weathering on the harder slabs of stone. This consistency would seem to indicate that this erosion process is a valid tool for dating the pyramids, as each stone tells the same history, no matter how hard or soft it is. While a 10,000-year history for the pyramids agrees quite well with the Bent Pyramid's repairs, it conflicts strongly once more with the traditional history of the region. Nevertheless, this era will be in agreement with the new dates we shall be finding later in the book.

Giza

For the next pyramids chronologically, according to standard texts, we come to those very pyramids on the Giza plateau. The Giza complex is light years from the pyramids of Meidum and Saqqara. Here, even the blocks of stone in the core are shaped, instead of being rubble, so the pyramids of Giza do not need the inclined internal structure for stability, like Saqqara and Meidum. The size of the masonry has also increased dramatically from the small bricks that are used on the Saqqara site; they now range from a minimum of 2.5 tonnes, up to the largest which weigh in at some 70 tonnes. Yet each of these massive stones had to be transported vertically up some 100 meters of sloping pyramid.

In addition, some of the pavement blocks around the Second Pyramid weigh in at up to 200 tonnes and the depth of this pavement is quite astounding. The Second Pyramid was built on an incline and therefore the south western corner had to be countersunk into the bedrock.

1. Stirlings to Stonehenge

Indeed, part of this corner of the pyramid was actually formed from a raised section of remaining bedrock. To the east, the problem was the reverse; the ground here sloped away and was deeply fissured. Thus, the foundations to the pyramid across all of this eastern area had to be raised up to make the site level and stable. The Bronze Age solution to this defect on the topography of the chosen site was 'simple': just form a thick raft of megalithic blocks, each weighing in at hundreds of tonnes, and then build the pyramid on top of that.

The feat achieved here is truly astounding, perhaps as great as the pyramid itself. The questions that this observation provokes are always the same; why were such massive stones used for the foundations, and how were they moved and fitted together so precisely? As usual, these questions are difficult to answer, but two things are certain.

Firstly, a designer would only use such methods if they were simple for his workmen to execute. If one looks at the third and fifth dynasty pyramids, the engineering solutions are all simple and man-manageable. This does, however, beg the obvious question as to how placing hundreds of blocks, weighing hundreds of tonnes each, was deemed to be 'simple' by the designer.

Secondly, the placing of the Second Pyramid in this precise location was very difficult for the designer and a tremendous amount of work was wasted in levelling the site. This clearly indicates that the position of this pyramid was critical and it directly supports the concept that these three pyramids were deliberately placed together, to mimic the outline of the belt of the constellation of Orion.

Much of this has been observed before, but there was one other thing that struck my mind, about the Great Pyramid's design in particular. How, in such an early building project, did the architect derive so much knowledge about designing a structure that would withstand earthquakes? Egypt is often jolted by low and medium strength earthquakes and any building, wishing to stand a few millennia, would have to withstand one or two in its lifetime. With the Great Pyramid, it would seem that many parts of the structure were designed to withstand such forces. Other pyramids were not quite so well equipped, but then perhaps the interiors of those pyramids were not so intricate or important.

Firstly, we have the items that have been talked about in other works. One could mention the separately-jointed roof slabs in the Grand Gallery, which appear to prevent the weight of each roof slab from pressing on its neighbour, so preventing forces building up along the entire length of the gallery. Also, there are the 'independent' walls of the King's Chamber, which are not bonded with the rest of the structure. This prevents the harder granite wall stones from interfering with any settlement in the softer limestone blocks that lie immediately behind. Plus, we have the 'girdle' stones in the ascending passage: vast stones through which the passageway tunnels bodily, apparently tying this feature firmly into the rest of the structure. Then there is the slight indentation in the centre of each outer face of the pyramid; this feature would help prevent any oscillations in the face of the pyramid itself. Rather like the crease or curve in the door panel of a car; it may look nice, but the real purpose of the crease is to stiffen the structure.

The final piece of evidence, and the one that convinced me there was something technical about all of this, were the layers of different-sized blocks used in the Great Pyramid. If we take a look at the core and cladding blocks of the structure, it can be clearly seen that there are distinct bands of large blocks progressing to smaller blocks, and then back to large blocks. This variation in block size is repeated in bands throughout the entire pyramid. It is a curious feature not seen on any other pyramid in Egypt and yet it will become more than obvious that everything that has been done on these sites is with good reason. If there are bands in the structure of this pyramid, then there must be a purpose for them; there must be some method in the madness of the designer. In this case, the banding is just another highly advanced and technical seismic safety device. The bands would have the effect of preventing any oscillations in the structure from resonating and therefore becoming worse, threatening the whole construction. This feature is there simply to damp out any seismic harmonics and it is similar to the design of tread patterns on car tyres.

Around any standard car tyre, the tread pattern, whatever its design, is spaced out in bands of long chunks of tread decreasing to shorter chunks, and then back to long. It was realised by designers many decades ago that such a design would reduce road noise. Not having access to computers at the time, the designers worked out the amplitude of each series of bands by throwing dice. Apparently, computer simulations have since demonstrated that the traditional method was quite close to the optimum. This variation in the amplitude of the banding is just the pattern we find in the Great Pyramid, and these bands are there for the same reason: to prevent resonance. In tyres, this design stops the tyres from 'singing' as a car is driven down the road. In a pyramid, it may prevent an internal chamber from collapsing during an earthquake. Such were the skills of these Bronze Age builders.

On top of all this, it is still a mystery – under the conventional version of history – as to why none of the pyramids at Giza had any internal decoration or hieroglyphs whatsoever. This is even more surprising when one considers the religious context in which these pyramids were supposed to have been built. The name of a person was very important in Egyptian theology, as it encapsulated the essence of that person. This would have been doubly important for a pharaoh striving for immortality as one of the gods:

> This essence was encapsulated in the name given to a child at birth. So long as one's name was being spoken, the Egyptians believed, immortality was assured. So protection of the name of the deceased was vital. The tomb, the mummy, the equipment, the paintings and reliefs were all designed to help preserve the name of the individual. The greatest horror was to have your name destroyed, cut out from the wall. [14]

This is the situation we find in the Valley of the Kings, where the name of the occupant is engraved and painted in every available location in each chamber. Alternatively, this cutting out of the name of someone who was disliked was the fate of several pharaohs, including the revolutionary pharaoh, Akhenaton, who had his name defaced all across the country. This shows how important leaving one's name for posterity was in ancient Egypt and how terrible anonymity was considered. Except, of course, that the entire Giza and Dahshur sites are devoid of any internal markings – we are faced with totally smooth, bare walls throughout! This is an utterly peculiar thing for a pharaoh in search of everlasting life to order from his designers and builders. In fact, it is not just peculiar, it is inconceivable. It would be possible to make an argument for the later fifth dynasty pyramids onwards, which have a profusion of hieroglyphs and drawings, as being tombs that have been plundered. There is no such argument to be made for any of the pyramids at Giza or Dahshur; the pyramids at these locations are *not* tombs.

Blueprint

The Giza pyramids, according to all commentators, have never held a mummy, and the walls of their chambers, although perfectly smooth and finished, have never supported a hieroglyph or painting; so, how do we know who built them and what they were for? The only direct clues to the builder of the Great Pyramid itself are some "builders' marks" above the King's Chamber, which apparently indicate that the pharaoh Khufu was reigning at the time of its construction. These hieroglyphs and cartouches of the pharaoh Khufu, however, are of dubious origins; despite the vigorous claims from both sides in the dispute, the case for or against their authenticity has still not been decided.

In addition to these problems, there are a few other facts that need to be taken into account. The New Kingdom pharaoh, Seti I, left a list of Egyptian kings for posterity. That list includes all of the fourth dynasty, yet the pharaoh Khufu does not appear on it. In his place there is to be found a king called Fura. Unfortunately, where the 'ball of string' or 'sieve' glyph should be (which is normally used for the 'Khu' in Khufu), it has been replaced by a symbol for the Sun-god, Ra. Thus, the traditional Khu-Fu becomes the relatively unknown Fu-Ra. The incumbent of the Great Pyramid now appears to have four appellations, depending on the text: Souphis, Khufu, Fura and Cheops. Therefore, deciding if Khufu really was the builder of the Great Pyramid is not so straightforward.

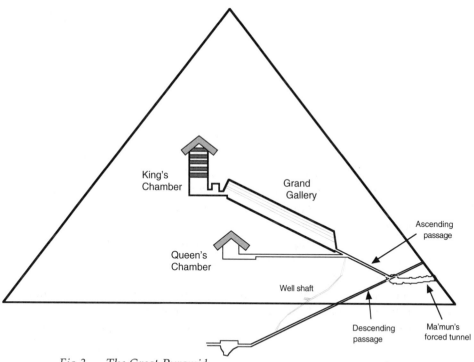

Fig 3.   The Great Pyramid

In addition to all this, there is a pyramid further down the plateau that *does* contain the cartouche of Khufu. This pyramid stands at Lisht, near Meidum, and it has no known associated pharaoh; although Seankhare, Nebtaire and Amenemhet have all been attributed to it. Curiously, although this pyramid had many cartouches of Khufu in the associated temple complex, these were dismissed as the result of pillaging stonework from the Great Pyramid. Ordinarily, such inscriptions would automatically be a justification for attributing the pyramid to this pharaoh; the Dahshur pyramids have been attributed to Snorferu on far less evidence. However, at this location it is presumed that the owner was just pillaging stonework; no doubt the thought of Khufu being represented at Lisht would do too much damage to the established chronology.

When considering the Great Pyramid's true purpose, a further puzzle is that the lower end of the ascending passage was apparently blocked off during the construction work, not after completion. Many theories have been proposed as to how these blocking stones in the ascending passage were placed in position after the pyramid was finished, but none is quite convincing. The ascending passage is the only practicable way into the King's Chamber for a burial so, if this access were blocked, any mummy that was intended to be entombed would have to have been placed inside the King's Chamber before the ceiling was installed and while the construction work for the rest of the pyramid was still being completed above. Such a proposal stretches credulity.

This unsuitability for the pyramid as a tomb has led some authors to suggest that the pyramid was a cathedral, a place of worship. Undoubtedly, the Giza site was in some respects just that. It has solar pointers to the main festival dates in the form of precessional causeways that point to the cross-quarter sunrises, and the site is littered with the tombs of lower dignitaries, as are Christian churches. But the fact remains that the pyramid is a poor cathedral in our terms, whether for the proletariat or just for the priesthood itself. It contains only two small rooms; most of the passageways are made for troglodytes; and the whole edifice was sealed, with the ascending passage being sealed and concealed with three huge blocks of granite. So, if the pyramid was neither a tomb nor a cathedral, what can it have been?

The 'ventilation' shafts, in the King's and Queen's Chambers, may give us the clue here. That these shafts and galleries were important is beyond doubt, as they are complicated constructions at precise angles. The northern shafts even have to snake their way around the Grand Gallery, a complicated air-shaft indeed. The ventilation theory was always somewhat dubious, especially as the Queen's 'ventilation' shafts were never fully cut through into the Queen's Chamber, or to the outside air for that matter. As an alternative, some authors have embraced the idea that the shafts were instead used for star-sighting. The argument then proceeds along spiritual lines, with the soul of the deceased pharaoh being guided by these shafts to the heavens. But this theory falls at the first hurdle if the King's Chamber was sealed without a mummy being interred.

Using a much more practical and physical interpretation, this same theory may also mean that this star-sighting was intended to be done on paper, by real people. If the star-sighting is achieved on paper then the pyramid is not a cathedral but more of a 'time capsule' or a blueprint for astronomical observations. In many respects, this practical interpretation also infers that this star-sighting was designed to be performed in the far future, at a time when the original plans to the plateau had been lost and the only way of determining which stars to observe was by breaking into the pyramid and measuring the shaft angles. The time-capsule theory, by its very nature, demands that the 'blueprint' be made indelible by its inscription upon, or construction using durable materials.

The theory, that will be further developed in later chapters, is similar to the star-sighting theory, in that the air-shafts do indeed represent construction lines on a geometrical plan, when seen in cross-section from the east or the west. So, the fabric of the pyramid may be considered to form a technical drawing with various lines inscribed upon it, but it is not a drawing that points towards stars. This rather radical hypothesis requires the pyramid to be sealed shut, of course: to be discovered only in the distant future when a suitable technology was available to decipher the plans. A roughly carved lower chamber at the bottom of the pyramid was installed to satisfy the demands of grave robbers, but the bulk of the brooding pyramid was waiting patiently for thousands of years for an enquiring civilization in the far future to come along and ask the question why?

This delicate plan was partly foiled by Caliph al Ma'mun, who, while quarrying inside the pyramid, dislodged the end-capstone of the ascending passage. The full story of the Caliph is narrated in *K2, Quest of the Gods*. The activities of the Caliph had sprung the trap a little too early. Nevertheless, the plan is still there, carved in monoliths of granite and limestone, and we now have the technology and understanding to decipher the plans and to eventually explain the entire pyramid complex.

The only structures in the pyramid that do not seem to fit this theory are the 'well-shaft' and 'Davidson's hole', which are both rather odd features. Possibly Mr David Davidson, who was a structural engineer from Leeds and after whom the hole is named, can help us here. He postulated that shortly after construction, at a time when the building plans were still available, the pyramid suffered structural damage from an earthquake. The new fissures opened up by the earthquake were, and are, clearly visible in the descending passage and they clearly occurred after its construction.

If the earthquake had also caused the collapse of the internal chambers, the 'blueprint' would have been destroyed and the whole project would have lost its entire purpose. To ascertain fully the internal state of the pyramid, the designers decided to cut a shaft up from the bottom of the pyramid; the rough lower chamber of the pyramid having been left open for access to the priesthood and to deter tomb-robbers. This new 'well-shaft' tracked, in its initial stages, up through the large fissures that had just appeared in the bedrock, so that these could be inspected. One of these fissures is known as the 'grotto'. The grotto is often said to be a man-made 'halfway house' in the well-shaft, but as Flinders Petrie points out:

> The so called 'grotto' ... is really a fissure in the limestone, through which the passage has been lined with small hewn stones to keep back the gravel found in the fissure. [15]

Knowing the design of the pyramid, the well-shaft diggers then pushed on, directly up into the base of the Grand Gallery. On an initial inspection of the internal chambers, things were not so bad as they had expected; the Queen's Chamber and Grand Gallery were unaffected. However, after penetrating through the portcullis slabs and into the King's Chamber, it was immediately apparent that many of the ceiling beams had suffered a complete fracture and were held up only by the thrusting pressure on the huge blocks. There was a distinct possibility that the roof would collapse and so further investigation was required of the complicated roof structure above the King's Chamber.

Accordingly, they cut a small hole from the top of the Grand Gallery into the upper 'relieving' chambers above the King's Chamber. Here, they found that the next set of ceiling rafters was intact, so things were not too bad. As it was impossible to replace the cracked beams, the inspectors daubed the cracks in the beams with mortar from above and below; perhaps for strength, perhaps to see at a later date if there was any further movement in the blocks. They then left the upper chambers, clearing up all evidence of their visit as they went. On exiting the well-shaft at the bottom of the descending passage, they made such a good job of concealing the entrance to it, that it was not discovered until the journey down the shaft was made in the reverse direction (from above) by Giovanni Cavigliar in 1765.

The theory certainly has a ring of truth to it: there was indeed a small tunnel cut into the first roof chamber above the King's Chamber, now known as Davidson's hole. Certainly, the beams in the King's Chamber were found to be cracked and daubed with original cement on both the upper and lower sides, by Sir Flinders Petrie on his survey of 1881. Also, both the well-shaft and Davidson's hole were made after the construction of the pyramid. We can tell this because they are not smooth-sided shafts; instead they tunnel directly through the core-stones of the structure. Yet both tunnels seem to home in on their required destinations, not only in the firm knowledge that there was a destination to tunnel to, but also seemingly having a precise knowledge of the location, within the structure, of that destination. These shaft-makers still had the plans to the pyramid!

This scenario not only sounds reasonable, but is quite likely to have happened, as the huge mass of the pyramid is liable to have caused some settlement in the underlying rocks of the Giza plateau. This settlement, or localized earthquake, would also be more prone to occur as the mass of the pyramid approached its maximum; and that would be well after the King's Chamber was sealed and buried under the millions of tonnes of the upper pyramid. The designer in this case would be forced to make an alternative entry into the chambers to examine them. This is a fairly convincing scenario, that serves to confirm that the Grand Gallery and the King's Chamber remained sealed until they were discovered by al Ma'mun in about AD 820. The final evidence, however, is the presence of Davidson's hole.

Davidson's hole, as we saw, was cut by someone knowing the plans to the pyramid, but this was not the act of a grave-robber, as the upper chambers of the King's Chamber seem to be purely structural. This examination was the act of a concerned architect. All this is further proof, if more proof were required, that there was never a burial or a mummy in the Great Pyramid and there never were any grave-robbers: the whole edifice was carefully inspected and re-sealed by the designer himself.

Building decline

Chronologically, between the magnificent monuments of Giza, the standard doctrine has acknowledged some rather peculiar constructions. In between the Great Pyramid and Second Pyramid, for instance, comes the pharaoh Djedfra, whose pyramid was constructed some 7 km to the north of Giza, at Abu Roash. The odd thing is that this pyramid has a substructure that was designed like the foundations of an early step-pyramid. In the opinion of V. Maragioglio and C. Rinaldi, this is exactly what it was, an early style step-pyramid. [16] There is another anomaly between the Second and Third

1. Stirlings to Stonehenge

Pyramids, where we have the unfinished pyramid of Bicheris, another pyramid which has step-pyramid-style footings. Both of these out-of-place pyramids were made of inferior, small stone blocks and mud-brick, and so little remains of these structures; they are quite unlike the Giza monuments. [17]

If we now continue with the standard chronology into the period after Giza – that is, into the very end of the fourth dynasty – the next constructions were miserable efforts, even in comparison with the intervening step-pyramids. The last of the fourth dynasty pharaohs, Shepseskaf, did not even attempt a pyramid; he was content with a small, traditional-style mastaba at Saqqara. This was the Fara'un Mastaba, and it contained only about 1% of the volume of masonry that was used in the Great Pyramid. Fifth and sixth dynasty pyramids, such as Amenemhat III at Dahshur and Neferirkare at Abusir – although now richly adorned with hieroglyphs internally – were yet shoddier constructions. Many of these loose rock and mud-brick edifices have largely crumbled back into the desert sands from which they rose, some being totally indistinguishable from the surrounding terrain, and they are located principally by the presence of their shafts and chambers.

The volume of masonry involved in these projects underlines the absurdity of the classical chronology. The fourth dynasty pharaohs managed to quarry and use two-and-a-half times as much masonry in one hundred years as all the other dynasties managed in eight hundred years. So, for a brief moment in time, the world's greatest buildings ever constructed were built and, as has been pointed out many times before, the classical chronology for the construction of the pyramids is therefore a little peculiar:

> (At Giza) ... there may be seen the very beginning of architecture, (and yet also) the most enormous piles of building ever raised, the most accurate constructions known, the finest masonry, and the employment of the most ingenious tools. [18]

While it lasted, the pyramid-building era was one of the most spectacular achievements of ancient, or indeed modern, times, with a total of 98 pyramids of all sizes being built. [19] That represents a great deal of effort and technical skill by a Bronze Age society; a society that produced the first and yet the finest architects ever known. Was the cult of the pharaoh so strong that in a few centuries Egypt produced such an elite and educated workforce and, simultaneously, the pharaohs commanded such loyalty among their people so as to construct such imposing monuments?

1. Stirlings to Stonehenge

Alternatives

The standard chronology of the pyramids has the Giza plateau somewhat out of place, in the centre of otherwise unimposing edifices. Either the technology of the Egyptians blossomed and quickly faded, or the standard chronology is wrong. An alternative theory, although tentative at this stage, is that the Giza and Dahshur sites were built first, before all of the other pyramids, but with outside assistance. Classical Egyptology also uses this ploy to explain the sudden flowering of a complete civilization, as if from nowhere; this is often explained in terms of a foreign invasion, but without entirely explaining where the invaders came from. Unlike the classical texts, however, I shall attempt to determine the source of the invading culture later in the book.

There then followed a long period of stagnation, during which the lessons of the past era were passed on, but the political and economic climate was such that no advantage could be taken of this knowledge. After many centuries, by the first dynasty, the political and economic climate had improved sufficiently so that the first steps towards an emulation of what was already sitting on the Giza plateau could be taken: the first imitation pyramids. In fits and starts, and with some failures, the Egyptians re-acquired some of their past knowledge, and with the help of Imhotep, the master architect of the third dynasty, they were at last in a position to build the third and fifth dynasty pyramids. The pyramid era lasted for nearly a thousand years, but eventually the economic cost of these constructions became such a burden on the society that even this was eventually abandoned, and subsequent pharaohs diverted their resources into the many fine temples and the tombs around the Valley of the Kings.

A tentative verification of this hypothesis – of there being an earlier date to the construction of the Great Pyramid, in particular – is that this pyramid had ascending shafts inside it. However, the ascending shafts were completely sealed and concealed until the era of Caliph al Ma'mun, in the ninth century AD. Any visitors before that date wishing to imitate the sacred Giza pyramids, would have been presented in each case with a descending passage entering from the north and an enigmatic, empty and – in the case of the Great Pyramid – an unfinished 'tomb' at its base. This is the pattern we see in 'subsequent' pyramids, a descending passage from the north and an empty, sometimes unfinished, tomb. This is just as if they had been copied from the Great Pyramid, as it would have appeared to the priesthood in dynastic times. Only much later in the pyramid era do we find variations on this theme creeping in, like the complicated layouts of Amenemhet III's pyramids.

1. Stirlings to Stonehenge

There is a myth that the pharaoh Khufu was interested in this very subject. He wanted to meet the magician Djedi, as it was rumoured that he knew the secrets of the hidden chambers of the Sanctuary of Thoth. He wanted to copy this plan for his own horizon (pyramid), so he could build a pyramid in the same fashion. The answer was to be found in a secret chest in the Sun-god's temple at Heliopolis, but the secret could only be found by the sons of Khufu. [20] This odd text could be translated as follows:

a.   The king Khufu is wanting to find out the secrets of a pyramid containing secret chambers. The Great Pyramid is the only pyramid that has been found to have contained upper chambers that were concealed in quite such a manner. This would appear, then, to be a tale of the pharaoh Khufu, who is trying to discover the secrets of what is classically ascribed as being his own pyramid!

b.   If, then, the Great Pyramid does not belong to Khufu, and if he or any other pharaoh, having failed to find the secret chambers, nevertheless built a copy of the Great Pyramid as it would have appeared to them, they would have been forced to build a descending passage below the pyramid and an enigmatic empty tomb; the pattern of many subsequent pyramids.

Stonehenge

While my father did not have much time available for archaeological work when I was growing up, there were still the odd shards of pottery hanging around the house and the occasional flint arrowhead, now donated to a local museum. It was fascinating to hold such ancient artifacts in my young fingers; to see the translucent quality of the stone. Had it killed a rabbit? Had it killed a man?

There were also many trips to the favourite sites of Avebury and Stonehenge – and this in the days when we could walk around and touch the stones of Stonehenge. They were magical moments for a child, even if it was difficult at that age to grasp the depth and age of the classical history of these sites. An image of the lumbering children's character 'Stig of the Dump' was something that instantly came to my mind as I ran around the stones, and perhaps that image of a hairy Neanderthal has influenced many of us as to the origins of these monuments. If so, it is a pity and something that has to be dispelled immediately; for these people were nothing like a Neanderthal race, as we shall see.

1. Stirlings to Stonehenge

While it is difficult to compare Stonehenge directly with the pyramids of Egypt, the henges of southern Britain are, nevertheless, a magnificent achievement for the Neolithic era. Stonehenge is the only such structure in the world and Avebury is the largest henge in the world. Stonehenge, in its heyday, comprised a massive ring of 30 sarsen stones, which were capped by a solid ring of lintel stones. This was a tremendous achievement, not only because these huge stones were transported from the Marlborough Downs near Avebury, some 30 km away, but also because of the nature of the stone.

Sarsens are very hard, siliceous, sandstone rocks that formed a layer across the region millions of years ago. That ancient layer of rock had become broken and fragmented with age, but because the sarsen stone is so much harder than the underlying rocks, the remnants lay as individual stones on the surface. Their toughness made them ideal for building, but difficult to work with. Yet they were heavily trimmed and shaped by hand from quite jagged rocks, into the rough ashlars that we see today. So, although most of the stones at Stonehenge look quite rough, there was in fact a lot of work put into each stone. If one looks at the Avebury stones, the difference in quality is easy to see.

Having said that, the Stonehenge designer, whom I shall call Zil (after the king reputed to be buried under the Silbury 'pyramid'), was still being economical with the workload required on the construction project. While walking around the stones, as I did recently one early morning by special invitation, one can actually touch them and feel the difference that the designer has made to them. Where it was really necessary, as on the central three Trilithon stones of the horseshoe-shaped formation, the stones are hammered into quite perfect shape; they even feel quite smooth. Yet other stones, like much of the Sarsen ring, have a very rough finish, and the famous Heelstone is left completely in its natural state.

The designer of Stonehenge was probably just an ordinary individual. Like us, he would naturally want to place the most emphasis and spend the most time on the really important sections of his design. From this simple observation one can say that the Heelstone was not of primary importance to Zil, and this is the first major diversion from the classical theories on this site. We shall see later that it was the Avenue alignment and the Trilithon stones that were most important at Stonehenge, not the Heelstone.

The Sarsen ring was a technical triumph as well as an organizational one. The upright stones all had protrusions on the top and the lintel stones all had matching indentations, so the upper ring had mortice and tenon joints all around the top to stop the lintels from falling off. In addition, the ends of each lintel stone had a similar tongue and groove jointing system with each of its neighbours, so the Sarsen ring would have been locked quite solidly into place. This is quite a concept for the Stone Age and it shows that the normal woodworking techniques of our modern era were well understood, even at this early time. Yet these techniques were applied to the design of Stonehenge, using immense blocks of masonry instead of simple wood.

The central horseshoe configuration – the Trilithon stones – were an even greater triumph. These massive sarsen stones were almost the equal of the largest stones in the Great Pyramid, each weighing nearly 45 tonnes in their trimmed state. The tallest pair are 6.6 m tall, and as one-third of each stone lies under the ground, this would make the total length an enormous 9 m. To place a capstone so carefully on the top of these stones is a remarkable achievement, especially as the resulting layout had to form a mathematical outline at the same time.

The inner circles of bluestones are now quite incomplete but, although they are much smaller than the sarsen stones, their transportation was another marvellous accomplishment. All of these bluestones have come from the Preseli Mountains in Wales, where they naturally lie scattered on the ground. It was thought, at one point, that the great glaciers of the Ice Age may have brought these stones to Wiltshire, but from the lack of any other such fortuitous transportations it has been grudgingly accepted that the feat must have been achieved by man.

This is yet another marvel of Stonehenge. The easiest route to Stonehenge is by boat from the Preseli mountains, all the way around the Cornwall peninsula, up the river Avon by barge, and finally a short overland haul up the Stonehenge Avenue from a landing stage on the river Avon. In support of this hypothesis, the Stonehenge Avenue marches out to the north-east; it then turns to the south and ends on the banks of the river Avon. This journey by boat is at least 650 km, but it is nevertheless easier than the direct overland route from Bristol, which encounters some inconvenient terrain. A recent attempt to duplicate this transportation resulted in ignominious failure, and the stone at the bottom of the Bristol Channel.

This is a staggering distance for such an ancient trade route with such heavy loads, and this journey was completed no less than 80 times, with each stone weighing up to four or five tonnes. One wonders what sort of vessel was used for the transportation of these stones? It would have to be a large and durable boat; one created with a reasonable knowledge of sail and rudder design for such a long sea journey. So what was all this effort in aid of? Why go all the way to Wales for bluestones, when sarsens were freely available only 30 km away? What was in the mind of Zil, the mythical designer? [21]

Archaeologists freely admit that they are at a loss to explain these things. Even Professor Richard Atkinson admits that facts about the site remain few and far between; we can only be vague about Stonehenge's general age. [22] So, not only do the finer details of the classical chronology for the site rest on shaky foundations, but so also do the very basic concepts. Like most archaeological dating, much of the chronology is based on the styles of odd shards of pottery, the shape of some flint and bone implements, and odd pieces of organic material at which attempts have been made at carbon-dating. It does not add up to very much and, as at Giza, we end up with monuments that are devoid of any contemporary inscriptions. They are therefore almost completely devoid of any reliable methods of dating.

We shall look at the question of radiocarbon dating in more detail later, but one of the first investigations of this nature into the site was performed by Dr. J Stone in 1950. This centered on bone remains in the Aubrey holes around the perimeter of the henge, and produced a date of 3400 BC. But, as we shall see, the burials in these holes are most likely to be 'recent' additions to the site. So we come to one of the central problems of archaeology: that is, can any particular artifact be reliably considered to be contemporary to the construction of that monument? Professor Atkinson continued this work in the 1950s, but concentrated on the Bluestone circle which again is a circle that appears to have been disturbed most by subsequent ancient excavations. In this case, most of the datable material from Stonehenge has been found in the areas that are the most disturbed on the site: from the henge ditch, isolated burial graves, and secondary burials in the Aubrey and the 'Y' and 'Z' holes. Any, or all, of this material could therefore be intrusive to the site and not at all indicative of its true age.

The most recent investigations inside the Sarsen circle were in the 1960s. Reading through the reports of the excavations on the site, I was struck by the absolute lack of datable material that has so far been found. I had expected a veritable wealth of organic remains to have been left on the site during its busy construction, yet this was not so. Many of the stones in the Sarsen and Trilithon circles have been excavated and lifted and yet, from all this effort, only four pieces of datable material have been found. [23] All of these artifacts were antler fragments and only one was from a lower strata in the hole. This is quite amazing; it means that on every occasion, the stone-holes must have been cleared of all the wooden props, wooden rollers, antler picks, animal bones and the general detritus that tends to

1. Stirlings to Stonehenge

litter most large building sites. Every sarsen stone was then levered into place and packed tightly with absolutely clean chalk and sarsen chips. The site must have been almost sterile and that *has* to be peculiar. Like Giza, it is apparent that the Stonehenge designer has left very little trace of the original construction era; perhaps this was even deliberate.

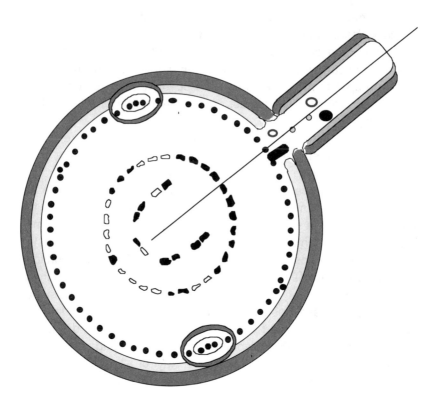

Fig 4.   Stonehenge

Avebury

Avebury is, in contrast to Stonehenge, a great earthwork rather than a great stone monument. The henge lies to the west of Marlborough, in Wiltshire, right next to the source of the sarsen stones. The diameter of the outer ditch is some 430 meters, nearly half a kilometer, which makes the monument large enough to encompass a part of the village of Avebury. If one goes to see the henge today, it is difficult to see the greatness of the achievement of these Neolithic workers, for the ditch has silted up considerably since it was constructed: it was originally some 10 meters deep.

The ditch was made in an ovoid fashion, fatter across the middle (east-west) than it was tall (north-south). This is curious, considering that other henges have been made to be exactly circular. Inside this great ditch, there was arranged an outer circle of 98 large sarsen stones, each stone being left in the natural rough state, exactly as they are to be found scattered across the Marlborough Downs. The ditch has four entrances, aligned roughly to the cardinal points, but rotated slightly in a counter-clockwise fashion. Inside this main circle there are two others: one to the north, one to the south. These are circular and comprise 26 and 29 stones respectively. Inside each of these circles lies a stone formation that has had no known significance up until this time, apart from the usual catch-all phrase of 'sacred stones for religious purposes and sacrifices'. In other words, we do not know their function ... yet.

The henge of Avebury probably stood intact and unmolested for thousands of years, with the local population understanding that the stones were special, even if they did not understand their true function. With the advent of Christianity, however, the new religion felt threatened by the old beliefs and, in order to try to brand the old henges as being undesirable, they were given sinister names: the Devil's Brandirons at Avebury, the Devil's Quoits at Beckhampton, the Devil's Chair for the Portal stones, and the Devil's Den at Clatford.

In the twelfth and thirteenth centuries, the threat of the henge became too obvious, with the new church and priory nestling just under the great ditch, and so the monks, in their wisdom, began vandalizing the site. Groups of locals were organized into work parties; they dug deep pits beside the stones, rolled the stones into them and buried them. The evidence that provided such a sure date was provided by a thirteenth-century skeleton under one of the stones. The stone had apparently rolled prematurely and took revenge on its tormentor by crushing the individual to death. Coins in his pockets placed a firm date on the burying of this stone of between 1320 and 1325.

It was to be the late seventeenth century that proved to be the real downfall of these monuments. New techniques for breaking up these tough stones and a new demand for stone buildings, turned Avebury into a local quarry. More pits were dug, but this time they were filled with combustible materials. The stones were pulled over to the pits and the fires lit. The hot stones were then doused with cold water and struck with hammers until they shattered. It is often only through the discovery of these burning pits that the approximate position of the original stone can be ascertained. In the face of this vandalism, Sir John Lubbock managed to buy part of the site and finally pushed a bill through Parliament to protect these ancient monuments. This was the Ancient Monument Act 1882. Yet public reaction still appeared to be against the act, deriding it as an infringement of the rights of the landowner.

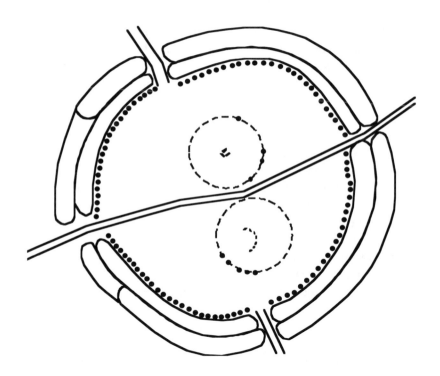

Fig 5. Avebury

There then followed the great excavation of the ditch in 1908-1922, which established the true scale of the earthwork. But still the site lay neglected and, in 1934, it was branded by Alexander Keiller as being the 'national archaeological disgrace of Britain'; much as Stonehenge is today. It was not until 1937 that Keiller finally began the task of restoring the site to its present condition, with heavy machinery being brought in to clear the site of farm buildings and trees. Archaeological excavations of the site only really began in 1939, when the sites of many buried and burned stones were finally located. Apart from some minor diggings in the 1960s, this excavation was the last major investigation into the site.[24]

Newgrange

The last great henge worthy of mention in this section is that of Newgrange, which lies just to the north of Dublin, on the river Boyne. Known locally as Bru na Boinne, or Bru on the Boyne, Newgrange is more like a large burial mound than a henge in the Avebury mould, but it is much more complicated than the simple mounds to be found in Wessex. Uniquely, it has a ring of both standing and recumbent megalithic stones around the perimeter, making it a true henge. Like Stonehenge, the site is surrounded by many Neolithic burial mounds. At first glance, one could easily mistake the area for south-western England.

The ring of recumbent stones at Newgrange is quite reminiscent of the perimeter of Avebury. There are thought to be 98 sarsen stones in the outer Avebury ring, but this number is uncertain as many of the stones are now missing. At Newgrange, there are 97 megalithic stones that encircle the henge, a number that is reasonably certain to be authentic as the stones have been covered by the collapsed barrow material for most of their history. Is this a coincidence? Should both of these henges have had the same number of stones around their perimeters?

A unique feature of Newgrange is the facing of quartz blocks on the southern side, a stone known locally as 'Sun Stone'. It also has a complicated interior of passageways and alcoves, a feature reminiscent of the long barrows of Wessex. The site has been dated as being older than the Wessex barrows under the classical dating system, the date being obtained from some carbonized mortar between the stones and turfs of grass that were used as fill. I shall look at this method of dating in more detail in chapter VII.

The main axis of the Newgrange henge points out towards a solstice sunrise; yet another feature that binds this site to the Wessex monuments. Unlike Stonehenge, however, Newgrange has been designed to receive the first rays of the winter sunrise, not the summer sunrise, but the concepts that are being used here are very much the same. The effect at Newgrange is probably the more spectacular of the two, with the first rays of the winter sunrise penetrating the darkness of the chamber and illuminating the stones for a brief five minutes, before the artificial cavern is returned to darkness once more. This dramatic event only happens on the five shortest days of the year, when the sun rises at its southern-most point in its yearly cycle. [25]

The sites of Wessex and the Boyne are not only similar to each other; it is my opinion that there must have been direct communications between the two locations. Not only is the function of the two sites the same, but the Newgrange henge is also very similar in design to the West Kennet long barrow, which lies immediately to the south of Avebury. Both these monuments consist of a large barrow of earth; both have a main access corridor lined with large standing stones; both have small alcoves off to each side of the corridor; and both have large stones ringing the entrance. The Newgrange site is technically the more advanced construction of the two, but there is no denying the similarity here. The Kennet barrow can easily be seen, in every respect, as a truncated copy of Newgrange.

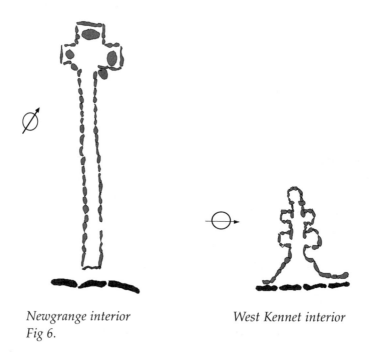

Newgrange interior
Fig 6.   West Kennet interior

Problems

If the two sites are linked, how did this Neolithic communication take place? The rather splendid museum at Newgrange places great emphasis on the Irish coracle for these sea journeys; a coracle being the traditional stick and skin boat used for fishing. It is also proposed that this coracle was used for the transportation of the quartz facing blocks to Newgrange from the Wicklow Mountains that lie to the south of Dublin. Tons of this material were apparently transported up the coast to the Boyne river and eventually to the Newgrange site, a distance of 90 kilometers or so.

This is a very similar scenario to the transportation of the Stonehenge bluestones. Firstly, it should be asked why these ancient designers should have much the same ideas and also why they would want to go to such trouble. Secondly, the proposed vessel for transportation is simply not robust enough. Was all this commercial coastal transportation really undertaken using the humble coracle and an oar? What of these communication links with Britain; did the influential dignitaries of the era really entrust themselves to a crossing of the Irish Sea in such a vessel?

Just as at the Wessex sites, the last major investigation at Newgrange was in the 1960s. Besides these government-sponsored excavations, there have been private studies of all these sites by interested individuals with unorthodox ideas. There have been mathematical investigations by Flinders Petrie; metrological research by Alexander Thom; and astronomical studies by Professor Hawkins, Professor Sir Fred Hoyle and others. But even from the alternative perspective, some of the theories seemed to be rather too contrived and some did not seem to fit at all. There appeared to be something wrong here. It was quite obvious to me that the rationale behind these monuments had to be more meaningful than this, and yet the explanation still had to remain simple in concept.

As I walked around and touched the stones at all of these locations, I could imagine the planning, the effort, the sweat and the tears that were involved in organizing all these people to come to live in the area and to build these great monuments. Looking at the depth of that ditch, the weight of that stone, the distance that it had travelled, there had to be a meaningful reason for it all. Saying that such a construction was merely a religious monument was simply a statement of ignorance; a method of reducing the intellectual workload. The designer knew what he was doing here, so why didn't we? Of course, divining the mind of someone who lived thousands of years ago is not an easy task, but it *will* become possible very shortly.

Chapter II

Overview

The task ahead looked daunting. There was a lot of spadework to be done and, the more material that was searched, the more information seemed to drop out of the equation. Even the nineteenth century books of Flinders Petrie, for instance, had noted that the King's Chamber in the Great Pyramid was constructed in nice round numbers of Thoth cubits (tc).

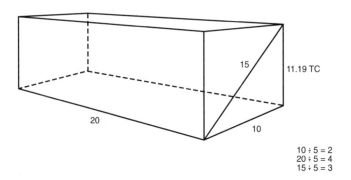

Fig 7. King's Chamber geometry

This was interesting but, for my fertile and slightly technical mind, what was even more interesting was that it had been shown that these even numbers to the dimensions of the chamber could be further reduced by dividing by 5. In doing so, and in a similar fashion to the geometry of the Second Pyramid, another of these unique Pythagorean triangles would pop out of the equation. These are special triangles that do not just happen by chance and their usage directly infers that the maths by which they are determined was understood. In addition, this particular set of measurements formed the most fundamental of all these special triangles. It was fascinating. There was no doubt in my mind that the designer here was playing a little game with the investigators, drawing them deeper and deeper into the plot.

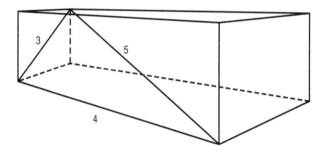

Fig 8   King's Chamber 3-4-5 triangle

What else can this tell us about the motives and reasons for these pyramids' construction? One could speculate once more that this is further evidence that the Giza pyramids were not tombs, for tombs do not need mathematics in such profuse quantities. It would seem to indicate that the designer's intention was something more technical, almost scientific. For a rationalist, a reasonable interpretation would be that this structure was not only a technical masterpiece of engineering, but a technical paper-trail as well. If the designer leaves enough clues around the building that there are mathematical formulae to be found, then someone is bound to sit down with a calculator and derive the function of every last nook and cranny in the whole edifice.

Following in the traditions of the sacred measurement-hunters, I began to research the numerics of the Great Pyramid, but was nevertheless determined to keep the investigation running along rational lines. I was not about to derive the history of the world and predict its future through measurements and maths. It was tedious – boring in places – but every now and then, something would drop out of a calculation that was interesting. The trick was not to believe that every coincidence was a true result. There were many false leads, but finally a picture of a purpose-built mathematical monument began to emerge. The finer detail of who built it and why, was still shrouded in a fog of myth and mystery for the moment; for even if the structure was mathematical and seemed to represent a technical drawing, it still seemed to have no purpose. At this stage in the investigation, the technical drawing made no sense.

Thoth

One fertile area to look at seemed to be wrapped up in the myths surrounding the Egyptian god Thoth, a god often intimately linked with the Great Pyramid. Thoth was the god of education and technology, so perhaps in this case, Thoth could tell us something about why an ancient designer would want to sit down at a desk and design a monument full of maths.

There are two creation myths in Egyptian theology. The more familiar comes from Heliopolis and is concerned with the four offspring of the gods Nut and Geb: Osiris and Seth and their respective sister-wives, Isis and Nephthys. According to the myths, Osiris and Seth engaged in the original 'Cain and Abel' struggle for power, with Seth being a symbol of evil gaining the upper hand, after murdering Osiris and casting him adrift on the Nile. There are various versions as to how Osiris met his end, but the *Pyramid Texts* say Osiris was killed near the banks of the river Nedyet. With the devotion and magic of his wife Isis, the body of Osiris was found at Abydos, entangled in a tree. Isis, through her magic, was able to stimulate the morbid body of Osiris enough to impregnate herself, while Osiris was resurrected from death to become the god of the underworld:

> In Egyptian religion it was not the earthly rule of Osiris that was significant, but the miracle of his resurrection from death, offering the hope of a continuity of existence for everyone in the underworld. [1]

The second creation myth was centered on the town of Hermopolis (Khemnu), the town dedicated to Thoth, and this myth was thought by the priesthood there to have predated the Osiris myth. This myth concerns the eight founding elements of the universe – the Ogdoad – represented by four gods and their sister-wives. The gods were known as Nu, Heh, Kek and Amen, and their wives Naunet, Hauhet, Kauket and Amaunet:

2. Overview

> The myth of creation involving the Ogdoad is almost scientific in its concern with the physical composition of the primaeval matter ... At some point, these entities (the Ogdoad) who comprised the primordial substance, interacted explosively and snapped whatever balanced tensions had contained their elemental powers ... resulting in the Sun. [2]

In a continuation of, or an intrusion into, the original myth, it was Thoth that flew, carrying the cosmic egg to the primeval mound at Hermopolis, from which the Sun was born. It is Thoth who is most central to our story. Thoth was the Moon god with the dual image of the Ibis, husband of Ma'at, the goddess of stability and justice. [3] Thoth was revered by the Egyptians as the inventor of maths, astronomy, and engineering. [4] His skills were portrayed in the following terms:

> ... his great skill in celestial maths, which made proper use of the laws upon which the foundation and maintenance of the Universe rested [5] ... he was the inventor of figures, and of the letters of the alphabet, and the arts of reading and writing. [6]

He was central to Egyptian mythology, and under the Graeco-Roman guise of Hermes Trismegistos (Thoth the three times great), he was said to be the originator of Theosophy, and finally a possible explanation for the Christian Holy Trinity. He was said to have:

> ... understood the mysteries of the heavens, and revealed them by inscribing them in sacred books, which he then hid here on Earth, intending that they should be searched for by future generations, but found only by the full worthy. [7]

Finally, Thoth is also firmly linked to the Great Pyramid, which is sometimes referred to as the sanctuary of Thoth. We know this because the Greeks had a habit of renaming heroes that they had acquired from other nations, and when they did so, they chose equivalent Greek names that had the same meaning (though not necessarily the same vocalization). As Plato says in the dialogue *Critias*:

> ... in case you are surprised at hearing foreigners so often referred to by Greek names. The reason is this. Solon intended to use the story in his own poem. And when, on enquiring about the significance of the names, he learned that the Egyptians had translated the originals

into their own language, he went through the reverse process, and as he learned the meaning of a name he wrote it down in Greek.

So the Greeks were in the habit of renaming characters from other civilizations in the equivalent Greek, if the name had a specific meaning. If not, the name was just transliterated and so kept the same phonetic sounds. When it came to the turn of Thoth, the Greeks renamed him as Hermes and it is quite apparent that they did so as a tribute to his great architectural skills. The root of the name Hermes is the Greek word Herma, which means a pile of stones. Such a name would be quite fitting for the god that was rumoured to have designed the Great Pyramid, which was sometimes referred to as the Sanctuary of Thoth.

Thoth can also be thought of as the founder of the esoteric and arcane 'underground stream', the 'eternal vine'. These are widely used concepts of something passing through the generations and millennia. Thoth is also a global concept, with similar benign educational gods appearing on many continents around the world: Viracocha, Quetzlcoatl and Con Ticci in the Americas, and perhaps even Zil of Silbury in Britain. But what information is supposed to be passed on in this underground stream and by whom?

Thoth is invariably said to be carrying a rod, which was known as the Rod of Argos, to whom it originally belonged. [8] It was either in the form of the Egyptian rod of dominion or shaped like a shepherd's crook, the latter being not only reminiscent of an Egyptian pharaoh's symbol of office, but also the Pope's crook. Since the concept of a sacred measuring pole will become central to the investigations in chapter IV, this is an interesting observation. The eminent Egyptologist, Wallis Budge, observed many years ago that:

> Thoth was called 'Lord of Khemennu ... he who reckons in heaven, the counter of the stars, the enumerator of the Earth and of what is therein, and the measurer of the Earth. [9]

Since the Great Pyramid has often been linked in recent years to the dimensions of the Earth, as a working hypothesis I am going to ignore the pharaoh Khufu in relation to the construction of this pyramid and, instead, ascribe this great edifice to Thoth. Thoth may have been regarded as a god, but perhaps his origins can be considered to be more akin to those of Imhotep, the great architect of the Old Kingdom. Imhotep was not just a competent designer but, like Thoth, he was also later elevated to the status of a god. In removing the pharaoh from the design of this structure, I hope to get away from the idea that this pyramid was designed as a tomb and instead, promote the thought that a great architect may have been playing a few mathematical games. The myths indicate that there was hidden knowledge in Egypt, which was related somehow to the pyramids; namely, the lost books of the great architect, Thoth. This was the basis for the mythical 'Hall of Records' that has been promoted so much as of late, and in effect this is what the search for pyramid mathematics is centered around.

Any transmission route for this secret knowledge or maths is more than likely to have been via the kings and chief priests within each culture, as these were the educated elite of each civilisation in times when education was a rare privilege. In this case, even if these traditions have survived the intervening thousands of years and their degradation through the inevitable 'Chinese whisper' syndrome, we would not necessarily have access to them. They could be there in the background and be the underlying conduit for all these ancient myths, but if that were the case, we may never be any the wiser as to their meaning.

There is, however, an alternative route. If the secrets were partly or wholly encoded within these great monuments, we can use this path instead, bypassing the myths completely. No designer in their right mind would rely on the passage of ephemeral myths for their great secret; in which case, all the information that is required in this quest would have been carved into solid and durable stone. We all now have access to the monuments of Thoth; they are no longer the preserve of the pharaohs and the priesthood. The Great Pyramid is now open to all, and we can wander through the sacred sanctuary of Thoth and see for ourselves this most secret of places. It is through the mathematical conundrums that these monuments contain that we have the possibility of jumping ahead of the priesthood and the kings, and finding out for ourselves what Thoth was trying to tell us. The plot will become much thicker.

Zil's Yard

This chapter started with a brief overview of Thoth because it is devoted to the search for, and understanding of, the measurement systems that the great architect Thoth was possibly responsible for creating. We have already seen evidence for the Thoth cubit in chapter I, but in addition, we shall encounter later in the book the Zil yard and the Quetzl cubit; measurements that, while being of different lengths, all achieve the same goal. The next of these measurements that we should look at is the Zil yard, for if Egypt can have very ancient and accurate measurements, why not ancient Britain as well?

Professor Alexander Thom of Oxford University was on this trail, back in the 1960s. After a long and detailed investigation, he stated that many of the Neolithic sites throughout the country had been designed using what became known as the Megalithic yard (my), as their units of construction; a unit measuring 0.83 m. This was, at first, hotly disputed by the establishment. The first contention was that Professor Thom was a professor of engineering and, as one old sage put it: 'Archaeology should be left to the experts'. [10] Secondly, it was disputed because such a theory led to some very thorny historical questions, such as: How is it that Neolithic man suddenly appears to have had better nationwide organization (in having common metrological standards) than the Saxons and Normans some 3,000 years later? What was the controlling organization that maintained these standards throughout the country; indeed across Europe? Although Professor Thom's thesis has gained more general acceptance in recent years, such awkward questions have not gone away; they have just been quietly shuffled under the table.

The results of Professor Thom's research gave some very good round-figure units for the construction of many of the Neolithic sites of Britain, and Carnac in western France. These round-figure numbers not only seemed to match the circumference of these henges, but also the stone spacings as well. The largest Trilithon stones at Stonehenge, for instance, were 2.5 my wide, a length that became known as a Megalithic rod (mr). The perimeter length of the Sarsen ring at Stonehenge measured 120 my, and since the ring consisted of 30 stones, the average stone spacing was 4 Megalithic yards (my). The theory certainly seemed to have a nice symmetry to it and it does seem to be a real artifact; something that was planned in the layout of these Megalithic sites, especially in the Scottish Highland examples. But, despite the success of the Megalithic yard in many cases, there is a small problem; it does not explain the design of all the Neolithic constructions. Most importantly of all, it does not seem to work for Avebury.

One of the most important spacings on the Avebury site is the inter-stone spacing, especially in the inner circles. Despite the fact that some stones do not conform to this exact spacing length – because the perimeter ditch is not perfectly circular – it has been widely accepted that the distance between each stone center at Avebury was supposed to be 11.04 m or just over 36 ft. [11] Indeed, the more regular spacing of the smaller northern and southern circles at Avebury conform quite precisely to this length. But the Megalithic yard does not fit this length at all; it gives us a rather odd

13.3 my or, when using the rod length, 5.3 mr. Avebury was the biggest henge in Europe, in the world no less, so if the Megalithic measurements do not work here, there must be a flaw in the system. The Megalithic yard cannot be the full story. Perhaps Avebury was built in a different era? Perhaps it used sacred instead of profane measurements?

There are many possibilities, but what would be really satisfying in this case is a new unit length that could not only resolve the Avebury stone separation into whole numbers and, at the same time, somehow form a link between the Megalithic system and the new system. Now that would be more conclusive of a real link between Avebury and Stonehenge. Creating whole numbers at any one site is an easy matter, but fitting that new system of measurements into existing theories and forming a compelling rationale behind that new system is much more difficult. So the task was set, and a lot of skin was worn off the fingertips before a result came into view. Finally, after much juggling of numbers, it was found that there is a good argument to be made that there was, perhaps, a second length in use at these ancient sites – one that I shall call the Zil yard – and this unit measures 1.004 meters. In support of this theory, take a look at the following table of measurements from both the Avebury and the Stonehenge sites:

Item	Zil yard	Zil rod	Meters
Stonehenge			
Upright stone width	2	-	2.07
Distance between them	1	-	1.03
Outer ring perimeter	99	18	99.4
Inner ring perimeter	93.5	17	93.9
Central horseshoe length	24.75	4.5	22.3
Central horseshoe width	16.5	3	16.6
Avebury			
Distance between stones	11	2	11.1
Ditch perimeter	1347.5	245	1350.0
Stones perimeter	1078	196	1082.0 [12]

So despite the success of the Megalithic yard around north-west Europe, suddenly, here is another unit of length that now fits the henges. It not only fits Stonehenge, but fits Avebury as well, especially when looking at the rod lengths in the table. That awkward stone spacing at Avebury is now reduced to just two of the new Zil rods. There are not hundreds of different measurement systems that will fit these stone spacings and it is unlikely that it was just coincidence that made two sets of units fit the Stonehenge

2. Overview

and Avebury data so neatly; this is quite possibly a real unit of measurement. So what has happened here? Were the experts wrong in proposing the Megalithic yard after all that patient and painstaking research work? If so, why was this alternative solution missed?

The answer to all these questions is quite simple. The whole reason that not only the measurement system, but also the entire function of the Avebury site, has remained a secret for so long is that everyone has underestimated the capabilities of the designer. Having found one suitable measurement system, Professor Thom was probably content enough. The lack of continuity at Avebury was probably one of many small problems at the time and so the possible second system went unnoticed. But why did the designer want two different measurement systems? This is not just a case of the different systems being used in different eras, as the Stonehenge data strongly indicates that both systems were in use simultaneously. The Sarsen ring, for instance, is composed of even numbers of units in both of these ancient measurement systems. A possible answer to this is that one system, the Zil system, may have been reserved for the most sacred of sites. The Zil system was a sacred measurement system and we shall see in chapter IV why this is a distinct possibility, as the Egyptians had the same idea.

The theory outlined thus far is that the main units of measurement in use at Avebury, Silbury and also Stonehenge were the Zil yard (zy), measuring some 1.004 meters in length, and its partner the Zil rod (zr) which comprised 5.5 Zil yards. There is some very good justification for saying this:

a.   Take a look again at the data in the table. Firstly, some of the smaller lengths look good in Zil yards at both Avebury and Stonehenge, with nice whole numbers. The worrying aspect is the longer measurements, which look less good. In fact, at first glance some parts of the Zil yard column look very untidy and this is probably why this new Zil system was overlooked in this metrology contest. But one should not give up just because of a little setback like this. It was to be my investigation into the Imperial measurements of Britain that gave the clue to the answer to this problem.

Take a look at the table again. Most of these odd Zil yard lengths are suddenly improved by using the Zil rod, a rod length that uses multiples of 5.5 zy. This is probably another reason why the Zil system was not stumbled upon previously, for nobody thought of translating the resulting yard lengths into larger lengths (rods) by using the rather odd multiple of 5.5. It is not exactly the first multiple that springs to mind when trying to simplify fractions.

b.   However, the 5.5 yard Zil rod has not been dreamed up by me just because it happens to fit the data; it also has some very good historical justification for its existence. The British Imperial rod, which has been in use for hundreds of years in Britain, was also 5.5 yards long, and this is where my solution to the problem originated. Although this Imperial rod was smaller in absolute terms, perhaps this evidence for an ancient 5.5 yard rod is an indication that the British Measurement System has a longer tradition than it has normally been credited with.

It is also not a coincidence that the perimeter of the Great Pyramid is also divisible by this rather odd multiple of 5.5 (1,760 / 5.5 = 320). This unit of length (the rod) is of fundamental importance to this quest and its meaning will become clear in the fullness of time.

c.   The Zil yard length has not been conjured up by the author either; it is a measurement based on the old Saxon yard, which was the same length. Of course, as Stonehenge and Avebury are older than the Saxons, it is the Zil yard that is the original here; the Saxons may have simply inherited it.

d.   Professor Thom, who first proposed the Megalithic yard system, was not too wrong in his calculations either. Firstly, the Megalithic yard does indeed function very well in many locations where the Zil yard does not and, in addition, the Zil yard is related to his Megalithic yard. Thus, it can be seen that 20 my equals 16.5 zy. This may sound like an awkward ratio, but again it simplifies itself if we talk in terms of rod lengths, so in rods the relationship becomes 4 mr equals 3 zr.

For this simple ratio between the Zil and Megalithic systems, I have doubled up the Megalithic rod to 5 yards not 2.5 yards; it makes the ratio simpler. But this is not the only justification for using this length for the Megalithic system; the Saxon rod was also 5 yards in length – 5 Saxon yards. Again, this may be a case of an ancient system that has slipped into more recent usage.

Perhaps it would be unwise at this point to say this is direct proof of what the designer of Avebury and Stonehenge had in mind when he constructed these monuments, but certainly the data looks promising. What is needed is some confirmation that these are the intended measurements for these sites. That will be shown shortly, but firstly it should be asked if this concept of a highly organized Neolithic society, holding and using elaborate measurement, systems is an appropriate one. Were these people as organized as that, or should we stick to the child's 'Stig of the Dump' mentality? This was a troubling notion and one that needed addressing before the research went any further. The simplest way of doing this was to look at the monuments themselves.

If one takes a walk across the plains of Wiltshire, as I have done on many occasions, one is struck not only by the natural beauty of the area in general, but also by the profusion of man-made earthworks – they are everywhere. The Winterbourne Stoke barrows, for instance, hide behind the trees on the eastern side of the Devizes to Salisbury road, just as it passes by Stonehenge. The first thing that struck me as I arrived at the top of the first barrow is that very little has changed here. These are small barrows, only a couple of meters high, but they have withstood the trampling of sheep and the roots of trees for millennia. This is a stable environment that can preserve the signs from the past in perfect condition, if man does not go about deliberately changing it. But to get a better view of the layout of the barrows there is only one choice: go by air.

Historical flight

I set off one autumnal afternoon in a light two-seater with my mother-in-law, Alexandra, on board, and followed the A388 from Ringwood to Salisbury. The wind was blowing furiously from the west and the poor little machine had to fly sideways to the road to have any chance of going in the right direction. As we were bouncing along, my mother-in-law looking surprisingly unfazed by the experience, I had one of those disconcerting moments; a definite feeling that I had been here once before. It was a flashback that was so real it was like going back in time and doing exactly the same journey all over again. It had been a venerable DC3 aircraft the first time; what became known all over the world as the Dakota. We were tasked with taking this majestic 50-year-old beast up to Middle Wallop, near Andover.

Perhaps it was the smells that were the most memorable aspects of that journey: a curious blend of leather, Skydrol hydraulic fluid, and 06A – the alcohol that was poured onto the windscreen to remove ice. It never seemed to do very much to the ice, but it had quite an invigorating effect on the pilots, as most of it seemed to pour in the cracks and onto one's lap: it cleared the nostrils if nothing else. The weather on the first flight was much the same in terms of wind, but on that occasion we were also flying into an approaching warm front that was swinging across the country from the north-west, lowering the cloud base more and more as we proceeded. By Fordingbridge, we were down to 1,000 ft over the ground. The forecast had not indicated that the weather would be as bad as this, but we were quite happy as we could always go up into the clouds and onto instrument flying. However, if we did this the mission was over, as Middle Wallop was a visual airfield only.

I was a mere rookie first officer in those days and tasked with the navigation of the flight. This was not as easy as it may seem because we were down to 500 ft now and the radio navigation aids were not working at that height. We came up to Salisbury well below the height required to transit the town, so we followed the ring road. 'Are you sure that is Salisbury?' asked the captain. It is true that from this perspective, and in the gloom of the mist under the clouds, the town did look not look very familiar; pilots are more used to looking at a view from above than from the side. 'Positive; there is the cathedral', I answered, pointing at the spire, lost in hazy darkness.

The rain had now become persistent, so I opened the valve that controlled the windscreen wipers. They were curious hydraulic contraptions and it was guaranteed that the valve would be stiff and open with a start. There followed a noise reminiscent of a crazed jack-hammer as the poor windscreen wiper blade attempted to thrash itself to death at 3,000 wipes a minute, before I managed to turn down the pressure a little. We peeled off the ring road when we saw the sign indicating the A30 and followed the road towards Andover. The weather was getting serious now; the visibility was poor, the rain continuous, and the ground from just 500 feet looked quite close.

Middle Wallop is an open field with no lights, so finding it would be a problem. I had set the stopwatch at Salisbury, and the next crossroads should come into view in 2 minutes 15 seconds, if my guestimate on the wind speed was correct. Exactly on time it came into view. 'How far now? Are you sure of our position?' The captain was not unduly worried but, at times like this, with the weather closing in around us, it seemed to be taking an age to get anywhere and he was beginning to think we had missed the airfield. 'One minute thirty seconds to go!' I shouted over the roar of the engines and the rain pelting the windscreen. Adding, superfluously, 'I thought they said the weather was supposed to be "fine" here.'

'Ten seconds, five, turn right now! Heading east. If you do not see it within two minutes, we have missed it.' I did not hold out much hope, for this is not how modern aviation operates. We have air-traffic control, navigation aids, lighting systems; it is all relatively easy nowadays. Of course, we learn all about manual operations at pilots' school, but how often does the situation arise where it has to put it into practice? Does it really work? The seconds were ticking by, twenty, thirty, forty ... 'Field in sight, one o'clock low!' We had nearly overflown it and the captain had to throw this queen of the skies into a hard right and left turn to position for a left-hand circuit, and land into wind. It was a long curving left turn and there below was ... Stonehenge, bang on time. The time frame had snapped back into the present and there, spread out below us were the fruits of thousands of years of sacred building projects. They littered the countryside for miles around, like confetti dropped at the church gate.

But perhaps that is a poor analogy, for it is quite apparent that these barrows have been deliberately planned in many cases. There are groups of two and three barrows, and groups of seemingly dozens of barrows. In several places they seem to run in a straight line, like those at Winterbourne Stoke to the west of Stonehenge. Here we have a group of three barrows and then two barrows, all in a straight line. Well, straight except for that little one at the end of the trio.

Indeed, by squinting a little, is that trio of barrows now rather 'Giza-esque' in its layout? We don't want to jump to conclusions here, but at the very least this layout must have been important because, just up the road to the north of Stonehenge, exactly the same layout is used in the Cursus barrows. Indeed, the two layouts even seem to use the same sizes of barrow in the same places: a large barrow, a slightly smaller one, and a little offset one. It is too soon to speculate further on this, but at the very minimum there was a cognitive design here, although perhaps the meaning is uncertain and has been lost in the ancient past. The question is, though, can we bring some of this meaning back by looking at the metrology of these sites?

We flew on to Silbury, situated to the north of Stonehenge. The Sun was autumnal and because of its shallow trajectory, it was setting at a leisurely pace into the south-western horizon. By a stroke of luck, as the Sun started to approach the horizon, it finally appeared from under the layer of medium-level stratus cloud above, instantly throwing the landscape into sharp relief. Every lump and bump in the topography produced its own patch of light and shadow, picking out the contours of the landscape in the finest detail. Avebury was like I had never seen it before, with every facet of its construction laid bare, and the photos – when they were later developed – were to be a revelation. There, off to one side was Silbury, with a shadow much longer than this Wessex pyramid is tall. But the shape of the shadow set me thinking because, being extended like this, it looked to be exactly the same angle as we see at the Great Pyramid at Giza. Is there a connection to be made here?

Chapter III

Pi Gate

Silbury

The question to be answered was obvious: if the mathematical constant Pi was used in the design of the shape of the Great Pyramid, could the dimensions of Silbury be based on Pi in a similar fashion? The Pi value being used at Giza can be derived from the perimeter length for the pyramid of 1,760 tc and the height of 280 tc, and the result is a value for Pi of 3.14286.

The value of 3.14286 is the decimal equivalent of the Pi fraction of 22 : 7 and, while a more accurate figure could have been used in the design, only 22 : 7 would have generated whole-number heights and perimeters for the pyramid being built. Like the jet aircraft designer who was making his aircraft using round numbers, the pyramid designer also liked using round numbers where possible. Therefore, any untidy constants like Pi would have to be rounded slightly, if they were to sit comfortably between whole numbers. The ratio of 22 : 7 is the closest whole-number fraction of Pi and it would seem that this is the Pi ratio that was used in the design of the Great Pyramid.

What would be the result of a similar calculation for the Silbury 'pyramid'? A quick look through the standard texts produced an initial result that seemed a little odd, until it was noticed that the standard diagram in the English Heritage book was drawn at the wrong angle, and the diameter of this pyramid was not 116 m. A further look at some other texts and some large-scale diagrams soon confirmed that the true angle of elevation for Silbury was more like 30° and this did give a Pi correlation. Because of the construction materials used at Silbury, the designer could not possibly match the slope angle of the Giza pyramids; by necessity, the Silbury

3. Pi Gate

'pyramid' had to have a more stable angle. If Pi were used in this design, then perhaps the designer multiplied the standard circle formula by 3.5, instead of the normal 2, to derive a flatter pyramid than Giza; one with slope angles of 30°. If this were the case, the two formulae that govern the slope angles of the Great and Silbury Pyramids would be:

> Great   Perimeter = 2 x Pi x height
> Silbury   Perimeter = 3.5 x Pi x height

This 3.5 Pi ratio to the Silbury 'pyramid' is not simply a figure that I have plucked from the air, it has a specific relationship to the metrology that has already been discussed. The Pi formula used in this calculation can now be simplified down to:

> Silbury   Perimeter = 11 x height

The number 11 is that magic Pi number again; the same number as we saw in the spacing between the Avebury stones. In this case, the Silbury 'pyramid' appears to be a Pi pyramid, just like the Great Pyramid. All of this indicates that there was most probably a precise plan to the Silbury 'pyramid'; they were not just placing blocks one upon another until they ran out of chalk.

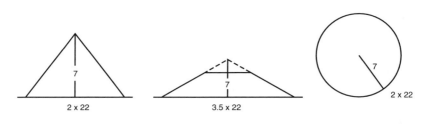

Pi ratio at G.P.   Pi ratio at Silbury   Pi ratio in a circle

Fig 9.

The implications of this were interesting: apart from some stellar alignments and a possible measurement system, nothing much more complex had ever been proposed for the Neolithic sites in Wessex. Perhaps it was too radical to think that the northern Europeans were capable of such feats so long ago. Perhaps nobody had seen any direct evidence previously. Whatever the case, it did seem to be something worth pursuing further.

The flight back south towards Stonehenge was uneventful, although the danger areas were obviously active. There are large no-fly zones over the Salisbury Plains and the army was busy demonstrating why they are there. Puffs of smoke appeared in little groups across the barren landscape, as the tanks pummelled their targets. A lone Hercules transport aircraft wheeled in a tight arc to the south and west of our position. I subconsciously double-checked our own position, making sure we were outside the zone – just in case.

I had intended to fly straight back to Bournemouth but, as we passed Stonehenge, the Sun was playing with the stones and throwing huge shadows out across the ring of the henge. It was interesting to see the henge in such stark relief; all the elements of this great monument that cannot normally be seen were laid plain. There was the earth ring around the stones, with a party of tourists in brightly coloured jackets gathered around the Heelstone. Out to the north-east ran the Avenue, two great tram-lines that marked the equator of the site, and there, nestling just inside the earth ring, were two small barrows that I did not know even existed.

As the aircraft came around again to the west for another photo run, the stones seemed to light up in the dying rays of the Sun. It was quite impressive. Alexandra tapped me on the shoulder and tried to say something. The noise from the engine made communication difficult, but I pulled the headset from one ear and shouted into the wind. 'Помедленнеи пожалуиста' (slowly please). Alexandra was not about to give up, just because of a noisy cockpit. 'Похоже на букву "пее" йз нашего Русского алфавита. Может они говорили по-Русски в то время'. I nodded sagely, not understanding a word. I can understand the basics of the Russian language, but that sounded far too complicated to me. I smiled and pointed in the direction of the south coast. That was real communication – I got the thumbs up and turned for home.

As we drove home, I casually asked my wife what Alexandra had been saying. The answer was to be as profound as it was unexpected. 'She was trying to say that, "It looks like the letter P. Did they speak Russian here?"' I looked blank, not understanding, concentrating on the road ahead. 'The Russian P, like this.' She drew two upright sticks and a cross bar in the condensation on the side window. The penny was beginning to drop: the Russian letter 'P' is the Greek letter 'Π', and Π is the symbol used for the mathematical constant Pi. It was quite obvious that there was much more work to be done here.

3. Pi Gate

Complexities of Pi

The earliest Egyptian records of Pi date from the seventeenth and nineteenth centuries BC. The Ahmes Manuscript at the British Museum, and the Golenishev Papyrus in Moscow, both deal with mathematical formulae.[1] However, the Pi used in these documents does not have a greater accuracy than 3.16, against the accurate figure of 3.1416. The Great Pyramid, however, seems at first sight to be using a Pi value of 3.14286, a much closer figure to Pi than the accepted, and much later, Egyptian value from the manuscripts. Yet the pyramids were, at the minimum estimate, some 1,200 years before this accepted first usage of an Egyptian Pi. How is this to be explained?

The conventional acclaim for the ancient and original discovery of an accurate value for Pi goes to Archimedes, born in Syracuse, Sicily in 280 BC. Archimedes obtained a fractional range of 3.142857 to 3.140845, which straddles the true figure and, without taking anything away from the great philosopher and engineer, he did spend his early years in Egypt and was in correspondence with Conon and Samos of Alexandria.[2] What a pity that we cannot visit that great library of Alexandria and see for ourselves what reference manuscripts were there for Archimedes to browse through. Unfortunately, the early Christians, in their disputes with the Gnostic Christians of Alexandria, destroyed the Mouseion library and the International Sarapeum library at Alexandria in AD 391.[3] The loss of these libraries to the intellectual world was incalculable and it took the best part of 1,000 years to overcome it.

As classical Egyptology finds it so difficult to accept the proposal that the value of Pi was known some 5,000 or more years ago, it has been strongly argued that the figure of Pi in the pyramids was achieved accidentally. This was either as a coincidence or as a result of using a wooden roller to roll out the ground plan of the site. This was because:

> ... the Egyptians had not formed the concept of an isotropic, three-dimensional space, (and) could not measure vertically in the same manner as horizontally.[4]

How anyone can say that the designer of the largest building in the world was unable to understand three dimensions is beyond understanding in itself. Yet this proposal has been made in all seriousness. In order to overcome this strange two-dimensional world in which the ancients apparently lived, they are said to have used a wooden roller to roll out the dimensions of the base of the pyramid.

3. Pi Gate

If one were to measure the height of the pyramid with a rod that measures one cubit: then use a wheel with a diameter of one cubit, and roll out half the number of units along one edge of the pyramid as the pyramid was high: then the distances and angles created by this method would indeed 'accidentally' form a pyramid similar in shape to the Great Pyramid. It would form a pyramid with a ratio of:

2 x Pi x height = circumference.

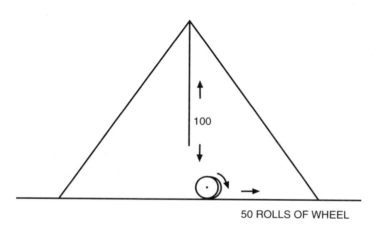

50 ROLLS OF WHEEL

Fig 10. Surveying the pyramid with rollers

A pyramid drawn to these dimensions would indeed have a slope angle of just less than 52°, much the same as the Great Pyramid, so in theory this method could have been used. But there are a number of flaws with this theory, apart from its unnecessary complexity. For instance, how were the plans drawn? With little rollers? Surely no-one would argue that such an elaborate construction as the Great Pyramid was made without a scale drawn plan? And what about Silbury? The roller theory would not work here. While the roller measure has is merits, it will shortly be proved to be fallacious. Both the ancient Britons and the ancient Egyptians did know the value of Pi, and they used and worshipped this natural constant in many locations in their constructions.

Having read of this proposal, however, the first question that came to mind was; why the fuss? What is so wrong with the idea of ancient Egyptians knowing the value of Pi? Why do people get so worked up about what is effectively a basic piece of mathematical knowledge? The

3. Pi Gate

Egyptians were a great nation – a nation that built the only remaining example of the seven wonders of the ancient world; the largest stone building ever constructed in the world to this day. Why shouldn't such a civilisation know something as trivial as Pi?

In addition to this, it is accepted, even in classical history, that Egypt went into a decline after the building of the Giza Pyramids. This fact is graphically demonstrated by the manner in which they either forgot how to, lost the will to, or perhaps even lost the economic ability to build pyramids. Even during the fifth dynasty, while pyramids were still being built, standards had slipped considerably, with mud-brick and rubble pyramids being built. Those marvellous tombs that litter the Valley of the Kings, whilst impressive, did not have one thousandth of the economic cost of manufacture that the Great Pyramid had. Given this decline, it is not hard to imagine that the value of Pi was lost at the same time. Did the Greeks not say that they *rediscovered* Pi from the Egyptians?

Stonehenge

So much for the background information. It appeared to be inconclusive, to say the least. The classical historians seemed to be at pains to say that the ancients did not know of Pi, and yet the Great Pyramid would seem to indicate otherwise. More importantly, what about those great Pi-shaped stones at Stonehenge? Getting access to the Stonehenge site was not easy, as tourists are not allowed inside the stone circle. Special permission can be granted occasionally, for very early visits under supervision.

Unfortunately, the weather was against me this time. In fact, it was rather reminiscent of the flight to Middle Wallop, with low cloud and a light drizzle in the air. The slope down to the office was wet and slippery; there was not a soul around but the office door was open so I made myself comfortable. After a few minutes one of the attendants came back from the site, I gave him my pass, and was led out through the subway to the site itself. Having not been on the site for so many years, I had forgotten what the stones were like up close. A number of them have been pinned together with rods and concreted back into shape, probably during the 1960s' restorations, and the largest of the stones was levered back upright from its drunken position earlier this century.

One thing struck me as being curious: most of the stones are quite rough in their finish and yet they must have been cut or broken into these shapes because they do not exist as neat oblong blocks in their natural state. If one looks at the stones on the Avebury site, one can see the

3. Pi Gate

natural shapes of the slabs there. By what means were these stones cut? For if they were just trimmed by hammer blows from small stones and not cut, there was an awful lot of material to trim off to make these shapes.

The second glaring anomaly was to be seen in the largest group of stones on the site: the two central pillars of the horseshoe formation and their lintel, the largest of the Pi-shaped Trilithon formations. That these two uprights were central to the Stonehenge theology is quite evident by the care with which these particular stones were dressed. They are simply the finest stones on the site, both in their shape and their smoothness. In comparison with the rest of the stones, this group of Trilithons are in a class of their own. The lintel of these two stones is similarly prepared; it has gently rounded sides and ends, in comparison with the other lintels, which are more squared off. This particular lintel is also highly curved to fit the shape of the horseshoe-shaped ring in which it resides (although it now lies on the ground).

Since these three stones have had the most care lavished upon them, it is not unreasonable to say that, quite simply, these are the most important stones on the site. The research seemed to be coming to an inevitable conclusion at this point. The physical shape of these stones was becoming glaringly obvious and now the finish of the stones indicated that it was only this particular group of three stones that were important. The final part of the investigation had to involve the measurements on site. What would these tell us?

It was unfortunate that this set of Trilithons had collapsed but they were the tallest on the site and, as the south-eastern upright had only quite shallow foundations, the formation was lucky to have stood as long as it did. It is strange that the fallen stone was so short and that it was denied proper foundations, but perhaps there is a practical reason for this – maybe a longer, flawless stone was simply not available on the Marlborough Downs. If this was the case, however, it does indicate that the height of the stone above the ground was important, otherwise the whole formation could have been lowered into the ground further to make it more stable. The recumbent Trilithon lying before me was clearly stating that its dimensions were important, and it was for this reason that the designer deprived it of adequate foundations.

But what were the original measurements for the largest of the Trilithon formations? Only now, with the new Zil measuring system for Stonehenge, can it be seen why these three stones were so important; why they were placed in the most central place at Stonehenge; why they were prepared and smoothed with the utmost of care; and why they had to be as high as possible, even if that meant compromising their foundations.

3. Pi Gate

The two upright stones stand some 6.65 m high and since the leaning upright stone was simply tilted back into its socket in the early twentieth century, it is reasonable to assume that this is the original height for this formation. The lintel that was previously in place on the top of the stones, measures some 80 cm thick (top to bottom). The width of each of the upright stones is some 210 cm. The gap between each of the upright stones is difficult to determine exactly, as the fallen stone has twisted slightly while falling, but a figure of just 25 cm would not be far wrong, and this measurement was taken, by me, directly from the stones themselves. We now have a total height of the Trilithon of 7.45 m and a distance between the centers of the two upright stones of about 2.3 m.

So here we seem to have a convincing demonstration as to why there are two measurement systems that coexist on this site. The individual stones themselves measure 8 x 2.5 Megalithic yards, which is enough to convince any normal individual that this is the measurement system that is intended for this site. If, however, we are initiated further into the real secrets of the sacred stones, then the measurement of the two stones together – translated this time into our new set of measurements, Zil yards – start to speak to us in a different language: the stones now say 7.4 x 2.3 zy.

Perhaps that is not too enlightening, for we need to be initiated into making one more leap of faith to see the real meaning in these stones. This leap depends on subdividing the yard unit. When subdividing cubits, from whichever country they originated, traditionally one always divided by six to generate the unit called a palm. This ratio only changed to seven for the magic Royal or Thoth cubit, which comprised seven palms. But in Britain, just to be different, traditionally the yard has always been divided by three to generate the foot. As we have been doing this since the beginning of recorded history in Britain, why can we not assume that the mythical Zil was doing the same? We have already seen that the 5.5 yard British rod seems to work well in the Zil system, so why not the unit of the foot as well?

In support of this idea, we can turn to the Borum Eshøj burial in East Jutland and the Borre Fen tomb in Denmark, where measuring poles were found in both cases. Both of these poles had incised marks on them, which are thought to be spaced out in units of $1/5$ Megalithic yard. However, $1/5$ of a my is not a unit that has any real historical significance, so the meaning of these rods is uncertain. If we were to translate the markings on these measuring rods into Zil units instead, we find that the spacings equate more closely to $1/6$ of a zy.

This unit of measure is much more significant historically, for $1/6$ of a yard is exactly half a foot; half a Zil (or Saxon) foot. It would seem much more likely that these rods were subdivided into Zil rods and they were buried with the deceased because they were sacred.[5] Not only are these burials a good indication of the sacred nature of these measurements, but they also indicate that the Zil foot length may be a real unit of measure. If we are bold enough to employ a unit of the Zil foot (zf) to this sacred formation, then the two pillars of Stonehenge now become:

22 x 7 Zil feet in height and width, or the Pi (Π) fraction.

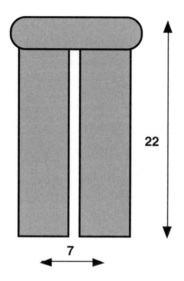

Fig 11.   Stonehenge Trilithons

So here we have good evidence that the ancient Britons knew the value of Pi thousands of years ago and, to preserve it, they built it into their stone temple of Stonehenge; but only for the eyes of the initiated few. It may seem incredible that the design of the symbol for Π is the same now as it was then, but we shall trace a few possible routes for the survival of this ancient tradition shortly. It does seem apparent that the original design for Pi has been sitting on the plains of Salisbury for thousands of years, and half of it still stands there to this day. Stonehenge is so much more than a solar or lunar calendar; it is a mathematical enigma, just as some people have suggested. If we were leaving a message for the future, there would be no point in writing down a sentence: speech changes, languages can be

3. Pi Gate

lost and so will the important message. But mathematical constants will last forever, in any language.

Here at Stonehenge, the message has already lasted for thousands and thousands of years, and this knowledge has been passed down through the generations and the continents. It is on another continent, in Egypt, that we can find further evidence that Pi was derived from the shape of the Trilithon stones at Stonehenge. In Egypt, the entrance to each of the vast temples that litter the east bank of the Nile, which postdate Stonehenge, is in the form of an enormous entrance gate; two massive uprights that taper towards the top, and a lintel between the two, forming a triumphal archway.

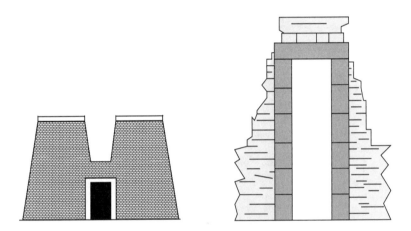

Fig 12. The entrance gate of the Temple of Horus at Edfu (left)
The side-gate from the temple of Karnak (right)

This would seem to be important because this shape is very similar to that of the Stonehenge Trilithon. So, too, are the side gates to the temples, which if anything are closer to the Stonehenge Trilithon layout than the main gate itself; these entrance gates are also made in proportions that are very close to 22 : 7, or Pi. The main gate is also known as a pylon, the word pylon being derived from the Greek piulon, meaning a gateway. So in this case, Pi is not only a letter of the alphabet, it may also mean just what it looks like, a gateway. Perhaps even the word pyramid is derived in a similar fashion.

The trail continues to run its course and we can now follow the route that the Pi symbology travelled on its tortuous path to Greece. It travelled firstly with the great Exodus of the Jewish nation from Egypt to Jerusalem in the fourteenth century BC. There, its sacred credentials were confirmed, as it was placed in a central position at the entrance to the first Temple of Solomon. We can trace the tradition at least this far because an account of it is reported in the Bible. Here, we find a detailed report on the construction of the great temple at Jerusalem and the Bible states quite clearly that at the gates of the Temple of Solomon, there were placed two pillars made of brass, each 18 cubits high; these were known as Jachin and Boaz:

> And King Solomon sent and fetched Hiram out of Tyre. He was a widow's son out of the tribe of Napthtali, and his father was a man of Tyre, a worker in brass ... For he cast two pillars of brass, of eighteen cubits high apiece; and a line of twelve cubits did compass either of them about. [6]

Placed on top of these pillars were two capitals (chapiters), or decorative tops, each being 4 cubits high. It was also reported that there was another set of capitals measuring 5 cubits high, but these were the terrestrial and celestial globes that sat on the very top, just as they still do at the Masonic Grand Lodge Near Holborn in London:

> And the chapiters that were upon the top of the pillars were of lily work in the porch, four cubits. [7]

So the height of the pillars and the capitals on the top was 18 + 4 cubits, or 22 cubits in total. In between the two pillars, on the chapiters, were nets and wreaths of chain work, the length of these nets was:

> seven for the one chapiter, and seven for the other chapiter. [8]

Thus, these nets were 14 cubits long, but they were arranged so that:

> He made the pillars, and two rows round about upon the one network, to cover the chapiters that were upon the top. [9]

The wording here is obscure in places, but it would seem to indicate that the fourteen cubits of netting were wound around the top of the pillars twice. So in this case, the length of the nets between the pillars is seven cubits on either side, and so in turn the distance between the pillars was seven cubits. It is for this reason that these two pillars hold such a central and important role in Masonic theology. Masonry as a society is generally thought to be a secular organization, but it is also one where sacred measurements appear to be central to the theological fringes of the organization.

3. Pi Gate

The Masonic god is known as the Architect of the Universe and so building metaphors are bound to be important in the craft, but when two biblical pillars conveniently spell out the mathematical constant Pi, in the sacred cubit measurements of the Bible, they are bound to become central to the resulting theology. It is, no doubt, for reasons of this nature that prominent people like Sir Isaac Newton were searching for the history of sacred measurement systems, as we shall see in chapter IV. So here we have, in the middle of the Bible, some sacred measurements; we have Pi (Π) written in big letters.

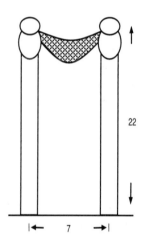

22

|← 7 →|

Fig 13. The Pillars of Solomon

The uprights of the pillars are twenty-two cubits high and the distance between them is seven cubits, and as we have seen, 22 : 7 is the fractional approximation of Pi. As I have indicated before, the only real way of preserving a message in stone is to write it in the only language that never changes, either with time or with distance. Write in mathematics and your message will endure for eternity. Once more we have the constant Pi, written for all to see at the beginning of one of the most published books in the world. This proves that King Solomon knew the value of Pi a long time before the Greeks and so the value of Pi has most certainly been in circulation for longer than we think.

It was to Greece that Pi made its next journey and it was the Greeks who understood the symbolism enough to embody the layout of the stones and the pillars into their alphabet, and so they formed the letter Pi: (Π), which was apparently a late addition to the Greek alphabet. There can be no better illustration of the shape and meaning of the Trilithon stones at Stonehenge, two uprights with a slightly overhanging lintel on the top: that is Π.

Some have argued that the adoption of the Greek symbol Π for Pi was initiated only in 1707 by William Jones, at the founding of the Masonic Grand Lodge in London. But Π has been an important symbol for much longer than this. The Greek alphabet was derived from a northern Semitic script, so we find that the first four letters of the Greek alphabet, in particular, are derived straight from the Semitic alphabet:

Greek: A Alpha   B Beta   Γ Gamma   Δ Delta
Semitic: ¢ Aleph   9 Beth   ¬ Gimel   ∇ Daled. [10]

It can be demonstrated that the transfer of this alphabet was from the Near East to Greece and not vice versa, as the letters themselves tend to have no intrinsic meaning in Greek, but they each have specific meanings in the Semitic languages. This means that Greek was derived from Semitic languages in Palestine and Egypt; indeed, the root of this alphabet appears to be Phoenician. A close cousin of the Greek alphabet still survives in Egypt today in the Coptic language of the Egyptian Christian church.[11] It would appear that the Greek symbol for Pi originated in the Near East and now we can see one possible route through to Greece: via Jerusalem. There is one other possibility though; that it came directly from Britain, but that will be discussed further in chapter VI.

These Pi gateways can either be formed from delicate pillars, like the pillars of Solomon, or from massive stone blocks like Stonehenge. Either way, the symbology between the Pi gateways of Edfu, Stonehenge, Solomon's temple and the letter Pi itself are more than obvious, for there can be no better alphabetic representation of the Trilithon stones at Stonehenge. No doubt this symbolism is already known in some circles, for why else would triumphal archways styled on the letter Pi have been constructed in most of the capitals of the modern world?

Sacred mile

All these investigations are very interesting, but they leave us with a major problem, especially in respect to the Giza site. One of the postulations, contained in earlier books, was that the perimeter of the Great Pyramid was a fractional ratio of the circumference of the Earth, a 43,200 ratio copy to be exact. [12] Yet this pyramid now also appears to be a whole number multiple of the Pi fraction 22 : 7, but these two requirements appear to be mutually exclusive.

While we can get any ratio of the Earth to fit the perimeter length of a given pyramid, it would be very difficult to do this and get whole-number answers for the perimeter length of that pyramid and the ratio itself. Not only do we seem to have whole-number answers on both sides of this conundrum, but now we also appear to have meaningful numbers on both sides as well. The perimeter of the pyramid is a multiple of the Pi ratio 22 : 7, and yet the proposed Earth ratio also has a good rationale underpinning it, as will be shown later. Perhaps, then, our expectations of the 43,200 Earth-to-pyramid ratio concept are wrong. Perhaps we have been chasing a red herring and the Earth-to-pyramid ratio is just coincidence. There is another explanation, however, and we shall come to that soon; meanwhile the 43,200 ratio needs further investigation at this point.

So what is this Earth ratio idea based on? Is it the figure calculated by Graham Hancock for the precession of the equinox? [13] Graham Hancock argues that, with a slight approximation of the precessional drift rate of the Earth's axis to 72 years per degree, two precessional 'months' gives us a total of 4,320 years (72 x 60). What is more, this can be expressed as 43,200. But this is all rather complicated. If we are to believe that this is a real ratio, then there should be an easier answer than this nonsense. Perhaps instead, the ratio could be related to the circumference of the Earth in much the same way as the modern Imperial Nautical mile (inm). The inm is derived by dividing the circumference of the Earth by 360 (degrees), and then dividing again by a further 60 (minutes). Using a figure of 24,873 statute miles for the circumference of the Earth, and dividing by 360 and 60, the result is a figure of 6,080 feet, or one inm.

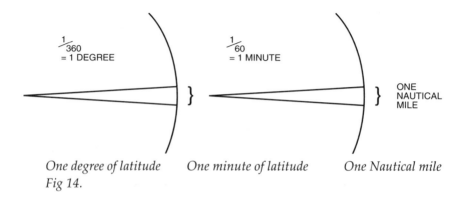

One degree of latitude   One minute of latitude   One Nautical mile
Fig 14.

3. Pi Gate

The modern inm therefore has a ratio to the Earth's circumference of 21,600 – which is derived from the 360 x 60. On the other hand, the Great Pyramid's circumference (the Thoth mile) has a ratio to the Earth of 43,200 – therefore the pyramid ratio of 43,200 is just double the inm ratio of 21,600. The simplest explanation to this peculiar ratio, is that the ratio of 43,200 has been derived in exactly the same way as the inm; except that in the Great Pyramid's version of the Nautical mile, each degree of longitude is subdivided by 120 half-minutes, instead of the normal 60 modern minutes. The new ratio is derived from 360 x 120, which equals 43,200. A neater and simpler answer would be difficult to find.

This does mean that one modern Imperial Nautical mile (inm) is equal to two Thoth miles (tm) and therefore the circumference of the Great Pyramid is $^1/_2$ inm. The reason this has not been highlighted previously is probably twofold. Firstly, the dimensions of the Great Pyramid are not an exact 43,200 ratio to the circumference of the Earth; there is a slight error, so the link is not immediately obvious. Secondly, if the pyramid is measured in yards, again the connection will not be apparent, as Nautical miles are never expressed in yards (it results in an odd fraction), so this number would not be familiar.

However, if this link is real, it does mean that the Egyptians were using 360 degrees to make a circle, as we do today. This is an interesting point, for who devised our worldwide standards, like 360 degrees to the circle, 24 hours to the day, and 60 minutes to the hour or degree? Undoubtedly, the 360 degrees in a circle came from the fact that a year is roughly 360 days long and this was the year length used by the Egyptians; they just included another five festival days at the end of the year to make up the difference. But extrapolating this to the circumference of a circle should not have been derived by a Bronze Age architect imagining the Earth revolving around the Sun every 360 days, as the Heliocentric model of the Solar System was not supposed to have been discovered until Nicolaus Copernicus and the Renaissance. The Bronze Age architect could, however, have watched the monthly rotation of the stars and imagined a 'wheel of stars' rotating around the Earth; a wheel with 360 spokes, one for each day. Even this is quite a concept for the era, but the architect of Giza apparently knew all of these conventions.

Double trouble

We now appear to have a double conundrum. The Pi ratio of the Great Pyramid still appears to be fixed in stone, yet the 43,200 ratio of the Great

3. Pi Gate

Pyramid to the perimeter of the Earth now seems to be even more of an immovable object. Is it possible to make the Thoth measurement systems fit in-between these fixed points and still produce whole numbers? This can be tried over and over again but, using an established measurement system, it is virtually impossible to get whole number-units for the size of a monument and also a whole and meaningful number for the pyramid-to-Earth ratio.

Perhaps a good illustration of the difficulty of forcing two scale systems together is the Imperial Nautical mile itself. The inm is defined as being the distance formed by one minute of arc at the Earth's equator, or $\frac{1}{21,600\text{th}}$ of the Earth's circumference, which is, as a reminder, half of the magic 43,200 ratio. Now the inm is great for navigators travelling around the globe, which is why it was devised in the first place. But because it is an alien unit, derived much later than the rest of the Imperial System, it does not fit into the Imperial measurements at all. The multiples arrived at are 6,076 feet to the Nautical mile and therefore 2,025.3 yards to the mile – not terribly useful. (The UK measure is 6,080 feet, but the Admiralty and International unit is 1,852 m or 6,076 feet!)

This conundrum is being heavily laboured because in many respects it is vitally important. To try to manipulate an established numerical unit to create a monument that can give whole numbers going up to a larger scale, and whole numbers going down to a smaller scale, is nigh on impossible. Indeed, if this were the intention, it would be easier to invent a new system of measurements; that way, the measurements can be adjusted to fit the results that are required.

That is exactly what we can speculate was done in both of these cases. This is why I have named the units the Zil yard and the Thoth cubit, because they were newly devised by Zil and Thoth – the mythical architects of Avebury and Giza – specifically for these projects. Proof of this theory had a long gestation period, but eventually it did surface. Of all places, the evidence for the sacred nature of the Thoth cubit was to be found in the design of the medieval shop frontages of Winchester, England.

Chapter IV

Thoth's Rod

Some basic research was needed into the background of the Egyptian and Imperial measurement systems, for there seemed to be a link here that was definitely worth investigating. The first stop was the county library and the official books of statutes; and what a peculiar maze that turned out to be! The library table soon became covered in volume after volume of arcane laws and regulations regarding the maintenance of our wonderful weights and measures system. Metrology is a little-noticed subject, yet it is one that has affected all our lives in some little way, especially in the Anglo-Saxon world, and often without our even noticing it. There have been many measurement systems around the world and down the ages, and the great tome sitting on the table indicated that the earliest we know of were Egyptian.

Apparently the unit of daily use in Egypt was the Egyptian Short cubit (sc) measuring about 44.9 cm in length. Like most of the cubit measures from the Middle East, this one was subdivided into six palm lengths, each measuring 7.5 cm. Moving on a few thousand years, the Greeks had a measurement known as a foot, which measured just 30 cm in length according to the standard texts; this was subdivided into just four palms. As the normal convention was that 1.5 feet made a cubit, one would suspect that this Greek unit of measure was based on the Egyptian Short cubit. It is simple to check this, because 1.5 Greek feet (at 30 cm to the foot) equals 45 cm, or just about the same as one Egyptian Short cubit. It would appear that the only change here was that the convenient daily-use unit has moved from the cubit in Egypt down to the smaller foot measurement in Greece.[1]

The next question was, if the Greek measurements were based on the Egyptian Short cubit, where does the Thoth cubit, the cubit from the Great Pyramid, fit in to all this? Well, the Thoth cubit is slightly longer than the Short cubit and it seems to be related to it by a factor of 6 : 7. An easier way to envisage this relationship is by saying that the Short cubit has six palms and the Thoth cubit has seven palms; palms of exactly the same length. This is confirmed for us in the book of Ezekiel in the Bible:

The cubit (used for the altar) is a cubit and a hand breadth. [2]

So the cubit being used for the altar in the Temple of Solomon was a Thoth cubit; it was one Short cubit (6 palms) plus one extra palm, making seven palms in all. This, of course, means that all three of these different measurements that we have looked at are related and the easiest way to see the relationship is again through the number of palms in each:

Greek foot	Short cubit	Thoth cubit
4	6	7
30 cm	45 cm	52.5 cm

This is setting a precedent here: it would appear that measurement systems can travel throughout Europe, and in this case they seem to have travelled from Egypt to Greece and Palestine relatively intact. A normal cubit length then – and this applies to many Middle Eastern countries and their respective cubits – was always supposed to be composed of six palms. Yet the number six is quite an unexceptional number. But now we see that the Thoth cubit comes in at seven palms in length and seven is a much more special number in many myths and legends. This, together with the Thoth cubit's intimate connection with the Great Pyramid, is probably part of the reason why the number seven has remained a special number to this day. This unique and sometimes sacred number of seven is not just the luck of the draw in some ancient numeric lottery; there is a good reason why it should be special, a reason that is directly connected with Pi and these ancient monuments, as we shall see.

The palm unit for these cubit measurements was further subdivided into four sub-units and these were known as fingers. Thus, the Short cubit had a total of 24 fingers and the Thoth cubit a total of 28 fingers. The number 24 is again not very special, but we might speculate that the total of 28 fingers to the Thoth cubit was much more so, because it may have evolved directly from the height of the Great Pyramid, which is 280 tc high. Thus, even the finger system of measures, which is a very awkward system to use fractionally, seems to have contained within itself a message about the pyramids.

As the sacred Thoth cubit was demonstrably used in the layout of the

4. Thoth's Rod

sacred temples and pyramids, it is likely that the Thoth cubit was a sacred unit that was primarily used for this purpose, and the Short cubit was a profane derivation of this unit. Since the Thoth cubit was deemed to be 'sacred', it is quite possible that this unit was entrusted to the priesthood for safekeeping and the Short cubit was destined for the everyday usage of the proletariat. The sacred nature of the Thoth cubit is confirmed from an ancient Egyptian text known as *The Story of Setne Khamwas*, who was the fourth son of Ramesses II:

> When you recite the first spell, you will charm the sky, the Earth, the netherworld, the mountains and the waters ... You will discover the fish of the deep, though there are twenty-one <u>sacred cubits</u> of water over them. [3]

The translator, Lichtheim, has noted that 'the sacred cubit appears to have been the Royal cubit (Thoth cubit) of 52.5 cm'. This division of the metrology into sacred and profane units is a similar scenario to the one I have proposed for the Zil measurements in Britain.

The thesis was looking promising at this point; I had a theory of sacred measurement systems being evolved in both Britain and Egypt. In Egypt, the sacred measurements were used on the Great Pyramid and the pyramids at Dahshur. As we shall see shortly, these were sacred monuments and only sacred measurements would be worthy enough for use in their construction. Then suddenly there was a spanner in the works: the other pyramids on the Giza plateau did not agree with the Thoth measurement system. The dimensions of the Second Pyramid and its chamber, for instance, could not be cajoled into nice round or meaningful numbers, so I set about devising other possible cubit lengths for this site.

Trying to find a common multiple for the chamber dimensions was a tedious chore, but eventually a couple of different lengths seemed to fit the bill. Unfortunately, the data given in the reference manuals was given in inches and contained an amount of rounding, so it was not until I was able to measure the Second Pyramid's chamber for myself that the problem could be tackled fully.

However, the measurements I obtained indicated that the chamber was in fact made in Thoth cubits, giving dimensions very close to 27 x 9.55 x 13 tc. (14.1 x 4.99 x 6.83 m). This seemed to indicate that the standard cubit length could be used to explain this chamber's dimensions, but there were two problem with this. Firstly, the chamber width of 9.55 tc was a real odd-number measurement. I had initially suspected that the chamber was 9.5 tc wide, but my laser measuring system indicated it was exactly 9.55 tc,

4. Thoth's Rod

which was a little odd. Secondly, the external dimensions of the pyramid itself did not resolve themselves into whole-number units whatsoever.

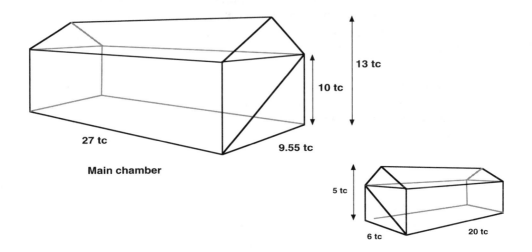

27 tc

Main chamber

9.55 tc

10 tc

13 tc

5 tc

6 tc

20 tc

Fig 15.   Chambers of Second Pyramid in Thoth cubits

While it is possible that the Second Pyramid was not designed to have all its dimensions in whole numbers, bearing in mind the evidence from the Great and Dahshur pyramids that somehow seemed rather unlikely. Every other pyramid that I had looked at appeared to have whole-number exterior lengths and many of them had lengths that were also associated with specific mathematical functions. It would be unusual for a pyramid to be constructed using a unit of length other than the Thoth cubit, but it would be stranger still to be using odd and fractional units for its exterior dimensions. This anomaly remained a mystery for some time, but after many false leads and much perseverance, I decided that the Thoth cubit *was* indeed the length in use in the Second Pyramid. This deduction came about because of an observation by Flinders Petrie, the antiquarian Egyptologist who has guided many of my thoughts.

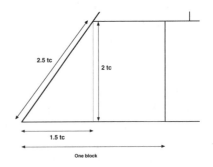

2.5 tc

2 tc

1.5 tc

One block

Fig 16.   Granite base of Second Pyramid.

4. Thoth's Rod

Petrie noticed that the granite casing on the Third Pyramid was an exact $\frac{1}{4}$ of the total height of the pyramid, and used that observation to calculate a more accurate height for this slightly oddly cladded pyramid. Petrie also noticed that the first granite course that forms the base of the Second Pyramid was exactly 2 tc in vertical height. He did not take these observations further and only failed to see the resulting symmetry, I believe, because of a lack of an electronic calculator to speed through the many possible results. [4]

The precise details of the wonderful symmetry in the geometry of the Second and Third Pyramids will have to wait until the sequel to this book – *K2, Quest of the Gods*. But the data there will demonstrate conclusively that all of the pyramids on the Giza plateau used the Thoth cubit: only some of them were more cunning in their design than others.

Imperial units

The measurement system trail now turns to a later era and another empire – Rome. The Romans appear to have taken the Greek foot, or something like it, and subdivided it into 12 units instead of the 16 in the Greek foot. These smaller Roman units were called unciae or ounces or inches: they all mean the same thing. Five of these Roman feet made a pace (a double pace – left foot, right foot and left again). There were 1,000 paces to the mile and therefore 5,000 Roman feet to the Roman mile. Again there is some confusion as to the exact length of the Roman foot, depending on where in the Empire the measurements are taken, but it is in the range of 29.4 to 29.6 cm, a whisker shorter than the Greek foot.

Although these Roman units were imposed on Britain after the Roman invasion in 55 BC, the tenacity of the indigenous units may indicate that these units were supported at the highest levels in the society. We can further infer an ancient lineage to these 'Imperial Measures', as they became known, because they appear to be based on the original Zil yard unit. But the system, as we know, it now has been corrupted by Saxon and Egyptian influences. This then brings us to the British weights and measures battles of the Middle Ages.

There have been several attempts by British monarchs to define a standard unit of measure. Before 1066, there had been some confusion over the length of the foot, yard and rod, due in part to the distinct and separate kingdoms that prevailed in the land tending to use different measurement systems. This was causing strife in the market places, as people could not tell if they were being short-changed by the traders. More importantly, the various kingdoms were finding it difficult to extract the required taxes from the people. Taxes were often paid in kind – in livestock, grain or beer – and this was difficult without standard weights and measures.

Amongst the many units of length in use in late Saxon Britain, there was the Saxon foot, which measures 33.4 cm, and this unit would seem to be a direct descendant of the Zil yard. Three feet normally make a yard and so the Saxon yard equalled 1.002 meters, against the Zil yard of 1.004 m. For longer measurements, the Saxons used a unit of 15 Saxon feet or 5 yards in length, which was known as the rod. This unit is either a simplification of the Zil rod, which comprised $5^{1}/_{2}$ yards, or perhaps it was a derivation from the Megalithic rod, which seems to have comprised 5 yards. Whichever the case, it would appear that the Zil system had survived at least as far as the Saxon invasion of Britain in the fifth century, despite the intervening tribulations of the Roman occupation. [5]

One of the first tables of standardized lengths in Britain was maintained by Edward the Confessor (1042–66), at his capital in Winchester, England. It has been shown from various abbey records in the area, and from measurements of the shop frontages in medieval Winchester, that a shorter foot and yard than the Saxon versions were in use there. This Winchester foot was a close equivalent of the modern Imperial foot. In an attempt to bring some order to this chaos, a statute dated 1196, in the reign of King Richard I, was made. It stated that:

> ... The iron rod of our Lord the King, containeth three feet and no more ... the thirty-sixth part of this yard rightly measured maketh an inch neither more nor less. [6]

Later, there was also a decree of Edward I (1272–1307) in the year 1305. This again commanded:

> Remember the thirty-sixth of the iron Ulna makes one inch. [7]

So despite the supremacy of the 'foot' measurement in domestic life, the standard measure was to be based on the ulna or yard. This was defined as the distance from the fingertips to the breastbone, or ulna as it was known. [8] The 'Iron Ulna' took the form of a real iron pole from which measurements for standardization were taken. The 1305 statute appears to have been another attempt to discontinue the Saxon foot that was still in use in various parts of the country, in favour of a national standardized Winchester (Imperial) foot of 30.5 cm in length.

This was finally achieved by the discontinuation of the Saxon rod of

4. Thoth's Rod

5.0 Saxon yards and its replacement by the new Winchester rod of $5^1/_2$ shorter Winchester yards. Note, however, that the lengths of the victorious Winchester rod and the rival Saxon rod were more or less exactly the same; it was only the lengths of the various sub-units that changed (the feet and the yards):

15.0 Saxon feet   x 33.4 cm   = 501 cm or one Saxon rod.
16.5 Winchester feet   x 30.48 cm = 503 cm or one Winchester rod.

So why did this happen? Why did the metrological system of the country have to be changed back to that very awkward multiple of 16.5 feet or $5^1/_2$ yards to the rod, when the Saxon system was much simpler? It seems to be absolutely nonsensical, until we begin to understand the concept and the power of these measurements. The answer to this conundrum has to be that there has always been an undercurrent of people in the country who feel that the British measurement system, like that of Egypt, is somehow 'sacred'. So, despite the changes that were instituted by the Romans and by the Saxons over a time span of no less than 1,000 years, the system was eventually changed back to the $5^1/_2$ yard rod of the old Zil system.

My research into the chronology of the British measurement systems up until the eleventh century (including the Zil measurements theory), appears to result in a chronology that may flow something like this. The Megalithic yard and its 5 yard rod were the normal profane units in use in ancient Britain. However, the priesthood, perhaps in fear of losing the Zil system altogether, promoted the sacred measurements and so, over the years, the sacred Zil yard and its $5^1/_2$ yard rod started to become more prominent in domestic life. Then came the Saxon invasion of the fifth century. The Saxons, being unimpressed with the sacredness of these units, grew tired of this awkward multiple of $5^1/_2$ yards to the rod and made it just 5 yards instead, the same as the profane Megalithic system.

The result appears to be a set of measurements that resembled the profane Megalithic system, but used the sacred Zil yard instead of the Megalithic yard. However, someone, somewhere, kept the old traditions alive and it is just as well for us that they did, because it has made the deciphering of the Thoth and Zil monuments that much easier. The holders of that tradition, many centuries later, then tried to restore the traditional Zil system of measurements and the $5^1/_2$ yard rod; but by this time there was a problem.

The population was now more settled and structured than before the Roman and Saxon invasions and the all-important land measurements of Britain were now firmly established in the units of the 5 yard Saxon rod. Any change to this rod length would have created chaos in the title deeds and land inheritance across the country. To prevent this, a compromise was reached and the absolute rod length was left the same as before. The only alterations under this new system of measures was to the lengths of the subdivisions, the yard and foot. Once more the rod was divided into $5^1/_2$ yards. It is not surprising, therefore, that any special length of the foot or yard was compromised at this point; some of the sacredness had been lost.

The traditional reasoning behind this change to the rod unit is somewhat obscure, as the new Winchester $5^1/_2$ yard rod did not tie in any better with the 5,000 foot Roman mile then in use. The only change was that the 4,416 Saxon feet in a Roman mile became 4,836 feet to the mile in the new, but smaller, Winchester feet. This clearly indicates that the Roman units were always independent of the local units and probably existed in an uneasy competition with them, each vying for dominance in this metrological battle.

This confused situation was made clearer in 1588, when Queen Elizabeth I increased the Roman or London mile from 5,000 Roman feet to 5,280 Winchester feet. When this length is converted into Winchester yards the result is 1,760 yards, another figure that should stand out as being familiar to our theme. In effect, the Winchester system of measurements had just won over their archenemies and the Roman mile was consigned to the history books. This new Elizabethan length for the mile had apparently been in use in various localities for generations; it just took several centuries to become a statutory definition. The statute was called 'An Acte againste newe Buyldinges', which prohibited the building of new houses within three miles of the gates of the City of London, but it also had the effect of nationalizing the new mile. [9]

So the yard and rod were supreme once more, restored to a place they had occupied perhaps several millennia before; but now they had a new partner, the 1,760 yard mile. This was not the 1,080 yard mile from the Zil system, a length gleaned from the measurement of the perimeter length of the Avebury henge; this was a new import, another sacred unit and this one came direct from Egypt. So, despite the best efforts of the people behind the scenes, the measurement system had been considerably distorted down the centuries and only now was it becoming clear that the British Imperial System is a combination of the Zil and the Thoth systems.

Imperial Giza

I have mentioned the influence of Egypt on the British measurements on a

4. Thoth's Rod

few occasions now, but in what way is the Imperial Measurement System connected with the metrology of Giza? Well, the Imperial yard system is as follows:

5.5	yards	=	1 rod
40	rods	=	1 furlong
8	furlongs	=	1 mile
320	rods	=	1 mile
1,760	yards	=	1 mile

In comparison, if we take the dimensions of the Great Pyramid and divide up the perimeter length of 1,760 tc using the standard British measurement ratios, the fractions of the pyramid become:

Scale	Divisor	Perimeter
Thoth cubits	0	1,760
Thoth rods	5.5	320
Thoth furlongs	40	8
Thoth miles	8	1

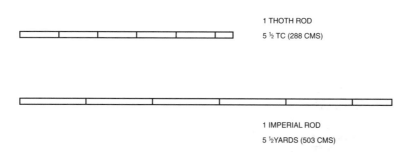

1 THOTH ROD
5 ½ TC (288 CMS)

1 IMPERIAL ROD
5 ½ YARDS (503 CMS)

Fig 17. A Thoth rod and an Imperial rod

Quite obviously, the Thoth mile and the Imperial mile are very similar; they are both 1,760 units in length. With the mile length being a slightly peculiar length that is not a simple multiple of thousands, it is unlikely that this similarity has occurred by chance. Either there was some metrological plagiarism here, or perhaps the two systems have been derived from the same mathematical concept; and as we shall see, that is a distinct possibility. So, the Great Pyramid and the British measurements appear to have been designed using the same ratios. Of course, the absolute measurements are not the same, only the ratios remain; but the fact that these ratios appear to have endured for so long and travelled so far is quite amazing.

Here is something else to consider. Since the Great Pyramid also measures half a Nautical mile around the perimeter, can it be a coincidence that it is now related to both of the British mile measurement systems (both nautical and statute)? Having one of our measurement systems related to the dimensions of the base of the Great Pyramid is interesting, but having two of our mile lengths related to it is very peculiar. Is this likely to be a simple coincidence, or is it more likely to be deliberate manipulation of the British measurement systems by influential people, who believed in the 'sacredness' of certain measurement systems and tried to incorporate them into the British statutes?

Of course, this similarity between the Imperial mile and the perimeter of the Great Pyramid does not, in itself, prove that the Egyptians were using the same subdivisions of rod and furlong. In this case, the next task is to find examples of these multiples in use at Giza. The result did not take long to find, for the rod unit of length does occur in at least two other places in the Great Pyramid, so this reinforces the theory that the two measurement systems are based on the same principles. The more comprehensive evidence for these Imperial ratios being designed into the pyramid is to be found in *K2, Quest of the Gods*:

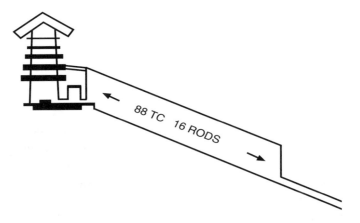

Fig 18.   *Length of the Grand Gallery*
          16 tr, or 88 tc

4. Thoth's Rod

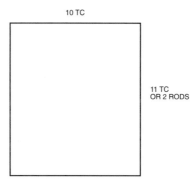

10 TC

11 TC
OR 2 RODS

Fig 19. Length of Queen's Chamber
2 tr, or 11 tc

So if two widely separated cultures have used this type of measurement system, why was this unnecessarily complex system first invented? From the British point of view, these perplexing measurements seemed quite natural; having 14 pounds to the stone and 12 pence to the shilling were just part of the initiation into the culture; no more peculiar than having milk delivered to the doorstep. To the rest of the world, however, it would seem that the figures of 1,760 yards to the mile and $5\frac{1}{2}$ yards to the rod were plucked out of thin air. Even our new link with the Great Pyramid does not obviously explain the fundamental ideas behind these units any more clearly. This mismatch of odd-numbered units in the Imperial System has caused many eminent heads to be scratched over the years. No less an authority than Professor R. Connor, who has been working on weight and measures for more than forty years, says:

> If we look again at the table of length, we might agree that the relation of inches to feet and feet to yard are not unreasonable, nor is that of the relation of rods to furlong to mile, but the entry '$5\frac{1}{2}$ yards = 1 rod' strikes a discordant note. For who in his right mind would establish a table of relationships using fractional parts? ... it can be taken for granted that the table was not set up 'de novo' (as new), but that two or more systems were being fused together to meet the needs of the times. [10]

This is all very logical: the foot and yard were part of one measurement system and the furlong and rod were part of another. Where they met formed that uncomfortable $5\frac{1}{2}$ yards to the rod. But this does not exactly explain all the other odd ratios in the system; for instance, the 320 rods to

4. Thoth's Rod

the mile and the 1,760 yards to the mile. There has to be a simpler and more comprehensive solution than this.

But there is another problem for the professor. As we have seen already, even that rather odd-sounding 5$\frac{1}{2}$ yards to the rod still manages to work quite well throughout the measurement system. The following are parts of the Imperial System expressed in yards and rods, yet both sides of the table are expressed in reasonably simple whole numbers. One has to admit that the whole system does have an underlying symmetry to it:

1,760	yards (1 mile)	divided by 5.5 = 320 rods,
220	yards (1 furlong)	divided by 5.5 = 40 rods,
22	yards (1 chain)	divided by 5.5 = 4 rods,
1	acre = 22 x 220 yds	which is 4 x 40 rods.

The ease with which the 5$\frac{1}{2}$ yard rod fits into the system has been recognized in the expert field as well. Professor Connor continues:

> The pivot of the table of length is the rod. It generates not only the furlong as a unit of length, but also the acre... [11]

But this is a contradiction of the previous statement: the rod unit cannot be both pivotal and the fusion of two different systems.

At last, though, there is a solution to this ancient conundrum. Additionally, it is an answer that is relatively simple, which according to the premise known as Occam's razor, is always the test of a good theory. The solution is that the whole table of units are based on Pi, as I have suggested before. The designer, therefore, had to *establish a table of relationships using fractions* (the awkward 5$\frac{1}{2}$ yard rod) because his starting point was Pi. Pi is not a nice whole number and it is also a fixed constant of nature, so there is not much that can done about its awkward fractional value. The value of Pi cannot be changed; it just has to be circumvented.

The easiest way to circumvent this problem is to use a slightly less fractional equivalent of Pi and the simpler ratio that was chosen for all of these monuments was 22 : 7. The number 22 in this ratio is fundamental to the way in which these systems were designed and, if the number 22 is divided up into simpler and smaller units, something interesting happens. Divide 22 by 2 and it produces the number 11, which is the number used in the Avebury stone spacing and in the Queen's Chamber. Divide by 2 again and the result is now our familiar number 5$\frac{1}{2}$.

There *is* a very simple solution to the peculiarities of the Imperial

4. Thoth's Rod

Measurement System; the peculiar sounding 5½ yard rod length is just a necessary by-product of the starting point for this measurement system, which is Pi. For Pi-based measurements to be resolved into simple multiples of units, we have to use a multiple of 5.5 somewhere in the measurement system. The British Imperial Measurement System was not, therefore, just plucked out of thin air – it was a system based on Pi. This was a system that was made for Avebury, but perhaps slightly corrupted by a system that was made for the Great Pyramid. The use of these measurements is a further proof that the fractional value of Pi was known long ago; long enough to be the founding concept behind this ancient measurement system.

Pi mile

There is one final question to be answered. When making this wonderfully new set of measurements, why would someone want to make them have such an awkward starting point; this odd mile length of 1,760 cubits/yards has still not been explained. Actually, this is probably another result of using Pi-based units; the result of using the 5.5 unit rod that is central to this system. The designer of the Great Pyramid was simply looking for a multiple of the Pi fraction 22 : 7 that would satisfy four requirements:

i)   The first ratio figure had to be a multiple of the number 22
ii)   The second ratio figure had to be a multiple of the number 7
iii)   It would be useful if the chosen ratio could be divided by simple 2s and 4s to fit the simple ancient maths
iv)   The chosen ratio had to produce a cubit/yard length that was small enough to be handled easily in everyday usage.

The following are some of the multiples of 22 : 7 that would have been available to the designer; each of these ratios is just 22 : 7 multiplied by a simple number:

   22:7, 44:14, 154:49, 198:63, 352:112, 638:203, 704:224, **880:280**...

The ratio chosen for the Great Pyramid was simply 880:280, which is a **40**-times multiple of the 22:7 ratio for Pi,

   22 x 40 = 880,   7 x 40 = 280;   ratio = 880:280.
   The circumference of a circle is multiplied by 2   (2 x 880 = 1,760).

4. Thoth's Rod

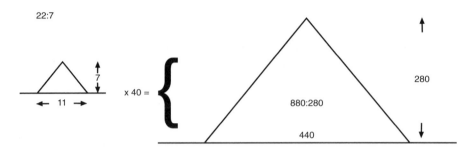

Fig 20.   Great Pyramid, a 40 x copy of 22:7

This just has to be the most logical reason yet given for the mile length in the British Imperial Measures. It is probably for this very reason that the number 40 was remembered as a special number throughout early history, in much the same way as the number 7 is to this day. Accordingly, we find that the flood lasted 40 days,[12] Moses spent 40 days on Mount Sinai,[13] the Israelites wandered 40 years in the wilderness,[14] and Jesus also spent 40 days in the wilderness.[15] Ian Wilson, in the *Exodus Enigma*, says:

> Although the exact reason is unknown, the number 40 seems to have been associated with individuals or whole peoples being put to the test.

Have we not been also put to the test? Can we now say that we are at least some way down the road towards passing that test?

Key to the megaliths

The question remains, however: did these measurements exist in very early history, or were they specifically designed for the megaliths? If so, was this just for convenience or were the Thoth and Zil mile units 'keys' designed simply as an aid to unlock the secrets of these great monuments? It should be obvious by now that these units were a deliberate ploy by the architects, our mythical Zil and Thoth.

This use of Pi in such durable monuments was to show future generations that their civilization knew this 'Secret of the Universe'. Languages may change, but a mathematical message will endure for eternity: Pi is Pi in any language. In addition, in order to decipher these monuments, it is helpful to know that there was a definite plan and to be able to understand the mind of the designer to some degree. With these new units we can do just that; most of the numbers that end in odd fractions can now be disregarded and the nice symmetries of the real conundrums are laid bare for all to see. These Pi-based units were most certainly keys and it is nearly time to turn that key and see for ourselves what lies behind this most secret of doors.

So, the Imperial Measurements are considered by many to be a 'sacred system' of measurements, a fact that has greatly extended the lives of these complicated and outdated metrological systems. Despite the added complexity of the Imperial system in comparison with the more logical Metric system, there is one country in particular that has clung onto these 'sacred' units: the United States. America has even rejected the metric system for space engineering, despite the international nature of the industry, so a sacred measurement system will eventually find its way out into our galaxy. The reason for America's rejection of the metric system has, no doubt, much to do with the Masonic tendencies that are apparent in upper American culture; because this organization is one of the prime supporters of the sacred measurement concept, with the Imperial System being deemed the most sacred of all.

Although these measurement systems have been, and still are, considered by many to be 'sacred', the use of that term has in reality never explained a great deal. What can we possibly mean by 'sacred', when this term is attached to something as mundane as a measurement system? Is it, perhaps, a theological measurement system supplied by the gods? But so what? What, in all seriousness, can be the religious purpose of such a system and why would the gods bother to send it to us? Only now, with our relatively clear picture of the workings of these systems, can we understand what sacred really means in this context. It simply means:

> Please hand these measurements down to future generations, because these measurements will help unlock the secrets of the megalithic monuments and therefore unlock the secrets of the 'gods'.

This tradition has worked just as planned. We have indeed used the sacred measurement keys and we shall now proceed to unlock the secrets of Thoth. Just imagine the designer thinking of this in advance; that if he created an unambiguously new system of measurements this system, or key, would be handed down from generation to generation for thousands of years, with the sole purpose of assisting a distant future generation with decoding the secrets of the Giza plateau and the Wiltshire henges.

4. Thoth's Rod

It is no accident that the author is British; one could debate whether a citizen of central and western Europe, working under the Metric system, would have ever spotted the ratios and links. One has to know the key. However, having said all that, once we have understood and used that key, let us consign it to the history books; put it in a display case in the Science Museum in London to be pampered and polished by the faithful. Our science and engineering will progress so much faster using the metric system.

The concept, however, of such a grand metrological plan simply transcends the ideology and foresight of previous future-thinking regimes, such as the Roman and the British Empires. Perhaps they thought of a 1,000-year reign; this plan is a 10,000-year message. So who was this great individual, this great 'god' of Britain and Egypt; this individual who wanted to announce his presence to men and women across thousands of years? And what was his message?

Game of the gods

The next paragraph is especially for any cricket fans; this sub-theory is that cricket was another key, created especially to unlock the secrets of the pyramids! Seriously though, for someone to transmit a key down the generations, down the millennia, there are only a few ways of doing it. What are constants throughout the ages that can be moulded to hold an oral or written tradition? Religion, weights and measures, astrology, maths; but how about sport?

Cricket, for England, is a fiercely traditional team game; one that is still holding onto its arcane field length of one chain, even though during this time our complete weights and measures system has been changed. The cricket pitch is, as every British schoolboy knows, 22 yards long. So despite the loss of the national weights and measures key, the sport key remains intact and ready to educate the next generation of sacred measurement hunters. Quite an effective key, is it not?

The history of the sport merely indicates that cricket originated, possibly in the thirteenth century, with the first games not being properly recorded until the seventeenth century. The seventeenth century, however, was the era of Mr Edmund Gunter, inventor of the chain system of measurement; a chain being just 1/10th of a furlong (22 yards). So we have a situation here where the introduction of the chain measurement length and the formalization of the rules of cricket appear to be relatively coincident.

While I am not suggesting that cricket is as ancient as the pyramids, this does not preclude a later manipulation, by Mr Gunter, to further seal the key of the Imperial Measurements into history. Many influential people have been sympathetic to this cause and have tried to reinforce the status of the Imperial Measurements, so Mr Gunter is not alone in this type of quest. Other notables include Mr Charles Piazzi Smyth and Sir John Herschel. Both were eminent astronomers and were passionately in favour of the Imperial Measurement System, which was apparently due to some form of Egyptian provenance. Even today, one author on a similar topic states:

> The system of measurement that is by far to be preferred is that which counts in feet and inches rather than in meters. Indeed, adepts in sacred geometry and metrology tend to regard the meter as nothing more than a 'fashionable folly.' [16]

So could cricket be a key to the Great Pyramid – the great mystery running through the history of mankind? People may scoff at this idea, but games have held mysteries before. They are little mysteries that have probably been a part of most of our lives without our even noticing. How about the common deck of cards? It provides an innocent enough game, but perhaps it is another key, this time to the standard calendar. The key to a humble deck of cards is as follows:

Item	Number	Meaning
Number of cards	52	Number of weeks in the year.
Number of cards per suit	13	Number of lunar months.
Number of picture cards	12	Number of months in a year.
Number of suits	4	Number of seasons.
Number of spots	364	Number of days per year.

To the last item, the joker was added; its value was known as 1.234.

Number of spots	365.234	Number of days per year.

Although this is not based on the Egyptian calendar, it is interesting. [17]

Newton

Of course, the possibility still remains that this is all based on some wishful thinking on my part. A temple is located, measured and then the result is subdivided into any measurements that are desired. Using this information, one can now build a convincing theory. But in defence of this idea, it is very difficult to get a 'new measurement system' to fit the facts quite so well. We have seen, in the Thoth measurements, the direct correlation with Pi; and with respect to the interior of the Great Pyramid, we have seen whole-number cubit lengths of 1, 2, 3, 4, 10, 11, 20 and 88 being used. There is one further proof, however, that could verify the theories expanded so far for the Giza site. The following is doubly interesting, firstly because the calculations were performed by Sir Isaac Newton and secondly, because they were done before the Great Pyramid was properly surveyed.

Sir Isaac Newton (1642–1727), physicist and mathematician, had a deep-rooted interest in the pyramids. He also had more than a cursory interest in the units of measurements of all nations, this being based on his desire to find the length of the Sacred cubit, a topic on which he wrote a small booklet. [18] As with the previous historical characters we have looked at, the reasoning behind his need to find the Sacred cubit is not made clear. The unit was purportedly the measurement system used for the biblical Ark of Noah and the Temple of Solomon in Jerusalem and, as will be demonstrated in the book *Tempest & Exodus*, the belief that Noah's Ark was measured in Thoth cubits is perfectly correct. In usual circumstances, this would be of little interest in theology; the measuring systems present in the Bible would only become an issue if one's theology were based more on sacred geometry, rather than Roman dogma.

I had heard of Newton's dissertation and immediately ordered it from the British Library. At great expense, it arrived through the post in photocopy format, a direct reproduction of Newton's original. The text was written in old-fashioned English, with the 's' printed confusingly as an ' f ' in the traditional way. Considering the age of the text, it was interesting to see the level of knowledge that Newton had of the Middle East; Newton's researcher, a Mr Greaves, must have done a sterling job in his field work. When I read through his dissertation, however, it appeared that Newton was working with some disadvantages in his quest. When making his calculations, he would have been unaware of the results we shall find shortly, because of a few minor problems:

a.   Newton made one or two small errors in his dissertation. This is not surprising given that his dissertation is all calculated by hand and all in fractions. With a small pocket calculator and a laptop with editing facilities, one would not be surprised if a month of Newton's work could not be run off on the calculator in an afternoon.

b.   The Great Pyramid was surveyed by John Greaves in 1639, [19] but unfortunately at that time the lower portions of the pyramid were buried under mounds of rubble and sand. The result was that, although his measurements of the chambers and the interior of the pyramid were quite good, the exterior measurements he found were well short of the true figure. Newton could not, therefore, compare his results with the external dimensions of the Great Pyramid.

Newton used these measurements by Greaves to find a cubit length of between 52.33 and 52.39 cm and he named this measurement the Memphis cubit. This compares with our figure of 52.35 cm for the same cubit length, our Thoth cubit. This cubit length was found primarily by the deduction that the King's Chamber is 10 x 20 cubits in size, Newton being credited as the first person in our era to have discovered this. John Greaves, in his travels, also did an exhaustive study of Rome, using small artifacts and temple measurements to find a more accurate figure for the Roman foot. The foot he found, as reported by Newton, was 967/1,000 'English feet' (29.48 cm). Newton also reports the Greek foot at 30.1 cm; these figures are both still widely accepted as being accurate.

Newton's calculations center on the comparison of his alleged Sacred cubit with known units. Looking at the Roman system of measures then, five Roman feet make a Roman pace, as we saw earlier, but Newton also reports that the ancients (Philander, Agricola, Paetus Villalpandus and Snellius) thought that 125 Roman paces made a Greek stadium. In this case, by deduction, there would have been a conversion factor between Rome and Greece, with 625 Roman feet making a Greek stadium against the usual 600 Greek feet to a Greek stadium. Therefore, one Roman mile would equal eight stadia. Newton, only having access to the Greek foot of 30.1 cm, thought that:

> It is probable that the nearest round numbers were used here ... but from the foregoing proportion of the stadium to the milliare (Roman mile), expressed very near the truth in round numbers. [20]

But Newton knew nothing of the Olympic foot; a unit confirmed in metrological circles by the measurement of the Parthenon in Greece and measuring 30.7cm in length. Thus, Newton thought that the conversion factor to Greece and the Greek foot was only an approximation. But knowing that the Greeks had two types of foot measurements, and knowing the size of this second Olympic foot, gives us the advantage. Firstly, calculate the size of the Roman mile (1,474 meters), divide that by 8 and 600 to give the size of the equivalent Greek foot and the answer will be 30.7 cm – the length of an Olympic foot. There *was* a direct correlation between Rome and Greece.

4. Thoth's Rod

Sacred cubit

Newton then goes on to try to prove that the Sacred cubit was a much longer unit of length than the Thoth cubit, but his hypothesis here is on more tenuous ground. Firstly, because it is based on possible misinterpretations of the Bible. Secondly, because Newton's desire to find a very long Sacred cubit perhaps colours his judgement. Had Greaves taken a bumpy coach ride down to Avebury, he would have probably found his longer Sacred cubit waiting patiently there. The Zil yard of Avebury is most probably the longer Sacred cubit. On the other hand, a compelling argument can be made that Newton's explanations tend instead to prove that the Thoth cubit was the Sacred cubit that he was looking for in Palestine, and not some hypothetical longer cubit.

So Newton was looking for a longer cubit than could be found in Egypt. He was put off from viewing the tc as being his Sacred cubit because he thought it was the 'vulgar' or shorter common cubit of the Jews. Newton thought this, despite the fact that there was an even shorter cubit already present in Egypt – the Short cubit. He also disregarded the fact that the Thoth cubit was used extensively in the sacred monuments of Egypt, including the Great Pyramid, which is the most prestigious pyramid in the world. This usage of the tc strongly indicates that if any cubit should be regarded as being part of a sacred measurement system, it should be this one. Newton's theory for a much longer Sacred cubit is as follows:

> a.   The Talmud reports that a man stands 3 cubits high, 4 with his hands outstretched. Newton took this to be a reference to the vulgar, or natural cubit, which he estimated as being between 49 and 59 cm. The natural, or vulgar, cubit is supposed to be the length of the forearm, yet having just 3 forearms' (cubits) length to the height of a man is somewhat out of proportion; 3.5 to 4.0 cubits is more reasonable.
>
> If the Talmudic reference is not to the natural cubit, it is more likely to be talking about a Sacred cubit, and Newton's best guess of 49 to 59 cm per cubit for this Sacred cubit does nicely straddle the figure of 52.35 cm per Thoth cubit. Three cubits measuring just such a length would make a man 157 cm, or 5' 2" tall; not too bad considering the generally smaller stature of people in the past. This has to be a reference to the Thoth cubit.
>
> b.   The Talmud and Josephus say that 4 sacred palm lengths make a Greek cubit, which measures 45 cm in length. Newton

presumed that by multiplying this Greek cubit by 1.5, this would give him the length of a profane cubit at 67.5 cm and, by adding another palm length, a Sacred cubit of 79 cm.

But the statement in the Talmud can be better explained if one surmises that it is actually the Thoth cubit that is being discussed. Four palm lengths are actually the equivalent of one Greek foot (29.9 cm). Perhaps, then, the compiler of the Talmud was confused by the term 'foot' and confused by a peculiar cubit that he had not come across before, which contained more than six palms. In which case, he may have changed the text from 'foot' to read 'cubit', to make more sense of the text. In this case, four Sacred palms would indeed make a Greek cubit (a Greek foot, changed to read cubit).

c. Newton thought the Jews brought the Sacred cubit from Egypt. If the Sacred cubit and the Thoth cubit were one and the same, one would expect this to be just the case, because that is where the Israelite exodus started. [21]

Moses, like Joseph, was one of the most powerful men in Egypt during the Israelite sojourn at Heliopolis. Indeed, he was raised by one of the pharaohs' daughters in the royal court; became a successful military commander who fought a great campaign against the Ethiopians; and was apparently in line to take the kingship. [22] So if there were any secret measurements that happened to be lurking about in the upper echelons of Egyptian society, Moses would have been certain to have known of them.

From there, these measurements could have travelled with the priesthood of the Israelites on the great exodus from Egypt, and eventually into Jerusalem and the Temple of Solomon. It is likely, therefore, that the sacred measurement systems eventually resided with the resulting Jewish nation, just as Newton thought. Indeed, in the book *Jesus, Last of the Pharaohs*, I speculate further that the biblical patriarchs were pharaohs of Egypt themselves. In this case, it would have been axiomatic that they would have known about any sacred measurement systems in Egypt.

But one must ask the question again; how is it possible that the tradition of Thoth's sacred measurement systems have persisted down the ages for so long? Why were so many of the major measurement systems of Europe seemingly based on the dimensions of these ancient monuments? How is it that the Egyptian measurement systems are seemingly based on the circumference of the Earth? What did the ancients really know about the dimensions of the Earth? It cannot be accidental that all these systems are inter-linked in this manner. Is someone playing games with us and with history?

4. Thoth's Rod

Knights of the Round Table

If the theory so far is that the sacred measurements of Egypt were brought to Britain in the distant past, we need to find a possible link between Egypt and Britain that is at least greater than 1,000 years ago. Not only this, we also need a link between the ruling aristocracy of Britain and the pharaohs or priesthood of Egypt. After all, this was supposed to be a sacred measurement system and not something that is likely to have been given to soldiers of the Roman Empire, for instance. So when was there such a link? There is one possible transmission route from Egypt to Britain; one which is shrouded in as much myth and mystery as the measurements themselves. That link is via the Biblical character Joseph of Arimathea and the often-associated and legendary King Arthur and his Knights of the Round Table. The two are often linked, despite the six centuries that apparently separate them.

A part of the enduring Grail romance myths is that Joseph of Arimathea, who was a disciple of Jesus,[23] fled to England just before the Jewish uprising of AD 70 and the eventual sacking of Jerusalem by the Romans. The first part of the myth comes directly from the apocryphal testament of Nicodemus, the publican that befriended Jesus and arranged for his burial; the testament is reproduced in a book printed by Pynson in AD 1520.[24] After Jesus' death, Mary, his mother, is reported to have gone to live with Joseph for some 15 years, until her own demise. Later, Joseph was reportedly the head of a delegation sent to Britain by the apostle Philip; a delegation that comprised just twelve saints, according to William of Malmesbury.[25] They escorted with them the Holy Grail, which was at that time manifest in Mary Magdelene, and also Josephenes, the son of Jesus, although he is often mentioned as being the son of Joseph.

I had been pondering these ancient myths for some time; they were very persistent down the centuries, despite the often cruel persecution by the Catholic church. I had known that the texts placed the exile of the family of Jesus as being initially in southern France, and so I had taken some time off work to research the Languedoc in southern France, which had been quite enjoyable but fruitless. The journey home took me back towards the west, through Bordeaux.

Bordeaux is a typical French town and, like the vast majority, it is still relatively untouched by modern developments in the city center. It has a mixture, typical of these southern towns, of great arrow-straight boulevards and a maze of winding alleyways behind; of exquisite and expensive shops in the main thoroughfares and overt poverty just meters away in the back streets. The town is not overly ancient or historic, but in order to find further information, as always, one heads for the main cathedrals. The tallest spire gave a panoramic view of the city and the river beyond, but gave away very little in the way of information, apart from a few Nazi inscriptions; a testament to a more recent invasion. As is often the case, one has to choose the correct churches and cathedrals to investigate wisely, for they are not all the same.

Around the backstreets, to the south and east of the town, and not far from the river, was a much more interesting church, known as the Eglise Saint-Croix. It was founded by Clovis, one of the Fisher Kings, and St Clothilde, in the sixth century. It was rebuilt in the twelfth century by the Knights Templar. Like most Templar churches, the interior was relatively plain, but the exterior of the church gave away its heritage in no uncertain terms. A large carving of St George and the dragon inside the Vesica Pisces took prime position on the façade; here again was that oval shape that is so important to adepts of sacred geometry. Further inside there were a number of huge, gloomy paintings, one of which appeared to show Jesus being treated for his wounds. Of even more interest were the stained-glass windows, which clearly showed an interesting scene that was not to be found in the Bible.

The pictures told a story of Mary, depicted in blue robes in the traditional manner, fleeing from Israel in a small sailing ship called the 'Mari Stella' or 'Sea Star' and she is quite clearly taking with her a young boy. The scenes fit the myth so closely that they have to be one and the same. Of course, we are talking about the next generation here and the Mary depicted would have been Mary Magdelene, not the mother of Jesus. In the texts, the story continues. They claim that Joseph, Mary and Josephenes landed initially in southern France, with the British delegation (including Josephenes) travelling onwards and arriving at Glastonbury, near Somerset, England, on Easter eve, some 31 years after Jesus's death. This date ties in well with the Jewish rebellion in Israel and the exodus of the many thousands of Jews from their homeland: an ancient ethnic cleansing that eventually formed the Diaspora – the expatriate Jewish population.

The myth continues that, on arrival in Britain, the local king, Arviragus, gave the foreign refugees some land in 'Ynys-Wytrin', a location that also became known as Avalon. This is again traditionally ascribed to the town of Glastonbury. It is here that Joseph is purported to have thrust his staff into the ground, whereupon it started to grow as a white hawthorn tree; a tree that blossoms in January.

Later, on an evangelical mission to North Wales, Joseph and many of his followers were imprisoned by the local king, but Josephenes appealed personally to another king, Mordrayous, to free them. After a few minor battles, the Welsh king was vanquished and Mordrayous took his land and his daughter, Labell. Joseph was released and founded a monastery near Glastonbury, where he was buried. The later kings, Marius and Coillus, gave the monastery further tracts of lands, which became the famous Twelve Hides of Glastonbury. This myth is enshrined in the still famous hymn by William Blake (1757–1827) *Jerusalem*, a hymn that starts with the immortal line:

'And did those feet, in ancient times...'

It is interesting, bearing in mind the line of our enquiry, that William of Malmesbury, in *The Antiquities of Glastonbury,* mentions two tombs that were built alongside the 'Old Church'; the first Christian church in Britain and the Western world. Alongside this ancient wooden church stood two stone pyramids, one 8.5 m high and the other 6 m. William understood them to have been tombs, as he reported a number of inscribed tablets on their sides, bearing the image of a king and the names of various nobles; it is also rumoured that St Patrick of Ireland was buried in one of them.

The source of William's story is uncertain, but among the books said to be available at Glastonbury at this time was *The acts and deeds of St Phagan and St Deruvian*, two second century saints reported by William as visiting Avalon. There was also a historical treatise by Melchin the Avalonian. Whatever his sources, though, one might speculate that it is unlikely that such a report should be fabricated, as the use of two enigmatic pyramids as tombs was quite an unlikely choice of resting place for saints in Celtic Britain.

However, the building of small pyramids as tombs was quite common elsewhere; in Egypt, for example. Deir el Medineh, which is the village of the tomb workers in the Valley of the Kings, has many such monuments, which were built for the tomb workers themselves. There is also a similar monument just outside the walls of Jerusalem, possibly belonging to the Egyptian wife of King Solomon – a pharaoh's daughter.

For this tradition to be transmitted to Britain, however, requires a messenger, and the only visitors in Britain with contacts to Egypt and Africa at the time are traditionally thought to be Roman. Yet apart from the pyramid of Caius Cestius, a wealthy tribune who died in Rome in 12 BC, the Romans are not noted for replicating pyramids around their empire; nor are they known for using the Thoth or Zil systems of measurement. Furthermore, the use of pyramids would have been anathema to the church of Saul. If these tales are true, then, these British pyramids would indicate that the Old Church was inspired by the church of James, not the church of Saul.

4. Thoth's Rod

The Table

The next trip took me to Winchester, a town rather closer to home. It was a long time since I had last visited the town, but the imposing bronze statue of Arthur, King of the Britons, was as impressive as ever at the entrance to the town. The building I had come to see lay behind the civic offices, on the site of the old castle. It was built in the twelfth century and it was originally the largest hall in the castle grounds. By the thirteenth century, it had been completely rebuilt by Henry III under an ambitious programme of reconstructions for the castle.

But luck was to run out for Winchester: the castle suffered widespread damage in a fire in 1302. Royal patronage of the site effectively ceased at that point and the royal apartments fell into disuse. The Great Hall fared slightly better: untouched by the fire, it became the center for legal and administrative functions for the county. The fabric of the castle itself finally came to grief, like so many others in the country, during the English Civil War, when Oliver Cromwell decided to prevent the Royalists from ever using the place again. This destruction all around left the Great Hall somewhat isolated; it was not until after the Restoration that Charles II decided to erect a palace on the site. The palace was never completed and the shell of the building finally burned down in 1894.

Thus, the rather chequered history of the site has effectively meant that all the castle has now been destroyed, apart from this one hall that has somehow sheltered its precious cargo of the Round Table for seven and a half centuries. This famous Round Table, linked in popular myth to King Arthur, was first mentioned in Wace of Jersey's *Roman de Brut* in 1155, and then again in Robert de Barron's poem *Joseph d'Arimathie ou le Roman de l'estoire dou Graal et Merlin.*[26] In this poem, Joseph was commanded to make a table in commemoration of the Last Supper, with one empty place for that of Judas; the empty place was a seat of great peril, to be occupied only by the true searcher of the Grail.[27] Also, in Sir Thomas Malory's *Morte d'Arthur*, when Sir Galahad sees a vision of the Grail, he sees a vision of Joseph of Arimathea standing at an altar.[28] Joseph is clearly being identified with the Knights of the Round Table and with the Grail.

So, could Joseph of Arimathea have brought with him from Israel the sacred measurements of Thoth? We have already noted that Moses could have brought many Egyptian religious influences with him on his flight from Egypt, and we can see direct evidence of many of those influences, even to this day. For instance, Christians around the world still finish all their prayers with an intonement to the Egyptian god, Amen, and the similarity between

4. Thoth's Rod

Thoth, who was known as 'Thoth the three times great', and the Holy Trinity is more than remarkable. Another nice illustration is that the Ark of the Covenant bears more than a passing resemblance to the Ark of Tutankhamen, as can be seen in the colour illustration. So, as an initiate and disciple of Jesus, who was in turn a descendant of the same family as Moses (both were descended from sons of Jacob), it is more than probable that Joseph of Arimathea was well-schooled in all these ancient secret rites, including any sacred measurements.

After the death of Jesus, the fledgling church became split between the fundamentalist Jewish church of James, Jesus' brother, and the new church of Saul (Paul). Saul was a Hellenized Jew from Tarsus; in Turkey, a Talmudic scholar. A fanatic by nature, Saul became a persecutor of the Nazarene church, consenting in the stoning to death of a deacon and:

> making havoc of the church ... committing them to prison. [29]

After a quick conversion on the road to Damascus, Saul set up his own Hellenized version of the Essene church, the new church of Saul. The disciples were amazed and could not believe this sudden transformation in Saul, saying:

> Is not this he, that destroyed them which called on [Jesus'] name ... that he might bring them bound unto the chief priests? [30]

With its new emphasis on salvation from sin, bodily resurrection into an idyllic afterlife, and its more relaxed line on dietary laws and circumcision, the new church of Saul became easily the more popular of the two. Saul exulted faith, while all James had to offer was the old Jewish tenet of adherence to the law. The popularity of the new church of Saul caused a certain amount of friction between the two sects, with James calling Saul 'the Liar', and saying that Saul:

> ... led many astray, and raised a congregation on deceit. [31]

Eventually, however, after striking a deal with the Roman Emperor Constantine I at the Council of Nicaea in AD 325, the church of Saul became the church of Rome, while the church of James and Jesus sank into obscurity. The identification of Saul in the historical record is given in the book *Jesus, Last of the Pharaohs*.

Even though the church of Saul was altered to suit a more Romanized way of life, the new religion was by no means initially acceptable to Rome, because it still contained fringe elements of the Jewish independence movements. So, especially after the sacking of Jerusalem by the Romans, as a Jewish refugee of whichever sect, the safer countries to flee to would be on the fringes of the Roman Empire. The far west of remote Britain would indeed be a suitable location and so, the Jewish family of Jesus emigrated from their homeland.

If Joseph did visit Britain back in the Roman era, he could easily have brought with him the secrets of the Essene church. It would be difficult, and perhaps under the circumstances not a priority, to bring a sacred measuring rod, but how much easier it would be to bring the sacred ratios of the Thoth measurement system: a system that was integrated with the similar Zil system of Britain to produce measurements that were used down the ages among the faithful, and were finally enshrined in the official statutes of the then English capital city of Winchester.

There remains, however, the slimmest of possibilities that Joseph did have time to bring with him that sacred measuring rod, and the evidence for this has come to us from none other than Adolf Hitler. So we jump forward in time to the end of that great conflict of nations. It is an established fact that the last U-boat to leave Germany at the end of the Second World War was U534, which left Kiel on 2 May, 1945. This last-minute sailing of U534 has often attracted the speculation that this was a special mission to take valuable contraband out of the ruins of the Third Reich to safer pastures in South America. Among the normal items rumoured to be aboard such vessels, like gold bullion to provide some much-needed collateral, there was also thought to be some more sacred cargo, the Spear of Destiny. [32]

For over a thousand years, the Spear of Destiny (the Spear of Longinus) has confounded historians. It is reputed to have been the spear that pierced the side of Jesus while on the cross, and it was said to have been transported to Europe by Joseph. Whether Hitler obtained the 'original' in his pillage of Austria, or one of the many copies, is uncertain. However, one thing is certain: here is an established tradition of a sacred rod being associated with Joseph of Arimathea.

Whether this rod is a real artifact or not, is somewhat immaterial; the tradition itself is a good enough indication that a sacred rod existed somewhere, at some time. Instead, the important speculation in this context is: was this rumour about a spear or was it a sacred measuring rod, like those found in the Danish burials mentioned earlier? The accounts of the first century historian Josephus, who wrote an entire history of the Old Testament, strongly suggests that this pole most probably resembled a rod and not a spear. In his *Antiquities of the Jews*, Josephus claims that each of the twelve tribes of Israel held a sacred rod:

4. *Thoth's Rod*

(Moses) desired the heads of the tribes to bring their rods, with the names of their tribes inscribed upon them ... These rods Moses laid up in the Tabernacle of God.[33]

The rods were being used by Moses to decide which of the twelve tribes would control the priesthood of Israel; it was said that the rod of the chosen tribe would start to grow. Here, then, is an ancient tradition of sacred rods being associated with the Israelite priesthood, which suggests that if there are any ancient rods from the time of the Jewish Exodus from Israel still in circulation, they are less likely to have been spears and more likely to have been wooden rods (made of almond wood, apparently). Whether these sacred rods were used for measuring or not is not reported, but given the Bible's obsession with the precise cubit measurements of the Ark, Tabernacle and Temple, this is not an unreasonable assumption.

U534 now lies in a museum in Birkenhead, in Britain, and while it is very interesting to look around the rusting hulk as a tourist, it has not yielded any secrets so far. Meanwhile, another spear was found after the war and returned to the Hofburg Museum in Vienna, so this is just one more branch of the mystery that will have to remain as speculation.

Zil's Table

At last, we come back to those enigmatic pyramids at Glastonbury. The tradition of these pyramidal tombs could just as easily have been transmitted from Egypt to Israel by Moses, and from Israel to Britain by Joseph. So the presence of two pyramidal tombs on British soil does have a tentative explanation. One imagines that all this is something that will have to be left to speculation, but it is fitting as a penultimate thought in this section that an ancient round table, feted as being based on the original, is still hanging on a wall in that fortunate Great Hall at Winchester, despite all the destruction that has gone on around it. In fact, it is believed to have been made inside the Great Hall, as it is larger than the doors of the hall. Made of solid oak from seven different trees, it weighs some 1.3 tonnes and measures 5.55 meters in diameter. The table has recently been dated, from its tree rings, as being made in about 1290, in the reign of Edward I.[34]

Myth starts to gel into something more tangible when we find that one of the 25 knights named on the rim of the table is called 'Lybyus Disconyus' or Le Beau Disconnu, the Handsome Stranger.[35] Is this not a reference to the perilous seat of Judas, to be used only by the true searcher of the Grail? The artwork on the table is sixteenth century, but it is widely thought to be based on earlier inscriptions. The current layout of the table indicates that there were places for 25 knights, with the primary position being set aside for King Arthur; who is drawn in this case in the image of Henry VIII. The back of the table, however, indicates that there were originally only 12 or 24 seating places, not 25, as this is how the table legs are arranged. The back of the table and the locations for the legs clearly indicate that this was built as a table, and so it must have become a wall decoration only in more recent times. Certainly it had moved from floor to wall by the opening of the English Civil War, as it was used as a dartboard by the musketeers of Cromwell, who peppered it with shot.

Now we come to the core of this piece of the investigation, because this ancient table is very interesting in respect of the new proposed measurement system for Neolithic Britain, the Zil system. Again, it was one of those moments when I was browsing the relevant documents and suddenly, something leapt off the page. At the time I was sitting on the floor of the Great Hall itself, as there is precious little seating inside, with the great but largely modern roof soaring above me and the table itself at the far end of the Hall. My daughter, just eighteen months old at the time, was toddling around the interior, testing the strength of the echo she could make. As was her way, she finally found a soft-hearted tourist to talk to and was busy trying to explain her many varied thoughts in a babble of baby language. The bemused tourist squatted down and started a long unfathomable conversation. Suddenly my attention was distracted, because here in the guide it stated that the diameter of the table was 5.55 meters. But this was rather interesting because when this figure is translated into Zil yards, it becomes exactly $5^1/_2$ Zil yards, or exactly one Zil rod in length.

In 'modern' times, that is, anything since the Roman occupation, this Zil unit of length is unheard of. The normal Saxon rod or Winchester rod of that era measured just 5.03 meters, or 5 Zil yards, not the $5^1/_2$ Zil yards of the original system. Coincidence aside, it would appear that here in the Winchester Great Hall, we have a copy of the original Zil standard measure, that has somehow withstood all the changes in the British metrology that have been going on all around it. How has this happened? Such a coincidence requires an equally dramatic theory to account for it; one that was composed there and then on the floor of the Great Hall.

What was needed here was a method of explaining how the Zil system of measurements, that $5^1/_2$ yard Zil rod that measures 5.53 meters, found its way back into the design of the Round Table, long after the Saxons and Romans had changed the metrological systems of the land into Saxon and Winchester rods. As the Round Table could be considered to be a sacred object in some esoteric quarters, the evolving theory could go something like this. After the construction of the Wiltshire monuments, the mythical King Zil also started the tradition of the sacred table. The table was round, just like Stonehenge, and it was designed so that it held within its dimensions the sacred measurements of the Zil rod. Knowing the importance of this table, the design has been copied through successive tables across the millennia, into the table that we see today. As each table could easily last 2,000 years, only a few copies need have been made, even in this long history. And so in this way the original units of Zil have been preserved down through the ages.

Such a theory may sound far-fetched, but there is one more thought on this subject that might just persuade the skeptics. If the table was really designed in Zil units, it would measure exactly one Zil rod ($5^1/_2$ yards) in diameter. If we multiply this diameter by Pi, we find that the table must have measured just over 17 Zil yards around the perimeter, which is exactly what it does. So far, so good. Now if those Zil yard measurements were each subdivided into 3 Zil feet, as we proposed in chapter III, then the perimeter of the table would measure just over 51 Zil feet. In turn, it is interesting that the table was originally manufactured from a total of 51 wedge-shaped segments of solid oak. [36] Being of Medieval construction, the segments themselves are not of even measurements, but this is still an interesting observation.

I gathered up my young charge and thanked the kind tourist, although in reality I think she was being entertained more than doing the entertaining. Strolling out into the bright sunlight of a fine afternoon, I contemplated the implications of this research. For one thing, if it was now understood there was a new chronology for the formation of these measurement systems, it seemed that some of the classical ideas on the chronology of the pyramids could be overturned.

Dating the pyramids

From the arguments outlined previously, it is reasonable to assume that the new measurement systems and the Giza Plateau were planned and constructed coincidentally. One was created specifically for the other. It follows, therefore, that the Thoth monuments must predate any structure that uses any of the Thoth measurement systems. In Egypt, for example, if we can find any first, second, third or early fourth dynasty structures using the Thoth system of measurements, then the established chronology given for these monuments are incorrect.

4. Thoth's Rod

So, is it possible to find such evidence of structures using the Thoth cubit before the building of the Great Pyramid? Yes indeed. The Pyramids of Dahshur and Meidum are traditionally ascribed to the early fourth dynasty pharaoh Snorferu, the father of Khufu, yet the pyramids ascribed to him appear to be built using the tc unit of measurement. Some of the measurements at Dahshur, and also at Meidum, are as follows:

Pyramid of Meidum:	Lengths (tc)		
Inclined entrance corridor length	110		
Level section of corridor	18		
2 x recesses in corridor	5		
Chamber width	5		
Causeway	410		
Bent Pyramid:			
Northern inclined entrance corridor	140		
Lower chamber	12	x	9.5
External base length	360	x	360
Valley temple	50	x	90
Red Pyramid:			
First two chambers	16	x	7
Third chamber	16	x	8
External base length	420	x	420
Height	200		

The figures given by the reference sources, although not as accurate as the data accumulated at Giza, are nevertheless compelling. The data for the Red Pyramid (without rounding), for instance, is base length 420.4 tc, height 199.7 tc. [37] These figures are quite accurate enough to be rounded to 420 tc and 200 tc with some confidence. Another reason for rounding with even greater confidence is the resulting geometry of these pyramids, for the outline of the Red Pyramid, in particular, is exactly the same as the Pythagorean triangle of 20 - 21 - 29. The Second Pyramid was also designed according to the angles obtained in a Pythagorean triangle, but there the base lengths involved did not seem to mimic the special Pythagorean numbers. With the Red Pyramid, however, the cubit lengths of the pyramid's dimensions mirror the Pythagorean triangle's numbers exactly, so the design specification for this pyramid is obvious.

It would appear, then, that the Pythagorean triangle was being used in this instance and to a high level of accuracy. But, in the light of the

4. Thoth's Rod

previous evidence, the use of the Thoth cubit in the Meidum and Dahshur pyramids firmly places the construction of these pyramids to a time at least after the designs for the Great Pyramid were drawn up. I shall attempt to demonstrate in chapter VI that the Dahshur pyramids were actually constructed coincidentally with the Giza site, for they are part of the same plan.

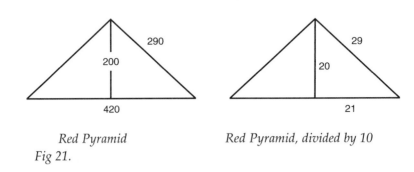

Red Pyramid   *Red Pyramid, divided by 10*

Fig 21.

So where does this leave this investigation? There seems to be an emerging scenario of an ancient plan here and, if someone were going to make such a plan, one of the first things he or she would need is a set of measurements. Now we can see direct evidence of these ancient measurement systems, ones that were based on complex mathematical principles. But having created these measurement systems, what is our mysterious designer going to draw with them? The first thing to be found was the symbol Pi, itself on the Stonehenge site, so we are looking at mathematics again. The only other evidence to be seen so far is a series of henges and pyramids, for which a number of possible solar and stellar alignments have been proposed.

But is this enough? There has already been plenty of evidence to indicate quite clearly that the technology being used here is well above that traditionally ascribed to these ancient civilizations. If we, as a technical civilization, wanted to build a great monument, would we stop at a mere solar alignment? Of course not, so is it not about time that we opened our eyes to the full range of possibilities that the designer had at his disposal? In the next chapter, our eyes *will* be opened.

Chapter V

Henge of the World

In every project, big or small, there are always the one or two make-or-break moments. The question was, should I proceed to pour in good money and precious time, again and again, or should I quit while the going was good? I could always say I had done my best; that it had been a fun hobby; that it was not something that I really wished to take too far; that it was time to retire gracefully before people thought that I was becoming too obsessed with the subject. Such ideas were beginning to look tempting; the subject matter was interesting so far, but it would hardly set the world alight in literary terms. Fate seems to demand these moments of self-doubt from us, before letting us proceed further. It seems to delight in testing our resolve and commitment. If one is persistent, though, sometimes fate will reward us and something new and exciting will land on the doorstep. There again, it may be just the result of determined hard graft.

Whatever the case, a package containing photographs arrived one morning. They were the results from the flying expedition a few weeks earlier and I was pleased to see that they had all turned out quite well. The shots of Stonehenge and Silbury were quite straightforward and the shadow formations did make them look quite interesting, but it was the picture of Avebury that stood out. I had not seen it while we were flying above, perhaps I had been too busy flying the aircraft and taking the shots out of the window. But here in the quiet of my office, something peculiar stood out from the pictures in my hand, like that strange face on the surface of the planet Mars must have stood out to Tobias Owen of NASA, in 1976.[1]

I knew then what Avebury was and, if the hunch was correct, the data would fit into place like a well-worn glove. I suppose I was optimistic that the data would fit the theory, but I was to be staggered when I saw how far this quest could actually be taken; the data and ideas just kept coming and coming. There was no longer any doubt about the role of Avebury, or the future of this research, for that matter. There was now going to be a book on the subject; whatever the steps necessary to produce it, there would be a book. Little did I realize at this stage, however, the twists and turns that would litter the road until its eventual publication. Discovering the truth about Avebury was to be minor part of the unfolding saga, but at least it became a major part of the book.

Here is that most central part of this lateral look at the history of mankind: the true function of one of the great henges of Wiltshire, the Avebury henge. This was never going to be a chapter that would leave the reader hanging at the end without a real answer, as is the case in so many other disappointing works; a chapter ending with some sort of catch-all phrase like 'it is a sacred circle'. No, as one of the biggest skeptics on the theory of an ancient technical civilization, I was immensely excited by this chapter. I think, therefore, it will probably persuade many of the people who read it of the true nature of this great henge. More than that though, anyone who is ultimately persuaded by the concepts of this chapter will, by necessity, have their ideas of British and world history changed forever. This is a bold statement to make in any book, but one that will be supported by the text to the satisfaction of many.

Scanning through the classical theories behind the construction and usage of this great henge, I was struck by the banal repetitions of primitive ideas and explanations of Neolithic life. Yet it is these learned opinions of the henges that have clouded our perceptions ever since. We are guided once more by those images of the hairy Neanderthal in the children's book *Stig of the Dump*. Take a look at the following example of the generalizations that we are fed about Neolithic festivals. Alongside this, it is inferred that this was the total social and intellectual capability of these Neolithic peoples:

> At Avebury the irregular shape of the off-center inner circles seems to have little relation to any calendrical or astronomical orientation. Stukeley, speculating in the 1720s, suggested that the northern inner circle was dedicated to the moon and the southern circle to the sun ... The role played by the circles at Avebury, [were probably for] ceremonial and ritual events. Festivals, perhaps, marking the changing seasons ... and that the upright stones of the circles were said to worship the earth gods, and formed an arena within which sacrifices were offered to ensure good weather and harvests,

perhaps to ensure fertility within the population as well ... The Obelisk has been interpreted as a phallic symbol, and therefore associated with fertility.

The high banks all round would have acted as a stadium, and people perhaps crowded onto them to gain a better view of the ceremonies within the circle. Possibly, only certain people were allowed inside, the chiefs, elders, and wise men who conducted the ceremonies. Young people undergoing special initiation rites, pregnant women wanting to make offerings to the fertility gods. Chanting, special dances, drums and musical instruments would have accompanied the rituals.

Animals may have been slaughtered, and perhaps their blood would have been poured over particular stones, dedicated to the gods with various powers. Harvest products could have been arranged around the stones, to the chanted words of an elder; and natural signs such as the wind, the sun, moon, stars and birds observed, in the hope of guaranteeing a propitious future harvest.' [2]

The type of portrayal above may be quite familiar, but it has been reproduced in full to illustrate a point. Why are we so comfortable with these images of Avebury and Neolithic life in general? Is it because these images are so alien to our modern culture that we can partition this era off; consign it to a barbarous past that has nothing to do with our modern lives? I suspect that this is part of the attraction. I would even go further and say that there are organizations in this world that would like to keep this idea going indefinitely, to keep us misinformed of our past. But hold on a minute; let's look at the text a little more closely. If we read again the last section, the one on the harvest:

> Harvest products could have been arranged around the stones, to the chanted words of an elder ... in the hope of guaranteeing a propitious future harvest.

In other words, a Christian harvest festival celebration: have we really come so far from these Neolithic times? If we can still act like Stone Age man in some of our own ceremonies, could Stone Age man not act just like us, and have some of the same ideas and beliefs? This may sound an odd thing to say, but come back to this section after reading the whole of this chapter, then read again the classical ideas on the rituals of the Avebury ring and see how primitive they really are.

5. Henge of the World

Sacred sites

First of all, why did I concentrate on Avebury and Stonehenge in this quest? Why not look first at one of the many other henges and circles that proliferate across central southern Britain, Ireland and western France? There are literally hundreds of prehistoric constructions to choose from. What makes Avebury, in particular, so different? Firstly, it is quite obvious that Avebury and Stonehenge are not of secular origins. The massive constructions that form the likes of the hilltop sites of Maiden Castle and Old Sarum are quite impressive but, while they may well have some mystical connections, it is quite apparent that they were primarily made for the defence of a small town or village.

Other barrows and henges were made specifically for a particular burial; for example, the Winterbourne Stoke and Cursus barrows near Stonehenge. One of the barrows in this complex was found to contain seven burials, which confirms beyond reasonable doubt its function as a tomb. Other sites, however, are more enigmatic, and one is left in no doubt that the latter type were purely religious in their design and use. This religious function must have, in many cases, filtered down into the quite recent past. For in many cases, in quite isolated henges like at Knowlton in Dorset, the new and recent Christian sect felt threatened enough by the power of these old faiths to put large Christian buildings inside the rings. Perhaps they were afraid of the old beliefs; perhaps they just wanted to draw power from and finally to supersede the old beliefs.

Avebury (overleaf) is just such a henge. It has never been thought to have been a defensive position, despite the depth and width of the ditches that surround the site, nor was there ever a Neolithic village here. The traditions surrounding these earthworks, and their siting, all point towards the origins of Avebury being of a purely religious nature, a religion so powerful and threatening that it had to be destroyed.

We should also consider these sites before all others, simply because of their quality and size. As we saw in chapter I, the Silbury 'pyramid' is the largest such structure in Europe and is quite comparable to the step-pyramid of Saqqara, both in size and the complexity of its construction. Avebury itself is the largest and most complex henge in the world, and likewise the mighty Stonehenge is again the largest such structure in the world. While none of these constructions can be considered to be in the same class as the great pyramids of Egypt, they are nevertheless great achievements for the era.

There is another reason in choosing just Avebury, Stonehenge and Silbury for special attention. If we take, for example, the henge at Mount

5. Henge of the World

Pleasant near Dorchester, we find that this site is superficially similar to Avebury. At Mount Pleasant, there is an earth ring and ditch, which is broken into four segments. The ring and ditch have entrance gates, placed roughly at the cardinal points, and inside the ring we find a small circle of concentric post holes, superficially similar to the small circles inside Avebury. But we can mathematically distance this construction from the design of Avebury, because of the units that were being used on this site.

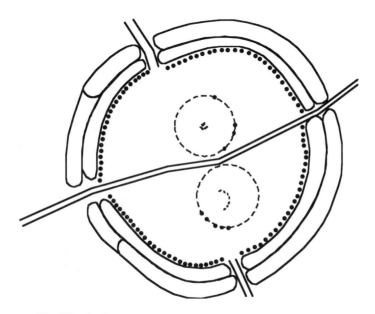

Fig 22. Avebury

If we try to force the Zil yard into the post-hole distances at the Mount Pleasant site, the mission fails completely. It is quite apparent that the Megalithic yard was exclusively in use here. At the same time, the whole numbers used and the ratios that the designer seems to have preferred are mostly even. We find repetitions in the numbers of stones and the lengths of units used of 4, 6, 8, 12, 16. This is in complete contrast to the Avebury site where the numbers in use are all Pi-based numbers, that is $5^1/_2$, 7, 11. So we can see that this and many other sites across Britain are not the same as Avebury. Perhaps the designer of these monuments did not have access to all the technical information of the monuments designed by the mythical Zil.

5. Henge of the World

Neolithic cartographer

This section in the book is working backwards in some respects because I already knew the function of Avebury. Part of the confirmation of this theory demanded a link – a direct correlation between Stonehenge and Avebury – showing that they are sister-constructions from the boards of the same designer. The traditional chronology of these sites does not allow for simultaneous construction so, if we are to prove that the same designer was involved at both sites, it would be nice to see a direct link between the two. This is actually quite easy; in fact, so easy one wonders why it has not been spotted before. Perhaps nobody was looking for it.

In the top right-hand corner of Avebury there is a small circle; originally there were two concentric circles. In the center of this small circle there is a group of three large, standing stones and, except for the Obelisk in the southern circle, these were the biggest stones on the Avebury site. These three stones were also unlike any others on the site: they were flat, rectangular and placed in the ground as a rectangle, rather than as a diamond. They measure some 5 x 4 meters each and were placed in a formation resembling the walls of an enclosure; accordingly, they became known as the Cove.

Many people have identified them as being an example of a dolmen, which normally consists of three upright stones and a huge capstone on the top. But this is not a dolmen; the layout of the lower stones is just not right and there is no evidence of there ever having been a capstone. No, this enclosure has another function. It consists of three stones that form a horseshoe-like arrangement, which points with its open end out towards the north-east, a horseshoe shape that is enclosed within a circle of stones.

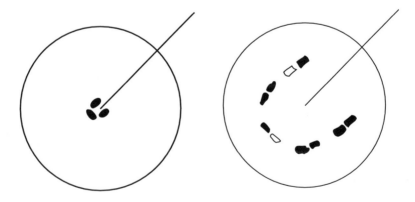

Fig 23. Avebury horseshoe   Stonehenge horseshoe

5. Henge of the World

Does this not sound a little like the central formation on the Stonehenge site? Flick back to the diagram of Stonehenge in chapter I: is there a resemblance? At Stonehenge, there are the Trilithons, the five pairs of standing stones that form a horseshoe shape in the center of the Sarsen circle. These pairs of stones were the largest on the site and formed a horseshoe arrangement that points out towards the north-east. Is this not exactly what we see here in the northern circle at Avebury: a little map of Stonehenge?

I sat for a while looking at this coincidence, wondering if this really had been planned. It seemed to me that, if the designer had really wanted to confirm this similarity between Avebury and Stonehenge, he would probably have tried to link the two sites, perhaps by using his measurement system. Looking at the two sites for a few minutes confirmed that they were indeed related, by their perimeter lengths. The link was eventually found when looking at the perimeter length of the Stonehenge site in comparison with that of Avebury.

Out by the earth ring and ditch at Stonehenge, there is a ring of post-holes just inside the ditch. These are known as the Aubrey holes after their discoverer, the seventeenth century antiquary, John Aubrey. These holes measure about 1 meter across by 1 meter deep, or in other words, measurements that just happen to be 1 Zil yard by 1 Zil yard. The function of these enigmatic holes was a complete mystery, as were most of the formations on these sites. But, by just looking at them, they had to be something to do with the mythical Zil/Thoth, for who else would dig a ring of holes and immediately fill them back in again? This would perform no rational function in the normal world, but it is just the sort of trick our cunning designer would devise to cover up another of his mathematical conundrums. As one commentator says in regard to these holes:

> Their purpose is unknown, though it is clear that they never held upright stones or wooden posts, which would have left impressions in the chalk at the bottom. Soon after they were dug they were refilled with chalk. Later they were reused for the burials of cremated human bones. [3]

The true function of this Aubrey circle was difficult to fathom, but if the thrust of this whole thesis was true, then it is likely to have a mathematical answer, not a religious one. Alexander Thom measured the ring in the 1960s, the reported result being a perimeter length of 328.1 Megalithic yards (my) or 271.7 meters. This equates to about 270 yards in the Zil system, or about 49 Zil rods (zr). The nice, whole and meaningful nature of 49 Zil rods (it is 7 squared) could indicate that this ring was actually a Zil construction. There was further confirmation that this was indeed the case, when it was finally noticed that 49 zr is exactly one-quarter of the perimeter length of the Avebury ring, the perimeter of Avebury being 196 zr. There was a correlation after all: the outer ring of Avebury is an exact four-fold copy of the outer ring at Stonehenge. So there is a direct correlation between circle lengths at Avebury and Stonehenge.

If the Aubrey circle has some definite meaning, then why this strange idea of digging and refilling these holes in the ground? It doesn't seem to make much sense: why not build a stone circle instead? The simplest answer to this is that perhaps the Aubrey holes were refilled in this manner because Zil/Thoth was running out of time. Perhaps the construction had taken far too long and steps were being taken to reduce the man-hours required for the completion of Stonehenge. So, whereas the most important stones on the site were carefully smoothed down, all the other stones were left in the rough. There was no time left for the construction of the Aubrey ring either, even though it is quite important.

The alternative and quite effective technique available to the designer was for holes to be dug and then refilled. This was done in the sure knowledge that, once the earth was disturbed on the site in this manner, the traces of this digging would remain in the ground for ever. This has worked just as planned and the holes were found with ease. But the priesthood would have known of this little secret and passed it down as a tradition and so, in later generations, some of the high dignitaries of each era wished to be interred on this sacred site, inside the peculiar sacred holes. Hence we find the traces of the cremated bodies in some of the holes, but traces that do not go to the very bottom of the holes.

In many publications, such a theory may well be the central subject in the story, with plenty of padding on either side to produce a fat book, but in this complete re-evaluation of these ancient sites, we have only just begun. It is at this point that we must try to purge our minds of any previous ideas we may have had about these sites, from whatever end of the spectrum they may come. Try to start with a blank sheet and work up from there. These ancient builders were men and women, exactly like us. Their education may have been a little different, but for the educated elite it was probably no less demanding. Think of them as having the same ideas, and perhaps the same knowledge of the world, as ourselves. Many people at this point may disagree with such a notion, but that is the very reason why the Avebury henge has not been seen for what it is for so long.

It needs an open mind to see the real Avebury.

5. Henge of the World

Heaven on Earth

The tale so far has taken us on a grand tour around the perimeter of these great mysteries, but the time has come for some more pertinent evidence: so we come to the real reason and purpose for building the great henge of Avebury. The answer to one of the central enigmas of British history, the answer that was so evident on the photograph in front of me, is very simply that Avebury is a representation of our planet Earth. And quite a good one at that!

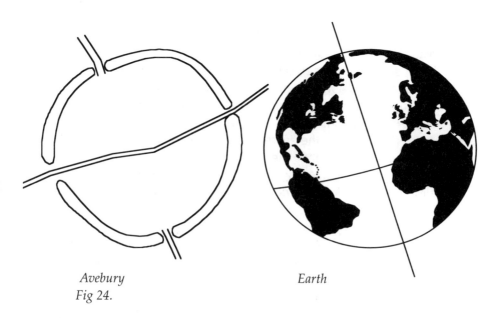

Avebury   *Earth*

Fig 24.

Is such a suggestion as preposterous as it sounds? We are talking about Neolithic man here; how could Neolithic man know the form of our Earth? This is where established dogma clouds our judgement. We must keep the sheet of paper blank until we have something to put on it, otherwise this line of reasoning cannot be taken to its ultimate conclusion. Instead, let us take a look at the evidence *in favor* of this suggestion, for there is plenty there to be found:

> a.   Notice how the east–west road cuts across the Avebury ring: this can be considered as being the equator of the Avebury 'Earth'.

> b.   Notice how the circle of Avebury is rotated to the left a little, at

an angle of about 23° from true north. It is unlikely that this is the result of imperfect surveying, as a line joining the centers of the two small inner circles mimics this leaning angle quite precisely; it has to have been designed this way. If one is prepared to take on board the controversial 'Earth' theory, however, one cannot help noticing that the Earth's current angle of obliquity, the angle at which it also 'leans', is some 23.4°.

c.   Note that the henge circle is not quite circular. It has traditionally been assumed that this was because the ancients could not survey a circle properly, yet there are many examples of perfectly circular henges in Britain, including the Stonehenge site and the smaller circles at Avebury. This new theory gives an entirely plausible reason for why Avebury was not made circular: it is because the Earth itself is not circular. The Earth, as it spins, bulges out at the equatorial latitudes and that is exactly what we find at Avebury: the east–west dimension of the henge is greater than the north–south dimension, just as it is on the real Earth.

Furthermore, the secret traditions of the priesthood would tell future generations that the henge had to be misshapen in this fashion. Not quite knowing the reason for this, later designers made all subsequent Avebury copies, such as Durrington Walls, Mount Pleasant and Marden, have distorted and exaggerated Avebury features. These henges tend to bulge out even more than Avebury does. It is apparent that the designers of these henges knew that this shape was sacred for some reason, but they did not quite know why. If Avebury bulges, then a henge that bulges even more must be even more sacred; the logic is simple and undeniable.

Durrington, in particular, seems to be an imperfect copy of Avebury. It even comes complete with two inner circles, one above the other, but the design is strangely distorted from the Avebury design. The most telling point that this is an Avebury copy, though, is that the designer could only manage wooden posts in his circles, not the massive sarsen stones of Avebury. The technology of Avebury had been lost, even in this era.

d.   The perimeter of the Avebury circle could be considered to be in a direct ratio to the circumference of the Earth, much the same as we saw for the Great Pyramid. This time, if we compare the two, we find that Avebury has very nearly a 36,600 : 1 ratio to the Earth; a ratio representing the number of days in a year. Not only is this a meaningful ratio, but there is clearly a picture of the Earth on the plains of Wiltshire.

e.   The small northern small circle at Avebury has already been identified as being a representation of the Stonehenge site, but why was it put there? The answer is now clear: it is because Stonehenge is in the northern hemisphere, both on the real Earth and also on our Avebury Earth. What we have is a picture of our Earth, floating in space, with a picture with Stonehenge clearly marked in its northern hemisphere. Stonehenge is a marker of some sort.

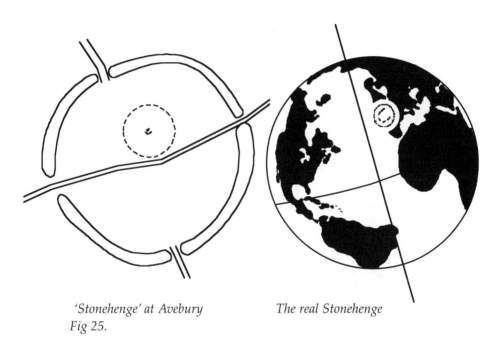

'Stonehenge' at Avebury   *The real Stonehenge*
Fig 25.

This is what one might call a really devastating theory, one that turns upside down all previous thoughts, not only about Avebury, but also about the history of mankind. These are our familiar Stone Age hunter-gatherers, people who have only just come out of the woods to do a little farming and settle in primitive stick and mud huts. It was always difficult to imagine these primitive people having the technology and organization required to drag the massive sarsen stones into these highly technical stone circles, like Stonehenge. Yet here we have them not only doing all this, but also drawing highly accurate pictures of our Earth, as seen from space.

5. Henge of the World

Such revelations can be uncomfortable on the mind. If this is the case, just think for the moment that the architect has had some assistance from the gods in making this design. For although this is a truly amazing hypothesis, it would remain just that if it were not for some nice little cross-checks that can verify this theory and set us thinking even more.

Complete picture

The task was now to find further evidence that this was indeed the intended picture that the designer had left for us to see, because what we have here so far would not really convince a critical mind. The designer of Avebury would have had to have left further clues to his prowess, otherwise nobody would believe him or that he had such a comprehensive understanding of our world. The quest was getting exciting because the theory was spawning further theories that were being verified in quick succession; for the designer had indeed left some further confirmation for us that this was the picture he wanted us to see.

The confirmation of this strange state of affairs is to be found in the small southern circle at Avebury. This circle has 29 stones and contains within it an odd 'D'-shaped group of stones. Needless to say, the function of these stones has never been even remotely guessed at. Traditionally, it has been assumed that there could be no way in which one could probe the mind of someone living so many thousands of years ago. At last it is now possible, but only just, for this particular feature took a great deal of lateral thinking even to start speculating about its true function. It may be interesting for the reader to try reasoning this one out independently without first reading the answer, but to achieve this it is imperative to keep reminding oneself that anything is possible. The secret of lateral thinking, in this case, is never to put limits on the possibilities that could be designed into these structures. This entails placing a great deal of faith in the capabilities of our designer, but the mythical Zil is not about to let us down in this respect.

To find the answer to the 'D'-shaped group of stones, we need to go back and look at the perimeter length of the small northern circle at Avebury – the one containing the picture of Stonehenge – to see if there is any hidden meaning to these stones. The diameter of the northern small circle inside Avebury was measured by A C Smith as being 97 m, and the circle was judged to contain about 27 stones. But remember, in doing this, Smith is attempting to reconstruct a circle of rough sarsen stones, of which only two remain intact; a further two have fallen or been moved; and the remaining eight stone positions that we reliably know about are only inferred through geophysical evidence. The locations of these inferred stones are derived from actual depressions from the stone holes that are still evident in the ground, and from resistivity surveys that locate the remains of 'burning pits', where the stones were broken up in antiquity.

The resistivity anomalies do not always coincide with the soil depressions, as the destruction sites of the stones do not always coincide with their original location, and so it is the soil depressions that seem to give the more regular spacing. The measurement of this circle is, therefore, by no means a precise science and, as one book says:

> Only four stones of this circle survive ... Their positions and spacing, with another stone recorded by William Stukeley in 1723, suggest that (the circle) originally contained 27 stones. [4]

So the exact number of stones is not known in this particular circle, it is only suggested. Because of the total lack of survey work to the south of this circle, there is no definitive answer to this problem, but if we look at a classical diagram of the circle, the number of stones was not 27. Of the four surviving stones, only two remain in their original positions. The other two have fallen and the modern surveyor has merely attempted to draw all the stones into this circle, including the fallen stone found to the south of the circle (stone 210), which appears superficially to be well south of its original position. This has caused the circle that has been drawn to be slightly larger than it should be and therefore it no longer matches the spacing of the depressions and burning pits to the north. We can clearly see this in the standard diagrams of the site.

Also, the center of this larger 27-stone circle is displaced to the south and west of the horseshoe enclosure, whereas logically it should be symmetrical with the center of this enclosure. Certainly, in the southern circle at Avebury, the central position of the circle was the large Obelisk, formerly the largest stone on the whole site. Should the large horseshoe stones not be the center of the northern circle too? The reason, as already stated, that the circle was drawn this way by modern archaeologists is that it then neatly bisects the fallen stone that is present to the south of the circle. But like many others of the fallen stones on the site, this stone has probably been moved. If we were to ignore this stone completely – it being the one stone that is pulling the circle out of center towards the south – a new smaller circle could be redrawn.

We can verify this theory by taking lines equidistant from each of the known stone locations, including the disputed southern stone. Lines of equidistance are a standard method of finding the center of any circle. Place two points anywhere on the perimeter of a circle, inscribe two arcs from each point with a compass, and a line drawn between the intersections will bisect the center of the circle.

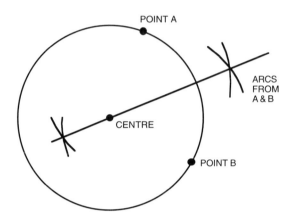

Fig 26. Finding the center of a circle

This process can be taken one step further, because if it is possible to find many points on the perimeter of the same circle, lines can be drawn from each one. Taking many such arcs will provide a variety of lines, all crossing at the same place – the center point of the circle. If, however, the circle is not quite accurate, the lines pointing at the center will miss each other slightly; they will form a small triangle which is known in the nautical plotting trade as a 'cocked hat' – a term presumably born in the days when naval navigation officers wore tricorn hats. This space marks an area of uncertainty, and the center of the circle will lie somewhere in the middle of this area; inside the cocked hat.

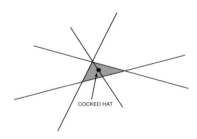

Fig 27. A cocked hat

5. Henge of the World

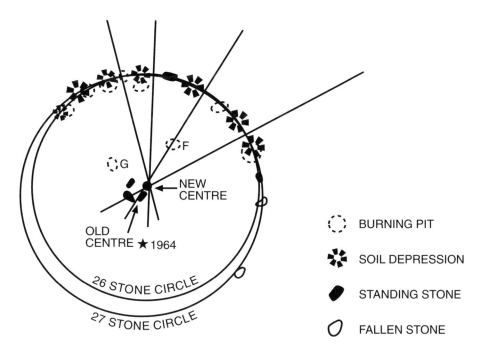

Fig 28. The 26-stone northern outer circle

Drawing a series of such lines from each of the stone locations in the north-east quadrant of the survey map of the northern outer circle at Avebury, produces just such a cocked hat, with the exception that any lines drawn from the southern stone (210) lie well to the south and west of all the other lines. From this, we can firstly deduce that the southern stone has been moved. Secondly, we can see that the center of this circle – the cocked hat – lies just to the north-east of the horseshoe formation, just outside its open mouth. Using this point for our new center point, the resulting circle does indeed touch all of the known stone locations and it is a smaller circle than is normally given for this construction; it is a 26-stone circle.

This brings us back to the riddle of the 'D'-shaped group of stones in the southern circle of Avebury. Before we can discover its true meaning, we have to be sure about what we actually see here, for the 'D' shape of standing stones is not a 'D' shape at all; it is really a ') ' shape. The current 'D' shape came about because of a misunderstanding about the site during the early excavations in 1939. The archaeologists seem to have presumed that any recumbent stones they found had to be fallen standing stones, for that was all Neolithic man could do: stand stones upright.

5. Henge of the World

This was despite the fact that the stones at the back of the 'D' shape displayed no signs of having ever been standing. Indeed, the photos of the excavations clearly show that the stones lay in shallow graves, and the weathering patterns on these stones indicated that they had been lying in this half-buried manner for a considerable time. Some of the stones had been rolled, by the site vandals, from these shallow graves into deeper burial pits; yet the original impressions of the shallow graves are still quite clear on the excavation photos and there is no sign of any holes for standing stones. The truth of the matter is that the back of the 'D' was originally designed as a line of small, flat, partially buried stones, like a line of stepping stones. This was done for a reason, but one that will become apparent only later. The large standing stones in the southern circle, therefore, formed a ') ' shape; a shape whose function we have still not explained.

It was time to revise the data so far. The northern circle at Avebury had, within it, a set of three huge stones that looked very similar to the group of Trilithon stones at the Stonehenge site. If the outer Avebury ring looked like a representation of the Earth, then these three stones of the Cove looked very much like a representation of the center of Stonehenge. We had a picture within a picture and, when looking at an atlas of the Earth, things started to fall into place very quickly. Avebury was a diagram of the Earth and, superimposed on that diagram in the northern hemisphere, was a picture of Stonehenge. Avebury was beginning to look very much like not only a representation of the Earth, but a map as well. But if Avebury was a map of the Earth, then what did the ') ' formation of stones mean? It had to be a representation of another ancient monument!

All the large-scale maps between Avebury, and Carnac in France, were pored over in minute detail, in the search for a Neolithic monument that had a crescent shape. It was a fruitless and frustrating search, for there was no such monument. It was one of those occasions when I had to relax and place everything on the floor, try and let the mind wander and see what it came up with. After a few minutes, the penny dropped. If the diagram of Stonehenge was in the northern hemisphere of the Earth, and the northern half of Avebury, then the crescent shape of Avebury should lie in the southern hemisphere. I was looking in the wrong hemisphere. But after I had scanned a large-scale map of the globe for possible ancient sites, disappointment soon set in. The southern continents on this side of the globe are not blessed with much in the way of famous ancient monuments. The task was looking impossible, but then my eyes were drawn off into the Atlantic on my world map by a curious set of islands: the South Sandwich Islands.

5. Henge of the World

The South Sandwich Islands are a group of forgotten islands in the far South Atlantic, which happen to have exactly the same shape as the ') ' shaped stones at Avebury. Avebury truly is a complete picture of the Earth. Just ponder for a minute the further ramifications of this bizarre state of affairs. If this theory is true, then Stone Age man, our familiar 'Stig of the Dump' hunter-gatherer from our school books – complete with fur-skin cape and wooden club – was not only aware of the form of the Earth all those thousands of years ago, but was also quite familiar with an obscure group of islands in the South Atlantic. Stone Age man may have known of the South Sandwich Islands long before any transatlantic trade was supposed to have started. Fascinating, is it not?

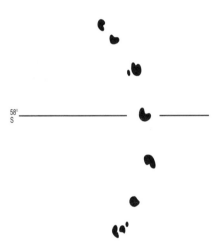

Fig 29. The Sandwich Islands

Of course, there will always be one or two skeptics. I can hear them already, beating their fists with rage at this preposterous assumption, for how can we be so certain that this little ') ' shape does refer to these remote southern islands? The answer is that the designer told us, in his usual fashion:

a.   The small representation of Stonehenge at Avebury lies in the upper half of the Avebury ring; this indicated that Stonehenge should lie in the northern hemisphere on the real Earth, which it does.

b.   In a similar fashion, the ') ' shape lies in the southern half of the large Avebury ring and so, in turn, the ') ' shape should also reside in the southern hemisphere on the real Earth. Accordingly, the South Sandwich Islands do reside in the southern hemisphere, and they reside almost exactly below the position of Stonehenge on an atlas. Thus, the real layout of the islands is exactly the same as we see at Avebury. The ') ' shape is in just the right position in relation to the small picture of Stonehenge at Avebury.

c.   The ') ' shape at Avebury is normally pictured as comprising seven stones; the ') ' shaped Sandwich Islands comprise seven islands. As I indicated earlier, the physical shape of the island chain is exactly the same as the ') ' shaped stones at Avebury; in this case the megalithic representation at Avebury is getting dangerously close to the real thing.

So, the layout of the Sandwich Islands is very close to what we see at Avebury and, in turn, the Avebury 'Earth' is very, very close to what we see in reality. While this is interesting, it could still be considered to be coincidence, especially in an educational climate that deems such things impossible. What we really need is something tangible, and mathematical, that we can really hang this theory on, such as a latitude or longitude. We are not to be disappointed; our cunning designer is running exactly according to plan.

a.   The northern outer circle, the one that surrounds the representation of Stonehenge, has in our new calculation just 26 stones. These 26 stones are placed 2 rods apart, which means that the circle is 52 Zil rods around the perimeter. It happens that Stonehenge lies just below the 52° parallel north of the equator; Avebury is 51.5° north and Stonehenge 51.3° north. We have our latitude pointer and Zil, the mythical designer has, at one stroke, clarified the function of this little enclosure of stones at Avebury. It really is a picture of Stonehenge.

Stonehenge lies just about on the 52nd parallel north of the equator and, at the same time, its Avebury representation lies inside a circle that measures 52 zr in length. In case the prospective researcher was still going to be unsure about all this, the designer of Avebury has ensured that 52 zr perimeter length is further confirmed for us by the number of stones in the circle. There are 26 stones in the circle, and 2 x 26 stones equals 52 degrees of latitude. It is simple really.

5. Henge of the World

e.   In the same fashion, we can now prove the true function of the ') ' shaped stones in the southern circle. The ring that surrounds this ') ' shape comprises 29 stones, and this time there is no dispute about the number of stones in this circle. These stones are again set in the traditional spacing of two Zil rods apart. The ring is therefore 58 rods in length, and this length is confirmed by the number of stones in the circle. As before, 2 x 29 stones equals 58 degrees of latitude. The South Sandwich Islands reside at 58° south on a globe of the Earth; in fact, the very center of the whole group of islands straddles the parallel of 58° S.

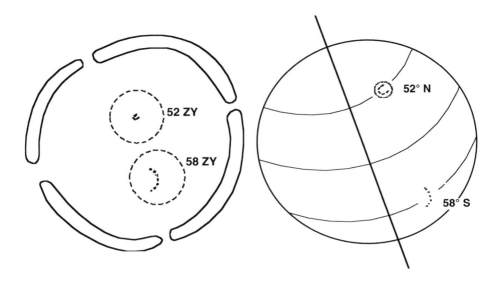

Latitudes 52° N and 58° S at Avebury   *Latitudes 52° N and 58° S on the Earth*
Fig 30.

Both Stonehenge and the Sandwich Islands are confirmed as being the correct concepts for each of these small circles at Avebury. They are confirmed by the latitudes at which they lie: simple but conclusive. The plot keeps getting more fascinating by the minute. How should we suppose that all this was achieved? Who were the incredible designers of these monuments both in Britain and Egypt? Perhaps we can now link them so closely in this investigation that we can say that they are one and the same person, just as William Stukeley thought, way back in 1740. Stukeley had postulated that the Egyptians had built Stonehenge; an observation for which he was much derided. But given the fantastic technical knowledge that we can now see residing in the design of Avebury, is this notion really so strange?

It is all rather revolutionary. Can we really accept that Stone Age man created an ocean-going ship and travelled the southern seas? Not only that, but can we also say that they took with them a sextant, in order that they might calculate the latitude of a group of southern islands? It is certainly a revolutionary concept and I can well understand anyone who is shaking their head in disbelief, but read the data again and look at the diagrams. Is this not proof of a long-lost technical civilization that was living on our planet many thousands of years ago?

Is this not also the source of those enigmatic ancient maps of Antarctica, that appear to show the southern continent long before it was deemed to have been discovered? The Piri Reis, Oronteus Finaeus and Philippe Buache maps all show the southern continents, but they were published 'impossibly' early; long before the documented discovery of Antarctica. In addition, the Philippe Buache map also seems to show the continent when it was free of ice; in other words, this eighteenth century cartographer was copying a very early map indeed. Could the Avebury designer have been the original author? Chapter VIII in this book will be arguing for a very early date for these monuments; a date which could well link into an Antarctica less encumbered with ice. [5]

And at the same time, of course, Avebury is pointing at some islands out in the Atlantic, beyond the pillars of Hercules, as Gibraltar was once known. Could this be a reference to Atlantis? Chapter IX will investigate this further.

Sandwich Islands

For a long time after I had evolved this theory and discovered these coincidences, I believed that this concept was entirely unique. Although other aspects of ancient culture have occasionally found their way into the modern world, I presumed it was going to be quite impossible to find any correlations in the present era involving the Sandwich Islands, because they are so remote and insignificant.

The Trilithon stones of Stonehenge may have been passed down through the millennia and evolved into the Masonic pillars of Jachin and Boaz, but the Sandwich Islands do not appear to be represented anywhere in the religious sphere. These islands were only supposed to have been discovered in the nineteenth century and even the enigmatic ancient maps

5. Henge of the World

just mentioned do not indicate the presence of these little islands, so how could these islands have entered into religious or secular life? Even the description of the mythical island of Atlantis was far removed from the reality of the little Sandwich Islands. This was obviously the end of this investigation; there was nothing further to be gained and the role of the Sandwich group would remain an enigma.

Then one day I had a four-hour delay at Mallorca airport: a flight had been cancelled, so we were not due out until five o'clock that evening. Looking for something to do, I took the opportunity to take the bus into town. The bus entered the city along the main esplanade, a long crescent of coastline with a very tidy-looking marina nestling in the bay and a jumbled array of hotels and shops on the right. Also on the right was the main cathedral of the island, Cathedral de Palma; an imposing sandstone construction propped up with a fine array of flying buttresses. It was more functional in its design than the fine slender columns that are a trademark of the French Gothic cathedrals, but it was nevertheless an imposing edifice for such a small island.

My usual first point of call in a city is the cathedral, so I made my way across the esplanade and up the stairs to the south porch. It was shut. So was the other normal entrance to a church, the west gate, but a notice indicated the cathedral was indeed open. After a square search, a small ticket office was eventually discovered on the northern side. It was fortunate that I had not given up, for this visit was not going to be without its rewards. As I wound my way into the body of the cathedral, I passed a display of reliquaries and treasures; the usual collection of clippings of hair from the saints enclosed in ornate boxes and vessels. Eventually I found myself standing in front of a huge pair of baroque candelabra, most probably fabricated in pewter.

They were made in the traditional Judaic style of a seven-branched candlestick, with the central candle holder being the tallest and the others arrayed downwards on each side. This particular example was rather large and ornate, but a simpler version fabricated in solid gold was originally the center piece of the Temple of Solomon in Jerusalem. It used to stand just outside the Holy of Holies, together with the 12 loaves and the 13 spices. This design is a very ancient and sacred piece of temple furniture; it is fundamental to the Judaic religion in particular and no Jewish home is complete without a copy of the original. The first century historian, Josephus, says of these candelabra:

> The seven lamps branching off from the lampstand symbolised the planets... [6]

5. Henge of the World

But if this lampstand represented the planets, why should it take this form, with the central lamp being the most prominent? While pondering this point, I suddenly found myself looking at the lamps in a different light, for it seemed to me that if the lampstand was tilted on its side, it transformed itself into a crescent shape... The lamps were no longer indicating the seven known planets; instead, they appeared be an exact copy of the Sandwich Islands themselves! There are always seven lamps on these stands and there are seven Sandwich Islands. The seven lamps form a crescent shape, with the central lamp being the most prominent; the islands form a crescent shape with the central island straddling the 58th parallel – the two layouts are identical. (See colour plate 20.)

This was too neat a correlation to be a coincidence. Here, at last, seemed to be evidence of an ancient knowledge of the Sandwich Islands; knowledge that had percolated down through the ages, in the form of a fundamental and sacred piece of religious furniture. This was a piece of sacred furniture that had sprung directly from Egypt herself. It had travelled, along with all the other holy practices and artifacts, with the Jewish exodus to Jerusalem. Thus, the Stonehenge Pi pillars of Jachin and Boaz, and the Avebury/Sandwich Island candelabra, were both a part of the fabric of the Temple of Solomon in Jerusalem. Here, at last, was another strong link between the British and Egyptian monuments. There were deep parallels and deep mysteries designed into this megalithic architecture and I was about to find many more.

Legends

There were many strange people who used to walk around sites like Avebury and mutter darkly that the stones talked to people, if only one took the time to listen, and if we could understand their language. Being righteous and sensible people, we would all snigger and laugh, perhaps calling for an ambulance in the worst cases. But what we have here is not necessarily the mutterings of madmen; it is just the lost traditions of these great mythical designers, Zil and Thoth. As an indication of their true purpose, the designers passed on a tradition that the stones talked but did not explain their message. So many people, since the dawn of civilization, have been walking around these stones, trying desperately to get in tune with them, trying to hear their message. Now we can do just that and we find that the stones are not just talking to us, they are singing at the tops of their voices. They are singing latitudes, angles of obliquity, perimeter length of the Earth, Atlantic islands; the list goes on and on. Now that we know the language of the stones; we are in a position to take this much further and we shall go shortly to see what message the great pyramids of Egypt are singing to us.

Fascinating as all this is, it does not explain the true function of Avebury. If we accept that a technical civilization built Avebury, the theory so far still does not tell us why these islands in the south Atlantic were picked out for special attention. If, however, we look again at the center of the ')' shaped group of stones, we find that the largest stone on the whole Avebury site was placed here, the Avebury Obelisk. This particular stone managed to survive the millennia until the eighteenth century, but was then broken up by the Philistines from the local church. Clearly then, this stone – this position in this island chain in the south Atlantic – was very special to the designer, but in what way? Why was Saunders Island so special?

Enough has been said here for the time being. The answer to what the Obelisk was doing, and what the designer intended us to see in this diagram, is contained in chapter X. The proposals in chapter X begin at last to scratch the surface of this problem. It is an answer that lies at the real root of this book and we have a long way to go yet to find the bottom of it: in the meantime, there will be more discoveries still to come.

But if this is all so obvious, why have these similarities between Avebury and the real world not been seen before? Modern man has known the form of the Earth for hundreds of years and yet not a breath has been whispered on this topic. Some of the answer to this has to lie in the fact that many people's perceptions of history have been clouded by concepts of their own superiority in this world. People still tend to place themselves in a position that is so much more enlightened than that of their ancestors, and those ancestors were, in turn, so much better than theirs; and this continues in an ever-decreasing chain back to a time in the distant past, where people had zero awareness and zero knowledge. Our concept of self is always a barrier to the truth, or what the Egyptians called the ma'at. The truth is, of course, that the ancients have always had the same cognitive ability as ourselves.

But there is a deeper reason as to why this line of reasoning has developed within our society. We are also blind to the abilities of the great civilizations of the past because our religious authorities have always been happier to keep us that way; to keep us ill informed of our history. Jesus himself confirms this in the Bible; his disciples asked him why he always spoke to the common people in parables. The answer to this simple question was not that the format of the parable made it easier for the uneducated people to understand the message of the gospel; or that the simple story-line would keep the attention of the proletariat long enough for the message at least to be heard. No, the answer to this simple question is more practical, and, perhaps more sinister than that:

> Because it is given unto you [the disciples] to know the secrets of the kingdom of heaven, but unto them [the people] it is not given. [7]

The import of this comment is startling; the church of Jesus is more akin to the position in modern Masonry than the open and welcoming church that we expect – not exactly a secret church, but at least a church with secrets. This line of reasoning is made even clearer in the Gospel of Philip, from the Nag Hammadi scrolls, where Jesus says:

> Now [the farmer] was a sensible fellow, and he knew what the food of each of them was. He served the children bread, he served the servants meal, barley and grass to the cattle, bones to the dogs, and slops to the pigs. Compare the disciple of god, if he is a sensible fellow, the bodily forms will not deceive him ... There are many animals in the world which are in human form ... to the swine he will throw slops, to the cattle grass and barley, to the dogs he will throw bones, to the slaves he will give elementary lessons, and to the children he will give the complete instruction. [8]

Many people may be tempted to dispute this source material because it is not from the central canon of the church. To verify its authority, however, we only need to compare the sentiments given in that paragraph with the treatment of the Greek woman by Jesus in Matthew and Mark; the two paragraphs dovetail exactly. The woman wanted a blessing for her child who was 'grievously ill', but Jesus refused her any help:

> But Jesus said unto her, Let the children first be filled, for it is not (right) to take the children's bread and cast it unto the dogs. And she answered him and said unto him, Yes Lord, yet the dogs under the table eat of the children's crumbs. [9]

There can be no doubt that the paragraph from the Gospel of Philip is taken from the teachings of Jesus and, at the same time, it is a further verification that the Nag Hammadi scrolls are as authoritative in these matters as are the texts that were chosen to go into the Bible. We can also see that the more complete text from the Nag Hammadi scrolls now makes it perfectly clear why Jesus was calling this woman a 'dog'. It was not a simple racist rebuke, just because she was a Greek; it was more because she was not of his religion and she certainly was not an initiate into the secrets of the church. Therefore, she was not entitled to the bread (the secrets) that was given to the children (the disciples).

Again and again, it is being made clear that the common people are not worthy of knowing the secrets of the kingdom of god. This is why the vast majority of Christians are quite ignorant of their religion; most do not even know the names of the brothers and sisters of Jesus. If little details like family names are censored, how are we to trust the rest of the teachings of the church? So, by this process of misinformation, the three Judaic religions (Christianity, Judaism and Islam) have always endeavoured to cloud our brains; both with notions of human superiority and also with incomplete facts. This is probably because it has always been in the interests of the religious authorities to prevent the ma'at – the truth – from showing through. Why should this be necessary? What would the clergy have to hide? Simple, they wish to hide their Egyptian origins and the nature of 'god'.

Although they tend not to advertise the fact, as we touched on in chapter IV, it is an established fact that all the Judaic religions sprang from Egypt some 3,500 years ago. So, it is axiomatic that these religions would have brought with them much of the liturgy and rituals of the ancient Egyptian rites. Many people do not want to believe this and stick doggedly to the standard ecclesiastical explanation that the liturgy of the church came directly to the Jews from god. That is a valid hypothesis, but not one that is borne out by the biblical texts. Compare, for instance, the struggle between the biblical Cain and Abel with the ancient Egyptian story of the struggle between Osiris and Seth; they are one and the same. There are so many similar illustrations that can be made, so perhaps in this case the orthodox theory on the origins of the Bible should be revised. Maybe it should be placed a few thousand years further back into the past; back into Egypt.

This 'new' theory is not very new, of course. It has been widely speculated by many religious academics, including Sigmund Freud (1856–1939), that the early Jewish religion was Egyptian. It has just been adapted down the years into the forms that we are familiar with today. [10] Is it a coincidence that Thoth was the Egyptian version of the Holy Trinity – Thoth the three-times-great? Such concepts and correlations between biblical and orthodox history are explored further in the sequel to this work, advertised at the beginning of this book. *Jesus, Last of the Pharaohs* attempts to follow the path of the Egyptian religion into modern theology, to show the true roots of our religions.

But whatever little snippets of the history of Thoth may remain within modern ecclesiastical teachings, it would never have been in the interests of these new Judaic religions to advertise their true origins; they wanted to be fresh and new. They would never wish openly to confess that there was, long ago, a civilization that was more advanced than theirs and, associated with it, a religion that was more knowledgeable than they would ever be. By necessity, the truth had to be hidden.

Chapter VI

Publication

Events were reaching a conclusion very rapidly now and I eventually sat down to write a manuscript on a battered old typewriter; one of those with the capability of holding a page or two in memory. It was a task that I had never envisaged doing before but it was a valuable exercise, however, because during the process of patiently writing everything down, I discovered some more startling revelations: new theories that linked the Avebury Earth concept into Stonehenge and Giza. These were theories that would form the second half of this rapidly escalating manuscript. Eventually, after much writing and rewriting, a manuscript was devised and printed in a set of quite presentable spiral bound volumes.

Perhaps rather naively, I then expected that the literary world would be suitably impressed with these efforts, and proposals would come flooding through the door. The postman had obviously not been made aware of this, because each morning he would look at our front door, shuffle a few letters in his hands and move on to the next house in the street. Eventually, there were one or two letters dropped through our box; a few grains of hope in this literary famine. Not only did the big players in the field not want to know, but neither did the smaller publishers or literary agents. Everyone either had full listings or suddenly did not handle works of this nature as soon as my manuscript landed on the mat. Frustrating was not the word.

Finally, there was a response. A kindly old gentleman said he could be of assistance and could I meet him as soon as possible! Without a second thought, I was in the meeting, which went extremely well. The gentleman was suitably impressed with my ideas and the world, it seemed, would soon be flicking through the next best seller on the newsstands. The old adage was as true as ever: if it seems too good to be true, it is probably just that. The confident talk at the meeting was one thing, but the reality of the situation was quite another. The editing of the manuscript never happened; publication was suddenly not as straightforward as had been promised; the finance for further investigations fell through. The whole escapade was turning into a charade.

Finally, in August 1997, the gentleman concerned went his own way. Then came news that another writer was involved in similar research – a project based around the concept of Pi Trilithons at Stonehenge. I shrugged off the coincidence and continued to promote the manuscript as before. But things were to come to a head in October of that year, when I heard another rumour on the grapevine. This indicated that all of the concepts I had outlined in the first five chapters of my manuscript – the only chapters I had let out of my sight so far – had been used as the basis of a proposal, by this new author, to a top publishing house. On the one hand I could believe it, and yet on the other, I couldn't. Surely this sort of thing doesn't go on in the genteel world of publishing! What tipped the issue was a consignment of maps that had been promised to me by the very same new author; maps of the Dahshur pyramids to assist in my research. It was a minor event in an unfolding drama, but when a package goes 'missing' – as this one did for two months – with daily updates by fax as to the progress of this mythical package, one instantly suspects that something is very wrong.

I had a deep feeling that if I was not quick, I would lose all this hard-won knowledge to a plagiarist. There is only one thing to do in the literary world to secure the copyright on a work: publish. But through whom? There was nobody interested. I decided there and then to publish the book myself, whatever the cost and whatever the unfinished state of the manuscript; anything to get the copyright secured. But where does one start? I had no idea. Since no publisher wanted to touch the manuscript, the first point of call was a printing company, who very kindly gave me a rough synopsis of the steps required; and there was much to think about. The list of requirements appeared to be never ending and yet, on top of all this, my day job had to be slotted in between. The pressure was on and there was no let-up for four long weeks.

Eventually, all the problems were resolved. The books were delivered and mail-order distribution began at a surprisingly brisk rate. It was an invigorating experience and, most importantly, the copyright on the book was established. It would be very difficult, if not impossible, for someone to follow in the same footsteps. However, the problems were not to stop there. The new writer in the field had somehow secured a major publishing contract with one of the biggest publishers in the country, and he brazenly stated that it was made using the same theories as were in my already published book. I continued to converse relatively amicably with this man, as it is not impossible for two people to have similar thoughts on these topics, but I was even more alarmed when he wished to quote from other sections in my book. The list seemed endless: eleven diagrams, seventeen pictures and copious quotes from within much of my book.

It did seem that he was in a hurry to pick up as much usable material as possible; a situation that was aggravated by the strange contract with the publisher which gave him just three months in which to write a 400-page book. In my limited experience, which tied in later with that of other authors, one needs to go over the material at least three times or even more, rewriting and checking for errors. This was an impossible task in this field, and the obvious solution that this author seemed to be using was to quote as much material from other authors as possible. A deal was eventually struck between us on the quotes from *Thoth*, whereby all of the Stonehenge and Giza data would be left alone. The hope was that the limited number of quotes in a best selling book would give my own work a much higher profile, yet there would still be some items of interest that would be unique to my work. In any case, this new author was only quoting me in two chapters out of a total of 58 in his book, so I didn't really have to worry about overexposure.

Echo

But there *was* reason to worry. The matter came to a head at an Egyptian conference in London, in March 1998. Lined up for the debate, in the faded glory of some ancient conference halls, were an assortment of authors and specialists, mostly drawn from the new and radical kind of alternative Egyptology. One of the speakers was the new man on the block; the writer I had been conversing with but had never met before. The first day of the conference went well and I sold a number of books; the atmosphere was convivial, and the new author was charming and friendly. On the second day, he proceeded to give a lecture on his forthcoming book which I listened to intently. I sat at the back of the hall with my eyes opening widely, not believing my ears or eyes. Here were large sections of my book, *Thoth*, being delivered by another author.

I could understand that someone may have had the same ideas as me, even though it was a coincidence that these ideas should surface at exactly the same time. However, to stand there and use my diagrams, my pictures, my words and the measurements that I had made with my own two hands on the pyramids of Egypt, was beyond belief. Here, too, were the diagrams that we had agreed would not be used; they had been lifted directly from the book without a please or a thank you. The lecture went on with numerous selections from my book. My blood was beginning to boil; my eyes saw shades of red for a while, before calming once more and considering the situation a little more rationally.

There was only one option now: the agreement on quoting certain sections of my book had to be redrawn in a tight and legally binding fashion. After checking the original agreement at home, an initial calm protest went off, which was ignored. A second stronger version was also ignored. The third letter went straight to the heart of the matter; direct to the publisher, Random House. The letter was no longer one of protest; instead, it forbade the use of any quotation, diagram or picture until the matter had been resolved and it caused an immediate flurry of correspondence. When you write to someone for two weeks with no reply, and then the third letter produces a response the very same day, you know you have hit a raw nerve.

This was obviously the route to produce quick results and they came in thick and fast. An offer to share 10% of the author's rights in the new book sounded promising, but when I asked for a glimpse of the manuscript to see how my work had been represented, the offer was modified. Suddenly, my potential share of this high-profile book increased to 25%, but the sticking point still seemed to be my insistence on a quick scan of the manuscript. Despite the previously numerous offers from this author of a manuscript for me to browse, for some reason this option was now totally unacceptable and the tempting offers to share the profits of this new book with me were suddenly withdrawn.

The sands in these negotiations were shifting with amazing speed, but, for the life of me, I could not understand the rush that the author and the publishers were in. Of course, businesses these days like to turn over their goods quickly to maximize profits, but we were not in the perishable fruit trade here; the book would not go mouldy sitting on the computer disks at head office. If there was a real problem with the product – a problem that could lead to legal proceedings if one made the wrong decisions – would it not be sensible to call time-out? Would it not be wise to take a few days rest, observe the problem from a new perspective and investigate it professionally? Not Random House! I received, almost return of post, a terse statement saying:

> In view of the incredibly tight production deadline ... I am writing to confirm that I shall now comply with your instruction that you now

refuse (the new author) permission to use any pictures, diagrams and quotes from the title *Thoth, Architect of the Universe*.[1]

It was not an entirely satisfactory solution to the problem and I was still baffled as to why they had rejected my proposal, simply to reduce the number of quotes from *Thoth* to a reasonable level. Why go from a position of having great sections of quotes in this new book taken from my work, to absolutely nothing? What was wrong with the middle ground? It just did not make sense, as I said in my reply to the publishers:

> As you say, it is unfortunate that it had to come to this, as there were many simpler options available to (you), my initial request being just one case in point. But that is business I suppose ... I expect that the good name of Random House will ensure that all those references are deleted from the new book by (your new author).

For good measure, a marked copy of the book *Thoth* was sent to the publisher, so that they could easily identify the relevant sections and delete them from this new book of theirs. The saga was more bizarre than I could have imagined; the author even threatened unspecified legal action against me if I ever contacted him again. Nevertheless, it did seem to appear that matters had reached a climax and had begun to fade away. Perhaps we could now get back to our normal lives. How wrong could I be?

Theft

A brief hiatus ensued: time for rest, relaxation and a welcome holiday. It was only the calm before the impending storm. The new book, by the new author, was eagerly awaited and eventually the shop we had ordered it from said it was now available. A special trip was made on a bright afternoon, and it was a journey charged with anticipation. I was fairly confident that all would be well, for we were talking about the reputation of an international company here – the biggest publishers in the Western World. They were unlikely to risk such a good name in the industry over a unknown book by an unknown author, but I was still slightly concerned as to how this new book had been rewritten within a few days. I was well versed now in the production problems of rewriting a book and then printing it. I had produced about five different versions of *Thoth* myself, and each rewrite was a laborious chore. Such things took weeks, not days. The whole situation seemed nonsensical.

6. Publication

The book was duly purchased, and with great resolve, my wife and I strolled down to the cathedral grounds in Salisbury without so much as opening it. The cathedral grounds here are one of the few places in the country where one can feel truly relaxed. They are wide and neatly trimmed, the mighty thirteenth century spire of the cathedral soars up majestically in front to meet the sky, while a huddle of grand old town houses crowd around and behind. There are no cars, buses or lorries here. The birds sing and you can hear them: a rare event in a city center. It is one of those places that dilates time; even the tourists seem to amble rather than rush. There is a serenity about the place; a calm that was about to be rudely shattered.

We sat down on a park bench, the afternoon sun warming our faces; our two-year-old heading off across the green with screams of delight to make new friends with some other children. I pulled the book from the carrier bag. Its dark and grim-looking cover proclaimed *Hall of the Gods*, published by William Heinemann (a division of Random House). [2] It looked foreboding. I opened the pages nervously, flicked through a few, and felt my heart sink. Here was my erosion theory; there, my concept of the Avebury 'Earth'; on another page was the section on Pi-based measures, followed by the neat little piece on the Uffington horse; and further on was my Giza planisphere. For goodness sake, the whole of my book had simply been reprinted!

I had a sick feeling in the pit of my stomach. How could they have done this?! What had happened to the promise of my work being quoted in only two chapters out of 58? For a start, there were only 35 chapters here and it appeared that I was 'quoted' in at least ten of them! With a cold sweat beginning to form on my brow, I tried to check the word usage in the text. Time after time, I spotted my own exact wording. I did not even have to compare the paragraphs – after all, I knew my own book like the back of my hand. The paragraphs were verbatim; this was nothing more than a cut-and-paste job!

I turned to my left to point something else out to my wife, who had not been saying much. Only then did I notice that she was trembling uncontrollably. It wasn't quite rage, for she was very controlled. It wasn't quite fear, because there was nothing to be physically afraid of. Clinically, a doctor might simply say it was just an adrenaline rush, but that does not even begin to scratch the surface of such deep emotions. There was only one word that could sum up the wave of emotions that such an event produces – theft; a literary violation of our household.

This was a cruel sword that had been thrust into the heart of our family; a blow that was contemptuous of the hours that we as a family had spent travelling across the globe; researching, calculating, organizing, writing and publishing our own book. The time, the money, the heartache, the hard work and the risk that was involved in self-publishing were undertaken so that the wider world could share these new concepts and ideas. It all appeared to be in vain. The final straw was the promise that this major publisher had made to withdraw all the quotations from my book. They make these idle promises from the comfort of their ivory towers and they go ahead and print anyway, without even bothering to check to see how much of *Thoth* had been plagiarised. It was as though I did not even exist to them. That was not just thrusting a sword into our family, it was twisting it as well.

It was decision time again. In the face of such shameless plagiarism, does one roll over and play dead? In the face of such giants of the industry, does one bow one's head in respect and simply turn the other cheek? Nobody likes to give up easily, but the opposition in this case seemed daunting. Would they really react to a mouse nibbling at their ankles? Could we afford to place a legal injunction on them and face the massive consequences if it failed? Could the legal bigwigs in a company of this size find some obscure twelfth century literary law that states that big companies can do what they like? Would they be able to string us along until we ran out of the money to pay for the legal advice and assistance?

We had to be sure of what we were doing; we had to be prepared to sell our house, if necessary; we had to be prepared to lose everything in the fight. It was not a decision to be taken lightly and I needed my wife's input to these serious considerations. I was about to ask her what she thought of all this when I noticed that she was flicking through the book feverishly, the pages trembling as she read them. 'Look, here is your section on Stonehenge, but we have faxes saying that this will not be used. Again here, he states that this section is all his research, his ideas and nobody has thought of this concept before!'

The pages rolled over in quick succession as she moved from chapter to chapter. 'This sentence is unbelievable! It says that he has never read a book that mentions this idea on the Sandwich Islands before, but he admitted in his letter that he thought this section in your book deserved further research! How on earth could someone descend to such depths ... we must fight them, Ralph, we must fight them.'

Declaration of war

That was enough for me. We called our toddler back to the bench. Luckily,

6. *Publication*

she was too young to understand our despair and was happily chatting away to two very long faces. With a certain lethargy, we gathered our belongings together and set off for home. That evening, I gathered my thoughts in front of the new computer, steeling myself for the coming conflict. I took a deep breath and started to type. The letter to the publisher was gloves off and knuckles bared:

Dear Ms. ****

I note that in the acknowledgements for this new book, (the author) writes;
> 'My sincerest thanks go to Ms. **** of William Heinemann at Random House for taking the huge risk in pushing ahead with this publication.'

I sincerely believe this to be the understatement of the year....

Let battle commence.

Chapter VII

Precessional Henge

The reason that I had requested the next three chapters to be left out of the 'other book' by the 'other author' was because, like the Avebury 'Earth' theory, these concerned new concepts that had not been published before. In addition, they firmly linked Avebury, Stonehenge and Giza together as being projects that were designed by the same individual or team. The three concepts in these chapters, when bound together in the one volume, made a convincing argument that something strange was going on with these ancient monuments. To print all three concepts together was to reprint my book.

The precessional henge theory was born directly from my observations at Avebury. Since I had overturned all the classical ideas about the site at Avebury, it was only fitting that I should now turn my attentions to the monument that lies just 28 km to the south of Avebury; the sister-monument of Stonehenge. Stonehenge is not only close to Avebury, it is also clearly marked out in the small northern circle at Avebury. There is a link between the two, as I have shown. It was obvious to me that if the physical layout of Avebury was so fundamentally important, then Stonehenge was likely to have something similar in its design.

The question was almost being set for me in advance: could the design of Stonehenge be compared in any way to that of the Earth? If I could show this to be so, the implications would be startling. Perhaps one site, like Avebury, having a similarity to the form of the Earth might just be considered coincidence, despite all the internal evidence to the contrary. But if I could explain Stonehenge in the same terms, then surely this must dispel any thoughts of mere coincidence. Numbers and angles of this nature just do not simply drop out of any construction; they have to be designed in.

Although Stonehenge doesn't look much like Avebury, it quickly

7. Precessional Henge

transpired that it does have much the same function. This became very obvious when I looked at the aerial pictures I had taken some months before. Perhaps one needs a peculiar mind to see these things, but to me it looked perfectly clear what Stonehenge really was. The reasoning behind this deduction went something like this. We have already seen the Pi Trilithons in chapter III, and this was the first indication that the Stonehenge site was sacred for its mathematics rather than its theology. As I continued to look at the site in this perspective, the next items one notices are the stones positioned in two pairs to the north and south of the site: the Station stones as they are known. The Station stones form the outline of a rectangle that defines both the center of the site and also the center-axis of the site. They are like builders' markers, set out in a rectangle before any of the serious surveying starts.

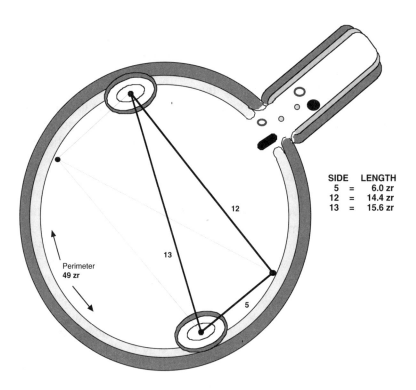

SIDE		LENGTH
5	=	6.0 zr
12	=	14.4 zr
13	=	15.6 zr

Fig 31. The Stonehenge triangles

The second indicator that Stonehenge should be known more for its mathematics comes from the arrangement of these Station stones; for

7. *Precessional Henge*

these innocent-looking little stones are as complex and as profound as anything that we have looked at Giza. It was startling to see the Pi Trilithons and realize that Neolithic man knew of this mathematical constant, but now we can also say that these Neolithic designers knew much of Pythagoras and his theorems. The rectangle formed by these Station stones is not any old rectangle; it is quite specific. To see why, we need some measurements. Flinders Petrie measured the distance between adjacent Station stones as 33.1 meters (33 Zil yards or 6 zr), [1] whereas Atkinson's 1978 data gives a slightly longer 6.04 zr between the centers of the stones. [2]

It is not recorded if Petrie was measuring between the centers of the stones or between their faces, and we have no way of knowing which the designer of the site thought was more important. In terms of Zil units, though, the measurements look logical. The diagonal across the rectangle (the diameter of the Aubrey holes circle) was estimated by Thom as 86.3 meters or 86 zy; Petrie gives 86.15 m or 85.8 zy; and again it is Atkinson who gives the longer measurement at 86.7 m or 86.37 zy. [3] The average of all these surveys is 86.03 zy.

All of these measurements were taken long before the Zil system of measurements had been contemplated, yet we can see how well this system seems to fit in. If we now draw a diagonal across the rectangle, two triangles are formed. Once again we find a mathematical oddity because both of these triangles turn out to be Pythagorean, just as Petrie suggested all those years ago. Fig 31 shows the measurements in Zil rod lengths. Note how the base length of the triangle now resolves into nearly exactly 6 rod lengths. This may well have been the original whole-number starting point for the site measurements, as it gives some interesting results.

These triangles are not quite the primary 3-4-5 triangle from the King's Chamber inside the Great Pyramid, but the sides of the triangles do reduce down to lengths of 13-12-5 and, in fact, these more complicated Pythagorean triangles are probably more difficult to discover. So we have two Pythagorean triangles sitting in the middle of Stonehenge, which in itself is quite amazing. But why are the lengths such awkward numbers? These are not the nice round numbers we have seen before in these monuments. Surely this indicates that this is merely a coincidence?

Not so: remember we have Pi and Pythagoras to deal with here, and neither of these functions is easy for making whole-number calculations: they both often produce odd fractions when dealing with triangles and circles. The reason we may have ended up with a few odd numbers here and there, is that the Zil system of measurement seems to have been designed for use in perimeter lengths, rather than the diameters of these

7. Precessional Henge

henges. A single measurement system cannot handle both diameters and perimeters in whole numbers, and so fractions are inevitable somewhere. The full answer to this question is given at the end of the chapter.

I think that the primary base length on this site, used by the designer, was the 33 zy or 6 Zil rod length in the triangle in fig 31. The Pythagorean lengths of 5, 12 and 13 can then be used to discover the true diameter of the Station stones and the Aubrey holes; this gives us 85.8 zy (86.14 m), exactly as Petrie suggested. Now if we multiply this 85.8 zy diameter by Pi (22:7), we end up with a perimeter length of 269.6 zy, which does not look too promising. But if this figure is divided by 5.5 to derive the rod length, the result is 49 zr, which just happens to be 7 squared. The perimeter length of the Aubrey ring is now in meaningful whole-number figures.

So not only was the design of Stonehenge based on some complicated maths, but it was also the root of the dimensions for the Avebury henge, as I demonstrated in chapter V. Incidentally, the critical angle that is formed by this 13-12-5 Pythagorean triangle is 22.6°; the fact that this angle is highlighted in this fashion will become important later.

At the same time as marking the site axis of Stonehenge, two of the Station stones also lie inside small barrows. These two barrows, to the north and south of the site, also conveniently sit at the extremities of the Pythagorean triangles, so they are also offset by about 22.6° from the axis of the site. An angle of nearly 23° is a familiar number to our theme; it is the Earth's angle of obliquity, or tilt angle, again (23.5°). It was quite apparent, even at this early stage in the investigation, that I was quite possibly looking at something terrestrial again – another Earth picture just like the one at Avebury.

Avenue

Another feature that needs to be explained is the angle of the Avenue, which, according to Petrie, runs off at 51° to the east of true north, and defines the equator of the site. [4] The orientation of this Avenue is uncertain under the traditional interpretation of the site. It has often been simply thought of as a processional way that leads down to the river Avon. In some respects this is exactly what it does and the bluestones themselves may well have been dragged up this very Avenue from a landing-stage on the River Avon, but there is more to their alignment than this. The more famous Heelstone lies just to the south of the line of the Avenue, and it is along this line that the traditional midsummer sunrise is supposed to appear: or does it?

7. Precessional Henge

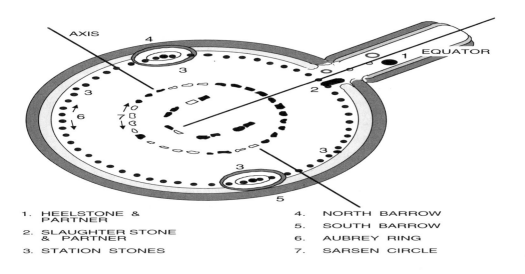

1. HEELSTONE & PARTNER
2. SLAUGHTER STONE & PARTNER
3. STATION STONES
4. NORTH BARROW
5. SOUTH BARROW
6. AUBREY RING
7. SARSEN CIRCLE

Fig 32. The axis and equator of Stonehenge

However, the Heelstone is only a jagged piece of rock, whereas the Avenue is a majestic double-lined procession route, leading right up to and through the henge. In addition, the 'important' Heelstone used to have a partner, a stone that lay slightly to the north of the Avenue. It is the line that runs in between these two stones that marks the center-line of the Avenue, so it is quite apparent that the line of the Avenue should be considered the more important alignment. The Avenue lies a full 1° to the north of the Heelstone, so what does the line of the Avenue mark?

Once again, we should clear the mind of all preconceptions and consider all possibilities, even the heresy that the midsummer sunrise may be nothing to do with the Heelstone, or possibly that it is a mere sideshow that obscures the main event. To say that this particular alignment is a coincidence may seem to be a bold statement, as most people know that this alignment with the sunrise is correct: don't they? As usual, the reality is quite different from the assumed answers to these problems. Here are comments on this misalignment in the sunrise that may not be familiar, or may have been glossed over because they seemed unimportant:

Let us proceed to another crucially important feature; the four Station stones ... (with these) a rather precise rectangle is formed, the short sides of which are *close* to being parallel to the direction from the center to the Heelstone. [5]

These comments are from Professor Sir Fred Hoyle, the famous scientist and astronomer, writing in his short missive on Stonehenge. He was comparing the equator of the monument, which is defined by the four Station stones, with the all-important alignment of the Heelstone. Note that the equator of the henge is only *close* to being parallel with a line drawn out to the Heelstone. This is because the equator of the monument aligns itself between the Heelstone and its missing partner, along the line of the Avenue. It does not align with the Heelstone itself. There is no getting away from this; the positions of the Station stones define quite accurately the center-line of the monument, and this <u>equator</u> of the henge is out through the center of the Avenue, between the Heelstone and its missing partner. Undoubtedly then, this alignment is more important than the Heelstone alignment, which lies some 1° to the south. Hoyle continues:

The bank ... was broken to allow an uninterrupted view in the direction of the midsummer Sun. A distant stone, the Heelstone as it has been named in modern times, was erected in this direction. [6]

This is the traditional image of Stonehenge: that the Sun rises over the Heelstone on midsummer's day. But this is not so, as we shall see, for now the doubts begin to creep in:

When I first read Professor Hawkin's book *Stonehenge Decoded,* I was struck by the angular differences between the actual measured sighting lines and the astronomical alignments ... Inadvertent errors of 0.2° to 0.4° might have been expected, but not the errors of 1° to 2° that I found. [7]

The critical question arises, therefore, of whether these large 'errors' of 1° to 2° could have been made deliberately by the builders. [8]

Professor Hoyle's scientific training does not allow him entirely to gloss over the inconsistencies here. He has to leave that element of doubt by saying 'close to', or indeed, by declaring the errors up front. All in all, it is a different story from the one normally told. So the fact remains that the midsummer sunrise does not align either with the Avenue or the Heelstone, and this fact has to be explained if we are to decipher the site fully.

7. Precessional Henge

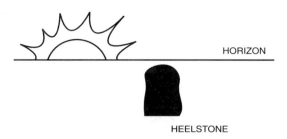

HORIZON

HEELSTONE

Fig 33. Sunrise at Stonehenge

So what is the Sun really doing? Professor Hoyle devotes some 15 pages to the precise calculation of the position of the midsummer sunrise, allowing for such events as atmospheric refraction and the elevation of the horizon. For all this effort we are very grateful, but I shall spare you the details. The outcome of this tedious chore is that the Sun first rises on a bearing of 048.5° east of true north. This compares with a site equator along the Avenue of 051° east of north, and the Heelstone which measures 052°. In this case, the Sun actually rises some 3.5° to the north of the Heelstone. (Professor Hoyle's 1–2° error did not allow for atmospheric refraction, and any pictures with the Sun rising from under the Heelstone are not taken exactly at midsummer.)

The question one really needs to ask is what do we define as a sunrise. Is it the first view of the Sun, as has been calculated by Hoyle, or should it be a half Sun or a full Sun just sitting on the horizon? This is not an academic question because at the midsummer sunrise, the Sun does not rise vertically into the air, like some equatorial sunrises. It is simultaneously tracking towards the south while it is rising and so, the later we take our 'sunrise' to be, the closer the Sun gets to the Heelstone. In fact, the modern 'sunrise' over the Heelstone that everyone looks for is not taken when the Sun first rises. It is taken when the center of the Sun is some 2° above the horizon. So, even despite aberration making the Sun appear larger than its true size (the harvest moon effect), it is not just skimming the horizon as we might expect; it is a full Sun's diameter above the Heelstone. Taking into account the full effects of atmospheric refraction (which artificially advances the sunrise), this Heelstone 'sunrise' is a full 14 minutes after the real sunrise – the 'real' sunrise being taken as when the first limb of the Sun climbs above the horizon, and when the first direct rays of the Sun are seen.

7. Precessional Henge

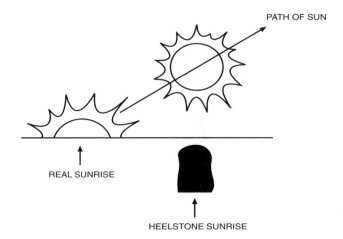

REAL SUNRISE

HEELSTONE SUNRISE

Fig 34. The two sunrises

This is a little peculiar, for it should have been quite easy, even for Neolithic man, to define the true midsummer sunrise; it is not a very difficult task. Stand a man with a vertical pole out on the plain in roughly the right position. Just as the Sun comes up (let us assume the first limb is the required event), shout 'left a bit, right a bit', until the rod aligns with the rising Sun. One might expect that using such a visual sighting, the rod could be placed on the ground within 20 cm of the required position. If the man stood about 100 meters away, the error involved in this simple technique is just $^1/_{10}$ of one degree.

All we have used to define this very accurate position of the sunrise is a pole and verbal commands. Yet we have achieved an accuracy some 30 times better than we see at Stonehenge. Why? What has changed? Fred Hoyle surmised many things that could have changed over the millennia, from ground subsidence, to trees on the horizon, to a thicker atmosphere causing more refraction; but only one item would really cause such a dramatic shift in the sunrise angle and that is a shift in our Earth's axis.

Wobble

This shift in the Earth's axis is not quite as improbable as it may at first sound. It has been accepted for some time now that the Earth's axis not only precesses, or 'wobbles', but that it also has a smaller 'wiggle' that is superimposed on the larger wobble. There are two wiggles that are superimposed upon the precessional rotation of the axis of the Earth. One

Plate 1. The step pyramid of Djoser at Saqqara, constructed in six steps.

Plate 2. The Silbury Pyramid at Marlborough, which was also constructed in six steps. The pyramid was then covered in earth to protect the fragile chalk cladding. For scale, note the person at the base of the pyramid.

Plate 3. Gate guardian from the tomb of Tutankhamen, showing the pyramidal apron being formed by the rays of the Sun beaming upwards.

Plate 4. Detail from the pyramid of Meidum. Note that the cladding is preserved in the lower levels, where the eroded rubble has protected it.

Plate 5. The pyramid of Meidum. Note the heaps of eroded rubble at the base. The intact original cladding stones can be seen where the corner has been cleared of rubble.

Plate 6. The Draco (Red) Pyramid at Dahshur, with the Vega (Bent) Pyramid in the background.

Plate 7.   Plate 8.

Comparison of erosion rates at the Great Pyramid. Both plates show the area that was always exposed to the elements on the left; the area that was covered by the cladding stones is on the right. Note the large difference in erosion between the two.

Plate 9. The round table in the Great Hall at Winchester. The table appears to have been constructed using very ancient measurement systems.

Plate 10. One of the diamond shaped stones at Avebury.

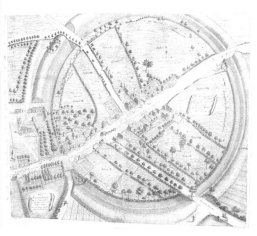

Plate 11. The original drawing of Avebury, by W. Stukeley 1743.

Plate 12. The Avebury ring near Marlborough, the largest henge in the world. Was it designed to look like a planetary body?

Plate 13. Stonehenge. Note the small barrows to the left and right; are these astronomical drawings on a Neolithic henge?

Plate 14.   Plate 15.
The Trilithons at Stonehenge. Note how most of the Trilithons are rugged, whereas the central Trilithon has the smoothest stones on the site. If this Trilithon had survived, it would have been the pride of the site; is this not the most important formation at Stonehenge?

Plate 16. Looking down the equator of Stonehenge, at the Avenue. The Heelstone, visible through the ring, originally had a partner-stone to the left. The midsummer sunrise was originally supposed to appear between these two stones, down the length of the Avenue.

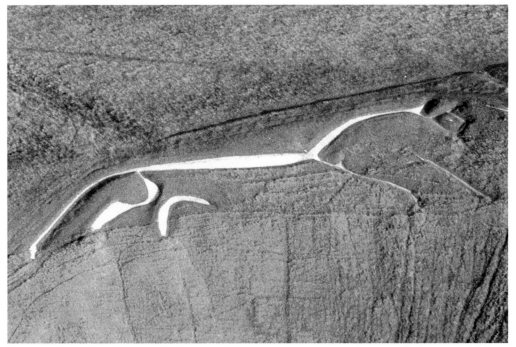

Plate 17. The White Horse at Uffington. The horse lies the same distance from Avebury as does Stonehenge.

Plate 18. Newgrange, Ireland. Was this henge based on the same design as Avebury?

Plate 19. The Grand Gallery in the Great Pyramid. Why was such a vast passageway deemed necessary, when the rest of the passageways are tiny?

Plate 20. Baroque candelabra, Mallorca Cathedral, Palma, Spain.

Plate 21. The three pyramids of Giza, taken from the south-west. The Great Pyramid is in the background.

is known as nuation, which simply means a 'nodding' motion. It is caused by the gravitational effect of the Moon and is quite small. The other is called libration, which means to oscillate, and is much larger. The deviation from our present 23.4° angle of tilt is slow and very difficult to establish with precision, as this libration can be affected by things as diverse as the build-up of ice at the poles during an ice-age, and the strength of flow of the ocean currents. One expert, the astronomer Milutin Milankovitch, from the former Yugoslavia, gives a value for the libration of +/– 1.2° with a cycle time of 41,000 years so, in this case, this wobble is quite a slow and unpredictable affair. [9]

This angle, however, does fit in quite nicely with the tilt axis deviation that is required to make Stonehenge 'work properly'. The midsummer sunrise is some 2.5° to the north of the alignment of the Avenue, as we saw earlier. This error has been exacerbated slightly because Professor Hoyle used 24° for the tilt angle of the Earth's axis instead of 23.5°; as this is the axis angle that is thought, by many scientists, to have been present in 3500 BC. If we used our current tilt axis of 23.5° instead of 24°, this error in the position of the sunrise reduces to 1.7° (for the formula used see the notes and references). [10] But if we liberate our minds again from the current chronology of the site, we are free to use any tilt axis of the Earth that we like, so the question then becomes 'at what tilt-axis would the layout of Stonehenge really work as intended', with the Sun just peeping over the horizon, directly down the line of the Avenue?

The tilt angle required would, in fact, be 22.5°. With that tilt angle of the Earth's axis, the Sun would rise at the midsummer solstice at a position 51° east of due north, exactly along the line of the Avenue. The Sun would be doing this at the site of a monument called Stonehenge, a monument which is situated on a latitude of 51.1° north of the Equator. Hold on a minute; there is a slight coincidence here. Standing a man out on the plains of Salisbury and shouting 'left a bit, right a bit' is one thing, but being able to measure the latitude on which to build the monument is quite another. But there may be even more to this than simply measuring the latitude of Stonehenge; as we can see if we take a look at the following table of sunrises and latitudes which are all calculated using an Earth tilt axis of 22.5°:

Position	Latitude	Sunrise angle (from true north)
Oslo	60 N	40°
Newcastle	55 N	48°
Stonehenge	51.15 N	51.15°
Luxembourg	50 N	53°
Milan	45 N	57°
Cairo	30 N	64°

7. Precessional Henge

Looking down the table, we can see that for any given tilt angle of the Earth's axis, there is only one position on the Earth where the latitude of the observer equals the angle of the midsummer sunrise. That position was, in this case, 51.15° north (or south) and at no other latitude on the surface of the Earth would this little coincidence happen. Was this planned? It may seem like a bold proposition, but Stonehenge seems to have been deliberately placed in this location for an astronomical reason; so what was it?

If the designer had this kind of knowledge and capability, then there is a good reason for pre-planning this little coincidence. For in doing so, the designer has now given us all the information we require to calculate the Earth's tilt axis at the time that these monuments were built. So, if there were to be any little discrepancies in the future – like the orientation of Avebury for instance – we can be certain about what Earth tilt axis we should be using in our calculations. Although the 'tilt angle' of Avebury can be estimated only roughly, because the entrance stones to the site are missing, it does actually seem to be closer to 22.5° than to 23.5°. If this 'error' seemed to be an issue with the theory then it need not be so any longer, as the angle of obliquity for the Earth at the time these monuments were built appears to have been 22.5°.

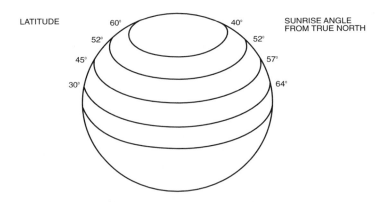

Fig 35. Earth's midsummer sunrise

Heelstone

As has been shown, it is the orientation of the Avenue that is of prime importance to the Stonehenge site, so why has the importance of the

7. Precessional Henge

Avenue been lost to us in favour of that rather rugged and poorly prepared Heelstone? There is probably a very long-standing misconception here, and one suspects that the Druids may have precipitated this misconception a few thousand years ago.

The problem was that, as the millennia moved on, the Earth's tilt axis changed slightly but the position and orientation of Stonehenge did not. So the 'picture' it drew looked slightly more odd to the observer as the years rolled on. The trusty Avenue was still in its same position, but the midsummer sunrise was now to the north of this important equatorial line; the trouble with this being that both the northern partner to the Heelstone; and also stone number 30 in the Sarsen circle, now began to obscure the view of this first sunrise and this, in turn, appeared to defeat the whole rationale for building the henge. The first flash of the sunrise was supposed to be visible and it was supposed to be down the line of the Avenue – the picture had become confused and it is no wonder that the ancients were equally confused about this odd situation.

Stone 30, the offending stone in the Sarsen circle, not only excluded a proper view of the sunrise, but also excluded a proper view of the northern partners to the Heel and Slaughter stones. Perhaps the later custodians of the Stonehenge site began to think that these two northern stones were not so important in the grand scheme; otherwise, why should the Sarsen ring obscure them and why should they obscure the important midsummer sunrise? Maybe it was for *this* reason that somebody, in the ancient history of the site, has pulled down the two northern partners to the Heelstone and destroyed them.

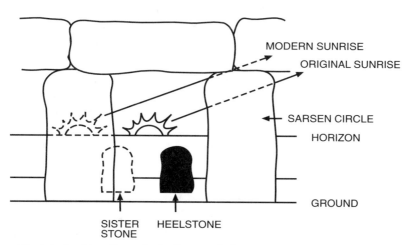

Fig 36. Looking through the Sarsen circle

149

7. Precessional Henge

But the Sun continued its slow march northwards and the midsummer's first sunrise now disappeared behind stone 30 in the Sarsen circle. The ancient Druids must have pondered over this misalignment for centuries and it would seem that, finally, they came to the conclusion that the midsummer celebration would now be of the Sun passing over the Avenue and Heelstone. A small barrow was then constructed around the Heelstone to emphasize its new primary role.

The situation had been resolved and the history of the site may then have proceeded something like this. The Heel and Slaughter stones now marked the 'orthodox' midsummer sunrise; or rather, they marked the Sun passing over these stones a full 14 minutes after the sunrise. This was now the orthodox view, so woe betide anyone who challenged that belief. Since the sister-stones of the Heel and Slaughter stones were now missing, the whole orientation of the Avenue had been subtly changed, and so this belief in the importance of the Heelstone has therefore prevailed and persisted to this day. It is as difficult to change this established 'truth' as it is to change any religious dogma: it had become established as a fact, even if it was not a fact. As Clement, Bishop of Alexandria, said in the fourth century, when discussing the beliefs of the church of James:

> For, even if they should say something true, one who loves the truth should not, even so, agree with them. For not all true things are the truth, nor should that truth which (merely) seems true according to human opinions be preferred to the true truth, that according to the faith. [11]

In other words, one should keep to the established orthodox doctrine, even if it is wrong. However, the original alignment of the Avenue was not wrong. The angles involved were extremely precise and accurate, but just in a different fashion from the one commonly thought. So what was really being portrayed by this angle of the Avenue; this sacred alignment of Stonehenge? This could not be simpler, but it has never been proposed before because of yet another underestimation of the abilities of the designer of these monuments. The true nature of Stonehenge has been glossed over, even though the angles involved must have been jumping off the page at people for centuries.

The position of Stonehenge on the surface of the Earth is defined as being a latitude of 51° 10´ north or 51.15° north, and the Avebury henge sits at 51.4°. So in this case, if we wished to draw the position of the Stonehenge site on a cross-section of the Earth, we would have to make a mark at an angle of 51.15° above the equator of that circle. It just so

7. Precessional Henge

happens that we can find these angles present, not only in the alignment of the great Avenue, but also in the arrangement of the Aubrey ring – the ring of holes that was discussed in chapter V. There is an Aubrey hole that lies exactly on the line of the Avenue and there is also another one that lies on the exact axis of the henge; so the 56 Aubrey holes are orientated with the Avenue and the Station stones, not with the Heelstone.

If we walk from the Avenue's hole northwards, we find an Aubrey hole that is exactly 51.4° north of this equator. This hole is in exactly the right position to mark the site of Avebury on this ancient Earth-map and it lies almost exactly on the true north line of the whole henge. Continuing anticlockwise, the barrows to the north and south of the site are displaced about 23° from the axis of Stonehenge, as has already been demonstrated; and so these barrows could be marking the angle of obliquity of the Earth, the leaning angle just like the lean of Avebury. The final piece of this journey takes us to the axis of the henge, which in turn could be regarded as the axis of the Earth – the line about which the Earth spins. In fact, what we seem to have here are all the angles required for the orientation of the Earth itself.

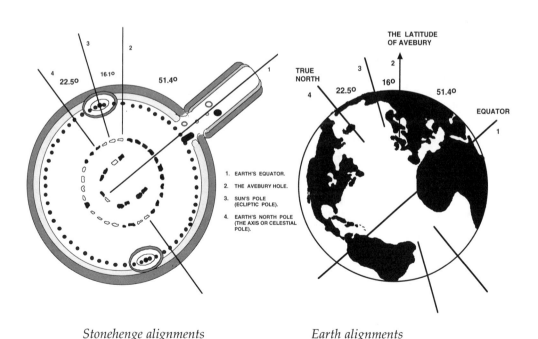

Stonehenge alignments
Fig 37.

Earth alignments

7. Precessional Henge

Precession

The terminology being used here is really quite simple and can be explained fairly quickly, but we should firstly look at some very simple astronomy. Astronomers have defined basic standards for looking at the stars. The first of these is the Celestial Equator. The equator of the Earth, if drawn out into space, forms a circle around the Universe, known as the Celestial Equator. The position of the Celestial Equator is constant over a normal lifetime and so an observer on the equator will see the same stars directly overhead on the same dates each year. At 90° to the Celestial Equator we have the Celestial Pole, the Earth's North Pole. Currently, this pole points at the star Polaris and, over a normal lifetime, this pole would also appear to be quite stable and point at the same star in the northern and southern skies.

The equator of the Solar System, however, is at a slightly different angle. It is defined as the plane along which all the planets revolve and is known as the Ecliptic. The Ecliptic can also be drawn out into space to form another circle. This Ecliptic circle is much more stable than the Celestial Equator and will remain constant in its position, not just over a lifetime, but over millions of years. At 90° to this circle there is another pole, known as the Ecliptic Pole, the Sun's pole as I have called it. This pole is, again, constant over millions of years. (To be precise, the Sun's pole is slightly inclined from the Ecliptic Pole, but the analogy gives a good picture of the situation.) So, we have the two poles that we shall be mentioning from time to time – the pole of the Earth, and the pole of the Sun – and they are displaced from each other by 23.5°, or the angle of inclination of the Earth.

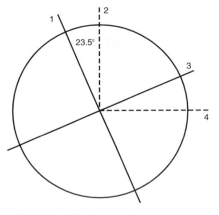

1.	CELESTIAL POLE OR EARTH'S POLE
2.	ECLIPTIC POLE OR SUN'S POLE
3.	CELESTIAL EQUATOR OR EARTH'S EQUATOR
4.	ECLIPTIC OR PLANE OF SOLAR SYSTEM

Fig 38.   The two poles

7. Precessional Henge

So, the Earth's pole is not quite a constant feature, and it has not always pointed at the star Polaris, because of the gentle circular motion known as precession. Precession seems to be a complicated thing to grasp, but think of it as being the same as the wobbles in a child's spinning top. A top not only spins, but its axis also wobbles in a circular motion at the same time. The axis of the Earth does exactly the same, but more slowly: it has a 25,765-year-long wobble. As the Earth wobbles, it describes a massive circle in the northern sky, that takes nearly 26,000 years to draw.

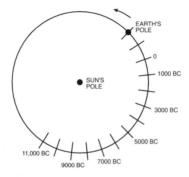

Fig 39. Position of the Celestial Pole over the last 11,000 years

In this case, we can divide up this circle into 26 divisions, with each division representing the position of the Celestial Pole every 1,000 years. So, during this long 'precessional circle', the Earth's pole performs a slow pirouette around the Sun's pole.

The Barrows

As I studied the aerial picture of the henge in front of me, it was quite evident that there was much more to these barrows than a simple Earth's axis angle of 23°. For not only are the Stonehenge barrows marking the position of the Sun's poles, they also seem to be representations of the function of these poles. The precessional cycle that we have been describing is all about the tracing of circles in the northern and southern constellations; these are celestial circles that surround the central position known as the Ecliptic Pole, or the Sun's pole.

It has already been shown that the centers of the barrows at Stonehenge are in exactly the right position to be representations of the

7. *Precessional Henge*

Sun's pole, but the barrows themselves are circles that surround this central 'Sun's pole' position. So here at Stonehenge, we have a circle drawn around the Sun's pole, which is exactly the same as can be traced in the real heavens. This is clearly the function of these barrows; they are nothing less than precessional circles, marked out on an extremely ancient map of the Earth. They are precisely as one would draw them on a real diagram of the Earth, as seen from a point in space.

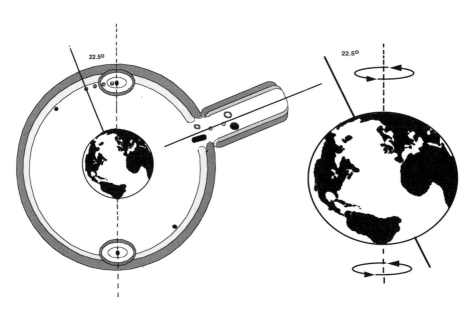

The Stonehenge barrows   *The Sun's pole (Ecliptic Pole)*
Fig 40.

This has to be the true function of the Avenue at Stonehenge: it sets out the baseline of this new Earth picture – it marks the equator of the Earth. Just as I have proposed for Avebury, we have yet another outline of the Earth; this time, one drawn on the plains of Salisbury. Can this all be coincidence? One would think not. In the case of Stonehenge, not only can we see the form of the Earth, but we also appear to have a cross-section through the heavens. Look at the diagram again: is this not the motion of the Earth's axis, perfectly drawn out on a Stone Age monument?! Perhaps it is time to change our entrenched concepts of the history of mankind; to question our history teachers more closely about what they actually know, rather than what they think they know.

7. *Precessional Henge*

Aubrey angles

Although this picture looks realistic, can we really accept that all the angles are quite so perfect as I have claimed? Can one of those little Aubrey holes really be a marker for the position of Stonehenge or Avebury on the real Earth? There are, after all, so many little Aubrey holes to choose from; it would seem to be easy to make any theory fit. Exceptional claims need exceptional evidence, so to give us more confidence in these theories there is, as usual, some further confirmation provided by the designer. This confirmation is provided by those very same Aubrey holes that we have already used.

The layout of Stonehenge is a little rough in places. Even if the monument was designed by a very competent designer, it was certainly constructed by slightly less articulate artisans, and so one or two of the alignments are not so precise as one would like. The Avenue angle, for instance, is defined by four rugged stones measuring some 1.5 m each in width and a roadway many meters wide, so the precise orientation of the Avenue is subject to some interpretation. It would be nice, therefore, if we could mathematically place the orientation of this Avenue to, say, the nearest $\frac{1}{10}$ of a degree to verify this theory quite precisely. Our diligent designer has given us all the information we require to do just that. This has been achieved with the neatest of crosschecks; one that can confirm the special nature of that Aubrey hole that marks the position of Stonehenge or Avebury on the Earth map, and also confirm the exact tilt angle of the Earth.

There are 56 of these Aubrey holes in the outer ring at Stonehenge. This number appeared at first to be rather too even and with too little, or no, relationship to Pi to be a product of our designer. Are these, instead, later additions to the site; a product of a designer who no longer knew the usual relationship to the number Pi? No, these are not later additions, for as we said before, who else would dig holes and fill them in again? The first indication that this was, in fact, an original part of the design is that it forms part of a mathematical progression. The perimeter length of the Aubrey ring at Stonehenge is 7 x 7 zr and the number of holes in the ring is 7 x 8. Just to the north of this site, the number of stones at the Avebury site is 7 x 14 and its perimeter is 7 x 28 zr. So, the 56-hole ring is based on a common denominator – the number 7.

Thus, the real mathematical reason for this 56-hole design is not that it defines some lunar risings or eclipses, as has been proposed in previous works; it is because, in using this spacing, each hole becomes situated 6.43° from its partner. In other words, each segment between two holes measures 6.43° (360° divided by 56 equals 6.43°). It happens that there is

7. Precessional Henge

an Aubrey hole that is directly in line with the center-line of the Avenue, which again is an indication of the special nature of this orientation. If we track north and west around the Aubrey ring, we find that there is another Aubrey hole just about in the due north position: the Stonehenge hole. If we count from the Avenue hole up to the Stonehenge hole, there are a total of eight Aubrey holes and therefore eight segments between these two points. Each segment subtends an angle of 6.43°, and 8 x 6.43° equals 51.4°, which is the latitude of Avebury, just north of Stonehenge.

If we do the same when heading further west, we find that there is another Aubrey hole situated on the line of the axis of the site. There are a further six Aubrey holes in this next segment, from the Stonehenge hole up to the axis, and six segments in between: 6 x 6.43 = 38.6°. It is not too surprising that the remaining latitude from Avebury northwards up to the North Pole is 38.6°.

So the Aubrey holes are there because they provide confirmation that the angles we are looking at are correct. It doesn't matter how inaccurately these holes are placed in the ground in reality, because mathematically they are perfect. We can see the maths and so we can also see into the mind of the designer. This little crosscheck only works in this perfect fashion because the 6.43° between each Aubrey hole is an exact divisor of the latitude of Avebury (51.4°) and, at the same time, an exact divisor of 90°. This will work only if there are either 28 or 56 Aubrey holes. Other combinations of numbers will divide nicely into the 51.4° but will not, at the same time, mark the axis: the 90° position.

This is not all. The magic number 56 is even more cunning because these same Aubrey holes will also define and confirm the new angle for the axis of the Earth: 22.5°. There are very convenient Aubrey holes that lie exactly on three of the pertinent points of the Earth diagram. Looking at the fourth and last of these points – the barrows – we find a problem. The center of each of these barrows lies exactly in between two Aubrey holes; there is no convenient hole to use in the calculation. Does this mean that something is fundamentally amiss with this whole idea? Not at all; this is not a reason to give up, for the data is looking far too good for coincidence thus far.

Struggling on, we should remember that the axis angle of the Earth that works for the Stonehenge site is 22.5°. Because of the position of the barrows in relation to the Aubrey holes, there are exactly 3.5 Aubrey segments between the axis of the henge (the Earth's pole) and the center of the barrows (the Sun's pole). It should be of no surprise by now that 3.5 x 6.42857, which is the exact angle of each segment between these Aubrey holes, equals exactly 22.5°. This has to have been planned, for even a 28-hole Aubrey ring would no longer satisfy all these demands; only a 56-hole ring will work, and a 56-hole ring is what we have. Such are the coincidences that we find on these sites.

Better still, if we recall the layout of the Pythagorean triangles in the center of Stonehenge from earlier in this chapter, the critical angle of these triangles was 22.6°. We might have thought that these triangles being Pythagorean was just another coincidence at the time, but it was not. Now we can see that these triangles were placed in exactly the right location relative to the Aubrey holes, so that the triangles bisect exactly 3.5 Aubrey holes. And 3.5 Aubrey holes equals exactly 22.5°.

It is unlikely that all of this could have happened by accident; the designer must have known that 360 ÷ 56 x 3.5 = 22.5°, and at the same time he must have known that a Pythagorean 5-12-13 triangle also produces a 22.6° angle. (The closest Pythagorean triangle to 22.5° by far.)

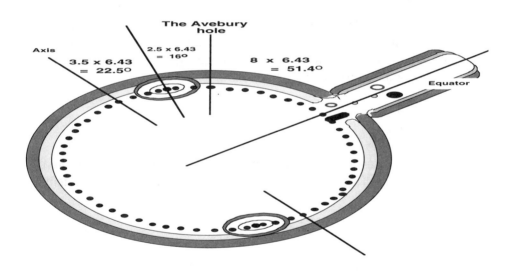

Fig 41. The Aubrey ring and the Avebury hole

The evidence is stark: the designer of Stonehenge was apparently conversant with some fairly complicated maths and astronomy. In addition, we can also see that the Earth's tilt axis has now been very precisely defined by the position of both the Aubrey holes and the Pythagorean triangles. The tilt angle of the Earth in the era of Stonehenge's construction is likely to have been 22.5°, and the fact that the Stonehenge designer knew of this may feel a little uncomfortable to those brought up on modern perceptions of history.

Of all these interesting little Aubrey holes, then, at least one of the four that we have identified is very special. This is the one that lies due north of the site; number 48 under the traditional classification. This hole represents the position of Avebury on this ancient 'map' of the Earth. One would expect that, being so special, it may have contained something unique, perhaps with something being placed at the bottom of the hole. Unfortunately this particular hole is one of the few that has not yet been excavated, according to the English Heritage 1995 Archaeological Report. It would be nice to see if such a prediction will bear any fruit.

If such a scenario were true for these ancient sites, then the archaeological world will never be the same again. How can we possibly equate the Neolithic tribes of Wiltshire with such a technological knowledge of the Earth? Yet if we disbelieve these theories, how are we to explain the coincidences that are to be found? Is it really coincidence that Stonehenge was constructed in the only location that will allow the sunrise to equal its latitude in this era? That it was constructed with angles and alignments that equal those of our real Earth? That it clearly predicts the motion of the axis of the Earth? It is difficult to keep saying repeating 'coincidence'; after the tenth rendering it starts to ring rather hollow.

Sarsen circle

So much for the layout of the outer rings at Stonehenge. What of the great Sarsen circle itself and the horseshoe Trilithons? What do these items signify?

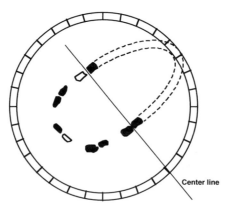

Fig 42. The oval

7. *Precessional Henge*

There is a conundrum here, but it is difficult to see exactly what it means in respect to the layout of the Earth. It is possible to demonstrate that there is a link between the Sarsen circle and the Trilithon oval; that they are part of the same mathematical layout, and we can link them in two ways. Firstly, we can extend the horseshoe shape into a complete oval, with the last two pairs of Trilithons in the open end of the horseshoe marking the center of this completed oval. Having done this, we find that the completed oval just joins with the Sarsen circle; they do not just touch, they merge exactly. This may not look the case on the diagram, but if we measure the center of such an oval, it is marked exactly by the center of the last two pairs of Trilithons.

The link between the circle and the oval can be taken one step further because we can compare both of their perimeter lengths. The perimeter of the Sarsen circle can be calculated with our usual Pi formula and it measures 99 Zil yards or 18 Zil rods. The oval, however, has a more complicated formula, and its perimeter length is given by the formula:

$$\frac{2 \times Pi \times \sqrt{a^2 + b^2}}{2} \qquad \text{a \& b are the radii of the oval.}$$

The radii of the horseshoe oval that must go into this formula are the shortest and longest lengths measurable. These turn out to be 16.5 x 24.75 zy, which are unlikely starting values for any well-planned oval. However, if we work out the perimeter length of the oval, it turns out to be an impressively round 66 Zil yards, which equates to 12 Zil rods. Once more we have a situation that can be explained only in terms of an advanced designer of the site, for who else in this era would be conversant with the oval formula? Who else would be able to make a Sarsen circle with a perimeter length of 99 zy, and place inside it an oval of 66 zy? This has to have been planned and not derived by accident, so the Sarsen circle and the oval must therefore have been cognitively linked in this fashion by the designer.

There is not much further we can progress with this particular line of thought, the only possibility being that perhaps we are looking at representations of latitudes and longitudes again. For if we wish to have latitudes and longitudes on the same diagram, these must, by necessity, be at 90° to each other. When drawing a three-dimensional image of latitudes and longitudes, we always draw one of the circles as an oval, as can be seen in the diagram overleaf.

Here we see the circle and oval imagery of Stonehenge explained in terms of latitudes and longitudes. It is not a complete explanation, but it is a distinct possibility.

7. Precessional Henge

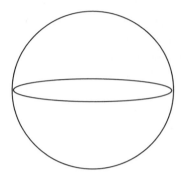

Fig 43. Latitudes and Longitudes

Precessional clock

With the uncovering of the Avebury and Stonehenge 'Earths', anything was becoming possible and the historical presence of an ancient technical civilization was becoming more and more probable. With this new outlook on history, it was only fitting to speculate on another radical possibility for Stonehenge; the site may have one further mathematical usage. The evidence for this theory, like so many times before, comes to us from Greece. The fact that ancient Greece can tell us so much about these sites is one more indicator that the ancient traditions of our architect survived relatively intact into quite recent history. The evidence for this additional tradition at the Stonehenge site comes from the Sicilian historian Diodorus (90 - 21 BC), who is, in turn, quoting from another ancient historian Hecataeus (*c.* 500 BC):

> Hecataeus and some others tell us that over against the 'land of the Celts' there exists in the ocean an island not smaller than Sicily. This island is inhabited by the Hyperboreans, who are called by that name because their home is beyond the point whence the north wind [Boreas] blows; and the land is both fertile and productive of every crop, and since it has an unusually temperate climate it produces two harvests each year. Moreover, the following legend is told concerning it. Leto (mother of Apollo and Artemis) was born on this island, and for this reason Apollo is honoured among them above all other gods; and the inhabitants are looked upon as priests of Apollo, after a manner, since they praise this god continuously.

7. Precessional Henge

And there is also on the Island both a magnificent sacred precinct of Apollo and a notable temple which is adorned with many votive offerings and is spherical in shape ... The myth also relates that certain Greeks visited the Hyperboreans and left behind them there costly votive offerings bearing inscriptions in Greek letters. And in the same way Abaris, a Hyperborean, came to Greece in ancient times and renewed the goodwill and kinship of his people to the Delians...

The account is also given that the god visits the island every *nineteen years,* the period in which the return of the stars to the same place in the heavens is accomplished; and for this reason the nineteen-year period is called by the Greeks the 'year of the Meton'. At the time of this appearance of the god he both plays on the cithara and dances continuously the night through from the vernal equinox until the rising of the Pleiades, expressing in this manner his delight in his successes. And the kings of this city and the supervisors of the sacred precinct are called the Boreades, since they are the descendants of Boreas, and the succession to these positions is always kept in their family. [12]

Here we have one of those intriguing passages from ancient recorded history, but what are we to make of it? Was this all made up? Was it distorted so much down the generations that none of it makes sense any more? Or can we find snippets of real history in amongst the prose? I think most people will identify some areas of reality in the text. For instance, it is easy to make a comparison between the land of Borea and the island of Great Britain. They are more than likely to be one and the same: the temperate climate, the northerly latitudes, the bountiful harvests in comparison to Greece. Even if this description was fourth hand, the details still fit well.

If truths like this can be found in the jottings of Diodorus, what of the rest of the text? For instance, the shape of that sacred temple has to be historically correct. It is described as being spherical (circular) and both Stonehenge and Avebury are not only circular, they are the biggest such constructions in the world. If legends of massive circular temples had filtered down to Greece, they are most likely to have been the great henges of Britain. What other site could this refer to? Indeed, the Greek reference to a *spherical* monument is rather interesting, for although both Stonehenge and Avebury are obviously circular, if they *were* originally intended to be representations of the Earth then they may well have been referred to as being spherical!

If we are to accept that this story does indeed refer to Stonehenge, then there is one other interesting deduction we can make. We also have the reference to Greek inscriptions being transported to Stonehenge in the ancient past, and the dagger carved onto one of the Sarsen stones does indeed seem to be in the Mycenaean style. It would seem that the Greeks were fully aware of Stonehenge, but perhaps there was some cross-fertilization here; perhaps some of the trade was in the other direction, from Britain to Greece. At this same time as these contacts were being made, was a certain inscription – a certain letter of the alphabet – taken from Stonehenge to Greece? The letter Pi (Π)? It is an interesting thought.

Finally, we come to another possible use for Stonehenge and this concerns the nineteen-year celebration period mentioned in the text. The modern translator of these texts makes light of the accuracy of Diodorus, by saying that:

> The author ... often wanders far from the truth ... He often dwells too long on fabulous reports.[13]

Yet, we have already seen that some of Diodorus's reports can also hold real-life observations, especially if one realises that Avebury may have been symbolically 'spherical'; so what of this nineteen-year celebration? Is it from a real and ancient recorded history of Britain or just from Diodorus' imagination?

The Greeks thought that the nineteen-year celebration was derived from the Metonic cycle. This cycle denotes the period required for the return of the phases of the Moon to the same calendar dates. Sir Fred Hoyle, instead, thought that it might have been related to the return of the lunar eclipse nodes. Both are plausible explanations, but the Metonic cycle is actually a 19.6-year cycle, and the eclipse nodes follow an 18.6-year path. We also have to ask whether a Neolithic society would want to mark these events. The return of the phases of the Moon does not really seem to be an exciting cycle to pick out for special attention and, while the return of an eclipse might be more so, the fact that a particular eclipse will recur in nineteen 'eclipse years' is hard to detect when there may be many other eclipses in between to confuse the issue. (The eclipse season recurs every 173 days.) No; while both of these explanations are possible, there is a simpler explanation to this nineteen-year celebration.

The nineteen-year celebration was, I believe, designed as a precessional clock. As we have already seen, Stonehenge embodies a precessional diagram in its layout, as denoted by the north and south barrows. This nineteen-year celebration cycle, which Hecataeus recorded,

7. Precessional Henge

allows us to count off the years between precessional cycles quite precisely. The hint that this is the case is given by Diodorus. He says that the nineteen-year celebration marks the *cycle in which the stars return to the same positions in the heavens*. He is undoubtedly talking of the precessionary cycle here, but his interval of nineteen years is ludicrous; the real precessional cycle is of the order of 26,000 years in length, not nineteen.

This is another case of a little knowledge being a dangerous thing. Not being a scientist, Diodorus was confused about the precessional cycle and simply reported what he had heard. Just as importantly, we may be tempted to dismiss his remark as sheer fantasy, if we ourselves do not understand its true meaning. For Diodorus *was* correct, in some respects. We could say that the stars do return on a cycle of nineteen years, for nineteen years is a handy number when thinking in precessional terms.

The root (as it were) of Diodorus's myth is derived from the fact that the square root of 360 (the number of degrees in a circle) is as near as makes no difference 19. So, if we paced out nineteen degrees around the perimeter of a circle (around the perimeter of Stonehenge), and then did that same process nineteen times in succession, we would arrive back at our starting point. Now, not only are the days in a year linked to the sacred number 360, but so is the precessional cycle; it is one of those tricks of our measurement systems. We can now use this technique as a clock, to count the number of years to go until the stars do indeed return to their original positions, just as Diodorus said.

This has been achieved at Stonehenge by the use of those magic little Aubrey holes again. The number of these holes at the great henge is quite fortuitous, for nothing else would work in quite the same fashion. The Stonehenge precessional clock starts with two markers, just like the hands of a clock; one big one, one little one. The little hand of this clock, instead of marking hours, in this case marks units of 360 years. The big hand in this precessional clock marks the smaller units, the minutes, in groups of 19 years.

The Stonehenge precessional clock is operated as follows:

a.   The two markers start at the same Aubrey hole; say the hole in the 12 o'clock position. The first celebration at Stonehenge is after nineteen years. At this time the large marker, the 'minute' hand, is moved three Aubrey holes in a clockwise fashion. It so happens that three Aubrey holes bisect an angle of 19°, one degree for each year – clever little things these Aubrey holes.

7. *Precessional Henge*

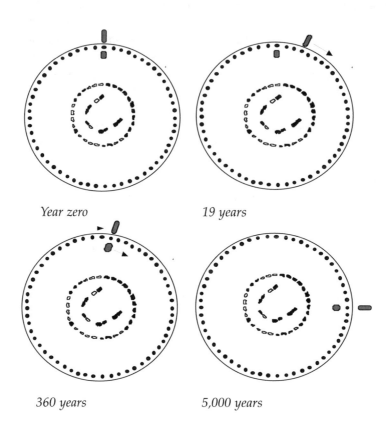

Year zero   19 years

360 years   5,000 years

Fig 44a. The precessional clock

b.   The minute marker continues around the clock face of Stonehenge, moving three holes every nineteen years. After 360 years we arrive back at the 12 o'clock position. But, because of the slight 'inaccuracies' in the system, the last three holes of the minute marker overshoot the hour marker and, collecting the hour marker *en route*, jump one hole to the right. 360 years (361) have been counted off and both markers are together again, but displaced one Aubrey hole to the right. So this slight inaccuracy in the system is not necessarily an inaccuracy at all; it keeps the two markers, the two hands of the clock, together after each rotation.

c.   If we keep up this celebration cycle of nineteen years, with the hour marker being moved on one hole every 360 years, then

7. *Precessional Henge*

when both markers come together at the bottom of the henge – the 6 o'clock position – a little over 10,000 years will have elapsed. Likewise, when both markers arrive back at the original 12 o'clock position, just over 20,000 years have gone by. This could well be a millennium clock at Stonehenge, marked out with nothing more complicated than a few holes in the ground.

d.   We also now have a precessional cycle counter. If 72 Aubrey holes are now counted with the hour marker, this will define one precessional cycle, or just under 26,000 years. So, after counting off 72 holes with the hour marker, the stars will have returned to their original positions in the heavens.

Megalithic triangle

While I have deliberately been using the Zil yard and rod in all the calculations thus far, the Megalithic yard (my) also appears to have been used in the design of the Aubrey circle. While the Zil yard and rod seem to give nice, whole-number answers to the perimeter lengths of the Aubrey circle in particular, due to the fractional nature of Pi the diameter ends up in fractional units. While doodling on the calculator, it suddenly struck me that the diameter of the Aubrey circle, and in turn the dimensions of the Pythagorean triangle drawn there, actually resolved themselves into Megalithic units.

Taking the diameter of the Aubrey circle at 86.3 meters, the diameter of the circle ends up as exactly 104 my. This did not appear to be very meaningful and I had already dismissed this measurement some months previously as being totally irrelevant, but it transpired that this was actually quite an important length. What I had failed to spot at the time was that the diameter of the Aubrey circle contained the 13-12-5 Pythagorean triangle and that the number of units in the 'diameter' of that triangle was 13. This same diameter, which measures 104 units in Megalithic yards, is actually a multiple of 13. This means that the dimensions of this triangle, when measured in Megalithic yards (my), resolves exactly into multiples of the units that are used in the Pythagorean triangle.

This triangle measures 104 x 96 x 40 Megalithic yards, whereas the Pythagorean triangle itself is composed of units of 13 x 12 x 5 units. If all these Megalithic measurements are divided by eight the result is as follows:

7. Precessional Henge

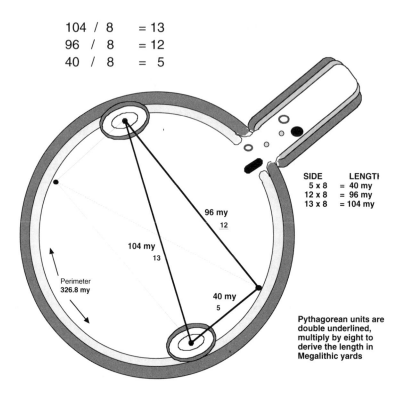

$$104 \ / \ 8 \quad = 13$$
$$96 \ / \ 8 \quad = 12$$
$$40 \ / \ 8 \quad = 5$$

SIDE	LENGTH
5 x 8	= 40 my
12 x 8	= 96 my
13 x 8	= 104 my

96 my
12

104 my
13

Perimeter
326.8 my

40 my
5

Pythagorean units are
double underlined,
multiply by eight to
derive the length in
Megalithic yards

Fig 44b. The Megalithic Pythagorean triangle

What this proves is that the Pythagorean triangle *was* a real part of the original design and that the designer knew of, and used, these complex mathematical functions. It also means that the Megalithic yard *is* a real unit of length, for all the scoffing at this proposition in academic circles. The trouble was that, previously, the only evidence in favour of the Megalithic yard was derived by pointing to certain monuments and saying that they appeared to be measured in whole-number units of Megalithic yards; all of which is not terribly convincing and is easily rebutted by those who like to exclaim 'coincidence' and 'prove it'.

Now, however, it *can* be proved. Here we have a unique mathematical function, the 13-12-5 Pythagorean triangle, which was manufactured on the Stonehenge site in units that are multiples of 13 x 12 x 5. In addition, these units were not derived by looking at this triangle as a starting point for the calculations, as I cannot find any evidence that Thom ever mentioned this triangle. So, the units of measure that Thom independently derived from various stone spacings are suddenly seen to precisely match this unique Pythagorean triangle. This is proof positive that the Megalithic yard is a *real* unit of measure and this is the very reason that this Pythagorean triangle was incorporated into the design in the first place. It is a mathematical proof for the length of the units that were being used on the site.

So where does this leave the poor old Zil yard? Actually, rather than invalidating the claim for another unit of measure, this may actually explain further the reason for having two measurement systems. The Megalithic system works well for the diameters of circles, as we have seen, while the Zil systems have been used on the perimeter lengths, as has been demonstrated. Between the two systems lies the rather odd fractional unit of Pi. The reason for two measurement systems is that, except in rare cases, it is impossible to get whole numbers for both the diameter and circumference of a circle; to do this one needs two measurement systems.

Now, the two measurement systems do not match accurately at present, but the amount of difference is so small that this is probably a result of our not knowing their unit lengths accurately enough. The exact conversion between the two systems would either require the Zil yard increasing from 1.004 m to 1.006 m, or the Megalithic yard reducing from 0.83 m to 0.828 m. These are very small differences and they lie well within the tolerances of the measurements available on the site. But, as already stated, the reason for the Pythagorean triangle being there on the Stonehenge site, is so that any future researcher can mathematically prove the exact length of the measurements that were in use. So, the obvious solution is to calculate these unit lengths from the Pythagorean triangle itself, but this can only be achieved to the accuracy of the measurements that can be made between the Station stones.

Unfortunately, the Station stones do not have exact pointed tops to measure from, and it is likely that at least one of them has leaned over slightly and one has fallen in the last few millennia. There are three recognised measurements of the Station stones and the scatter of their lengths betrays a 55 cm difference of opinion, which is quite large. Again, some of the researchers may have been taking the center of the stones for their measurements, while Petrie says he was using the inner faces of the stones; this in itself will give about a 30 cm difference in the length of the circle's diameter. The problem of defining an accurate measure for the Megalithic and Zil yards is becoming obvious, but since the lengths being measured are quite long, the variations in the resulting unit lengths is thankfully quite small. The results for all three surveys and both of the measurements systems are as follows:

7. Precessional Henge

Survey	Metric diameter of Aubrey circle	Megalithic yard length	Zil yard length
Atkinson	86.70	0.833 m	1.011 m
Thom	86.30	0.830 m	1.006 m
Petrie	86.15	0.828 m	1.004 m

As can be seen, the variations between the two units of length are not only well within the errors of measurements on the site, but they are almost defined by those very errors. As I have tended to used Petrie's data, the Zil yard became 1.004 m as a direct result of this; but if Thom were the more correct in this contest, then it could as easily have been 1.006 m.

Despite this extra revelation, however, the correlation given earlier in the book between the two measurement systems is still valid. The ratio given was 3 : 4 in rods; three Zil rods equalling 4 Megalithic rods. In yards, this means that 16.5 zy should equal 20 my, and if we multiply this through, this gives a Zil yard of 1.004 m (1.006 m), or conversely a Megalithic yard of 0.828 m (0.830 m). Only a more accurate measurement of the Station stones and the whole of the Aubrey circle can resolve these differences and derive a definitive length for both of these measurement systems.

Thanks to this Pythagorean triangle, a definitive answer to some of the metrology of these sites can at last be given. But there are other questions that still lie unanswered, like the era for their construction. What can the layout of these sites tell us about this?

Chapter VIII

Royal Planisphere

The story so far is that both Avebury and Stonehenge have some definite geophysical meaning, the quite startling concept that I had developed of two ancient monuments being no less than accurate representations of our Earth, drawn as if seen to be floating in space. The pictures these monuments portray are not only cartographical maps of the Earth, they also give every indication of being 'pictures' taken from a distance; they come complete with indications of the Earth's axis and the rotation of this axis around the Ecliptic Pole of the Sun. If poor, neglected Avebury and Stonehenge can have such meaning embodied into so few stones, what then can we expect from the millions of stones piled up on the Giza site? It must be quite apparent already that the internal and external dimensions of the Great Pyramid are infused with mathematical meaning, so can we find any more meaningful answers carved from these stones? Indeed we can, but most of that will have to wait until chapter X.

In the meantime, it was also obvious to me that if the layout of the Wiltshire monuments was so important, then the site layout of the Giza plateau might be equally profitable to investigate. Was the plateau three separate projects with pyramids scattered at random, as we are led to believe, or was there a definite plan to the whole site? For many reasons, I felt sure that there was a central plan to the whole plateau, not least because the Mexican pyramids at Teotihuacan have exactly the same layout (see chapter IX). But if the site was all designed at the same time, the question then becomes: does this central plan, at the same time, have any hidden meanings? Quite possibly it does.

It has been clear for some time that the secrets of the pyramids were contained in the stars, but it has always been a mystery as to how the

8. Royal Planisphere

pyramids and the stars were linked. This has been a question that has exercised the minds of many eminent thinkers through the centuries, and some of the earliest people to be interested in these correlations were the Greeks. The earliest surviving star charts are those of Claudius Ptolemaeus (Ptolemy) of the second century AD, containing some 850 stars. It would appear that Ptolemy's almanac was derived from Hipparchus, who lived in the second century BC. Nevertheless, it was thought that Ptolemy had the ability to revise and update the star positions on the chart. It is also thought that Hipparchus undoubtedly got some of his information from Alexandria and the central library of Egypt; yet it is interesting that his almanac also appears to contain the layout of the stars of the Southern Cross; which, being in the southern hemisphere, are not visible from Egypt.[1]

It is only in the modern era that a major step forward was taken into the identification of the role of Giza, with the idea that the three major pyramids at Giza form themselves into the shape of the three stars of the belt of the constellation of Orion.[2] This observation seems to be correct; in the belt of Orion, we have the two larger stars of Alnitak and Alnilam, and then displaced from them is the smaller star called Mintaka. The accuracy of this correlation has been called into question as of late, but I myself don't think that the idea was to replicate the position and intensity of each star to the third decimal place of accuracy. All one needs is a representation that clearly replicates the belt of Orion, and that can easily be recognised as such.

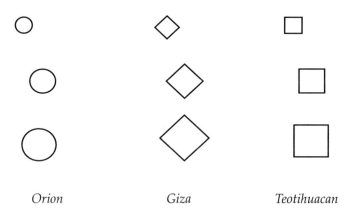

Orion   Giza   Teotihuacan

Fig 45.   Correlation in forms

8. Royal Planisphere

The celestial dance

At the same time as recognising the similarity with Orion, it was also noticed that the constellation of Orion played a central role in the theology of Egypt. This clearly demonstrated that if the Egyptians were going to mimic any stars in the heavens, it was most likely to have been those that form the constellation of Orion. Figure 45 demonstrates how the Mexican pyramid complex at Teotihuacan has great similarities to this same basic design, as was postulated in *Fingerprints of the Gods*, and I will attempt to show further evidence shortly that these correlations are no coincidence.

One of the central themes in these new, speculative books on the history of Egypt was the actual date of these monuments because – as I have already attempted to show – the classical history for these structures rests on very unstable foundations. These new books have attempted to derive a date for the pyramids that is dependent on precession, and for very good reason. If our mythical designer, Zil/Thoth, had wanted to leave a message in his monuments about the era in which they were built, there is really only one way in which to mark a date in the past so that future generations can decipher it.

If something simple like a season of a year was marked, it would not take many years before the mark became confused with other years. To mark an effective date in the past, a mark has to be made on something that has a very slow rhythm indeed, one that is much slower than that of the seasons. Precession fits the bill precisely. Precession has a 26,000 year rhythm and so many *thousands* of years would have to pass before there was any confusion about which cycle in the rhythm was being marked.

Although precession is perfect for leaving a mark in ancient history that can be deciphered mathematically to within 50 years with some ease, there is a small problem with this technique. I briefly explained precession in chapter VII and it really is that simple: the Earth just wobbles like a spinning top. However, the effects of this wobble can be quite confusing, depending on where the observer is standing. If the observer is looking at the spinning top from an external position, the wobble is quite simple and obvious. But try to imagine the view if the observer were standing on the equator of the top and spinning with it: how would the wobble make itself apparent now? Effectively, we on the Earth are just like the observer on the top; and there are three subtle effects caused by this wobble that can be easily observed.

> a.   The most obvious effect is that the North Pole star is not constant. The position in space that the axis of the Earth points to

drifts in a big circle around the constellation of Draco every 26,000 years.

b.   The star constellation that rises with the Sun at a particular time of year also changes. It drifts through the astrological constellations, passing through all twelve of them in 26,000 years.

c.   The height in the night sky of a particular constellation changes; it goes up and down with the passing years. To observe this, however, the season of observation must be changed as the years go by.

Here, we have the three main ways in which a designer can encode precession within his structure, through pointing at one of these effects. By this method we should be able to observe and measure the amount of precessional drift that has occurred since a building has been made, simply by taking measurements from the buildings themselves. Knowing the amount of precession that has taken place allows us to derive accurately the amount of time that has elapsed, as the main precessional cycle is reasonably predictable and stable.

It has been postulated that the pyramids can be dated by using the effect outlined in point 'c' above; by looking at the King's north shaft in the Great Pyramid, which points out at 45° from the horizon and would therefore be pointing directly at Orion's belt in the era of 2500 BC.[3] However, this idea in its current presentation has no form of verification; one could pick any star, any shaft, any season and any era to make the hypothesis work. As we have already seen, these monuments were certainly designed to contain checks and cross-checks to verify to us that each idea is correct. Where are the cross-checks in this case?

If this is not the correct technique for dating the pyramids, can the situation be salvaged in any way? Can we find another way in which to date the pyramids? Yes; and part of the proof of this theory lies in its simplicity. Of the three methods I listed above for observing the precessionary wobble of the Earth, the simplest has to be point a. If the observer looks down from above on to the top of the spinning top, it will be quite obvious what the top is doing and we could simply draw a diagram of that circular motion of its axis. To do this with the motion of the Earth, a good starting point would be a map of the stars on which to draw these celestial circles.

* * *

8. Royal Planisphere

Giza horizon

In the mythology of Egypt, it was common for the gods to have composite images and so Ra was often known as Ra-Atum.[4] Another of his images was of Ra-Horakhti, or 'Horus of the Horizon', or even Atum-Ra-Horakhti. Also, on the stele of pharaoh Amenhotep II (who has a temple close to the Sphinx), Amenhotep refers to the 'Pyramids of Hor-em-Ahket', or 'Pyramids of Horus in the Horizon'.[5] Finally, the stele of Thuthmoses IV, which stood between the paws of the Sphinx, refers to the Sphinx as 'Atum-Hor-em-Akhet' or 'Father god of Horus in the Horizon', and also to the Giza plateau as 'Horizon of Heliopolis in the West'.[6] So, as has been pointed out in *Fingerprints of the Gods*, the symbolism here is of the gods and the Giza plateau being compared to a horizon; but what sort of horizon, and why is this important?

The Giza plateau could be considered to have its own horizon. Giza has pyramids – which were often called 'horizons' – but it also has a stellar horizon; a horizon at the edge of a planisphere, or star chart. In this symbolic position, Giza is, as we shall see, a representation of the layout of this star chart or planisphere, with the constellation of Orion sitting at the base of the chart. The horizons referred to could, in this context therefore, be equated to the Celestial Equator and the Ecliptic Equator; for in the simplistic language available to the Egyptians, these celestial planes equate very closely to being 'horizons'. However, one of the reasons that this planisphere solution has been missed so often in the past is the obsession that is generated by the magnificence of the Giza plateau. For it is not Giza that is most important here; surprisingly enough, it is the pyramids of Dahshur that are in the central position on this planisphere.

I had been toying with these layouts for some time, but it was only because of my research at Stonehenge that the penny began to drop, for there was a great similarity here. In order to start the layout of the Giza planisphere, we must overcome any preconceived ideas that the pyramids at Giza and Dahshur were built, individually, as tombs. I already had enough data to indicate that the biggest pyramids in Egypt were part of one grand building project from the pen of the same designer, and that this project had more to do with maths than tombs. This similarity between Giza and Dahshur can be seen, for instance, in the large blocks of stone above the entrances to the chambers in the Red and Great Pyramids; both are modelled on the 3-4-5 triangle.

But it was the similarity with Wiltshire that gave the hint that it was the geographical layout of the pyramids that was important. The idea began to evolve in my mind that all these pyramids together did indeed form a planisphere, a star chart. A similar idea had been postulated previously, but the author came to no specific conclusions because of the particular stars that he chose. So, which stars are indicated by which pyramids on this chart? The references to horizons gave the clue.

Another problem that made the task more difficult was the proliferation of pyramids in the area; as we saw in chapter I, nearly 100 pyramids were constructed during the pyramid-building era. We must therefore, like at Avebury, differentiate between the original pyramids and the subsequent pyramids that were built by the pharaohs. These additional pyramids were built because the pharaohs knew that the pyramids were special, but it would appear that, just as at Avebury, they did not know quite in what way. So, through the subsequent millennia, the pharaohs built dozens of pyramids within the boundaries of this 'star chart', somewhat disrupting the layout.

However annoying this result is, it should not be too surprising. If Thoth, the designer, had wanted to keep a 'secret of the Universe' concealed within the structure and the layout of the pyramids that he built, there would be no point telling everyone about it. By necessity then, the layout of the pyramids would have to be a secret. What may have happened is that the designer told the priests and pharaohs a riddle; one that spelled out the importance of the pyramids, yet gave nothing away directly of their true function.

As is above, so is below.

This is a simple riddle that sums up the layout of the pyramids succinctly and precisely. Thus, on the desert sands of Egypt we have the situation where, 'as the stars are above, so are the pyramids below'; 'heavens mirror', as Graham Hancock aptly and succinctly called it. But however simple it is to state, the ancients and some of the more modern investigators have been scratching their heads over this riddle for generations because it is not easy to make comprehensive correlations between the pyramids and the stars. Whichever way they are forced to make a match, too many pyramids end up having no associated stars and vice versa. The reason for this difficulty in the case of the Dahshur pyramids, in my view, is simply that these two pyramids are not representations of stars at all; they are 'points in space'.

The next thing to do is to get rid of all the more recent pyramids from the charts; the ones that were not a part of the original plan. As it happens, this is not too difficult. The original pyramids were quite superior in their construction, and all of them would have still been in perfect condition today if man had not gone around stealing the cladding stones. The later pyramids, by comparison, were shoddy affairs and many have crumbled back into the desert sands without too much help from the quarrymen. However, there is one of these recent pyramids that is slightly different and stands out for special attention; that of Meidum.

Meidum is a bit of a conundrum because it has at least three construction periods, encompassing three or four very different styles. Starting from the outside and working inwards, the sequence is as follows. Firstly, there is a finely dressed but weak outer casing. Inside this is the stronger step-pyramid with a rubble core and, right in the center, the roughly made tumulus or chamber. Finally, there are the very finely jointed and very large megalithic blocks that underlie both the pyramid and the mud-brick mastaba outside. Meidum is therefore curious in that the only part of the structure that one would naturally ascribe to our mythical designer, the massive megalithic blocks, are at the bottom of the construction. These blocks almost look like a huge platform or foundation for something that was never properly finished. Nevertheless, the pyramid above is quite inferior to the pyramids of Giza and Dahshur, so this one will be left out of the star chart.

The only pyramids that are left for this planisphere chart are those of Giza and Dahshur. This is not many stars, as star charts go, but it is quite sufficient for a precessional dating and it is the same number of monuments as we find in the similar Wiltshire layout. All these pyramids comprise the same megalithic building technology; they were all constructed in sacred cubits, and were all sturdy enough to have survived pretty well intact, into the modern era. So let us look at what these pyramids are supposed to represent.

Firstly, the Giza layout has already been identified as being a representation of the belt of Orion. In any star chart, the first thing that is needed is a reference point – a suitably bright cluster of stars from which you can orientate yourself and, from there, derive the positions of other stars; the belt of Orion fits this requirement precisely. This only leaves the pyramids of Dahshur to complete this precessional dating; so what do they represent? There are two pyramids worthy of our attention on this site: the Red Pyramid and the Bent Pyramid. Their function appears to be as follows.

Red Pyramid

The Red Pyramid has a completely different slope angle to the pyramids of Giza and this indicates quite strongly that it should have a quite different interpretation placed upon it. The Giza layout is all about stars; the Red Pyramid, being so different, cannot therefore be a star. Instead, it is a representation of a point in space, the – Sun's pole –

and this is why it is known as the Red Pyramid. The designer went to great expense to bring core stones of an iron-rich, rust-coloured sandstone all the way to Dahshur and, like everything he did in Egypt, this was not without good reason. The Sun's pole can be thought of as an extension of the axis of the Sun out into space, hence the Red Pyramid is red; it is a representation of the pole of the Sun. As the Sun's pole points out towards the constellation of Draco, a much better appellation for this pyramid would be the pyramid of Draco.

Bent Pyramid

The Bent Pyramid is misshapen. The lower portions mimic something near to the angle of the Great Pyramid, while the upper portions mimic the Draco (Red) Pyramid. Why has this been done in this way? Many people have confidently stated that the change in angle of the Bent Pyramid was due to construction problems and they cite some cracks that have been found in the structure as evidence. But it is known that the Great Pyramid has suffered some internal cracking and no changes were made to the design; so why was the Bent Pyramid any different? In addition, under the traditional dating system the Great Pyramid was built after the Bent Pyramid; having already had to reduce the angle of the casing blocks at Dahshur, why did the designer use the steeper slope angle once more? A few cracks in the structure of the Bent Pyramid are not a full explanation here.

The best proof that the Bent Pyramid was designed to be this shape from the beginning concerns a little mathematical symmetry, and maths has much more persuasive powers than ifs, maybes, and a few cracks. If we were to extend bottom portions of this pyramid upwards into a complete pyramid, the pyramid so formed would have a base-length to vertical-height ratio of exactly 10 : 7.

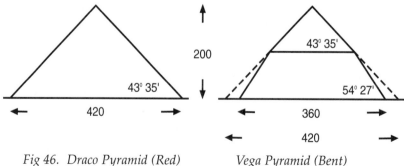

Fig 46. Draco Pyramid (Red)   *Vega Pyramid (Bent)*

8. Royal Planisphere

It is apparent that there was a logical plan for the slope angle of the lower portions of this pyramid. However, if we do the reverse and extend the line of the outer casing stones from the upper portion of the pyramid down onto the ground, the shorter but wider pyramid formed is exactly the same shape and size as the Draco Pyramid (Red Pyramid). The height of the Bent Pyramid is the same as Draco and so is the slope angle at the top. The Bent Pyramid is exactly the same as Draco, therefore, but with the lower sides trimmed off a little. [7]

But proving that the design was intentional does not answer the question of the function of this pyramid. So the question remains – why were the two slope angles of the Bent Pyramid thought to be so important as to be designed into the structure in this fashion? The answer has to be that the different slope angles mimic different pyramids. The Bent Pyramid is, therefore, an amalgam of two concepts. The lower portions mimic the Great Pyramid in slope angle because the Great Pyramid is, as we shall see later, also a representation of the planet Earth. In this case, the Bent Pyramid may be related to the Earth in some respect. Quite possibly, it was for this reason that the base length of the Bent Pyramid was made to equal 360 cubits, to mimic an earthly year. Likewise, the reason for a small satellite pyramid being built immediately to the south of the Bent Pyramid. [8] The ratio of the base lengths of the Bent Pyramid to the base length of this small satellite pyramid is 3.6 : 1. In the same fashion, the ratio of the diameter of the Earth to Lunar, our Moon, is also 3.6 : 1. In other words, the Bent Pyramid and its satellite appear to be a representation of the Earth/Lunar (Earth/Moon) system.

But the angles of the upper portions of the Bent Pyramid are the same as the Draco (Red) Pyramid, so the Bent Pyramid must also be related to the Sun's pole in some manner, just like the Draco Pyramid is. But perhaps the Bent Pyramid is not related to the Sun's pole as such, but just the concept of a pole or axis. If this is so, then the Bent Pyramid is partly a representation of the Earth and partly a representation of a pole; it can therefore be thought of as being the Earth's pole, or the Celestial Pole. As the Earth's pole, in the era we are looking at, pointed close to the star known as Vega, a better appellation for this pyramid would be the Vega Pyramid.

Giza planisphere

Lying on the desert sands of Egypt, we have a representation of the

8. Royal Planisphere

constellation of Orion in the form of the Giza pyramids; but now, in addition, we also seem to have representations of the Sun's pole and the Earth's pole. If so, we can now investigate the layout of these points on a star chart to find a date for these pyramids, because we have all the data that is required for a precessional dating.

Firstly, it should be noted that the angle formed between a line drawn through the stars in the belt of Orion, and a line drawn from the Sun's pole down to Orion on a planisphere, is about 65°. In the same way, the angle formed between a line through the pyramids of Giza, and another line joining the Draco Pyramid to Giza, is also about 65°. The planisphere chart, it would seem, is beginning to resemble the layout of the pyramids.

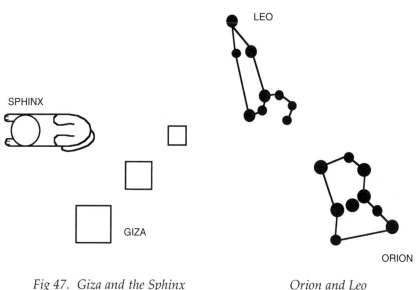

Fig 47. Giza and the Sphinx   Orion and Leo

However, this is certainly not a modern representation of the planisphere layout because, if we look at the angle from Giza (Orion) up to the Draco Pyramid (Sun's pole) and on to the Vega Pyramid (Earth's pole), it is a very different angle to the one we have today. But we should expect this because the Earth's pole moves in that great precessionary circle around the constellation of Draco, and it is by this very movement that we can calculate a date for the pyramids. It is this change in angle between the pyramid layout and the modern planisphere layout that will give us the age of the pyramids.

There is some additional proof that this is the picture that the designer intended us to see. Notice that, in addition to the alignment of the stars and the poles that we have just seen, we also have, at Giza, the position of the Sphinx. The Sphinx has long been associated with the constellation of Leo, and the position of Leo on a star chart is to the 'left' of a line running up from Orion to both of the celestial poles. This is exactly the same as we find at the Giza site; the Sphinx is out to the left of a line running from Giza to the Dahshur site. This is just a further confirmation that the star chart is orientated correctly and I shall show a further use of the Sphinx shortly.

Stonehenge planisphere

As further confirmation that this was the intended layout, it was not originally the Giza site that inspired me to see this planisphere layout; but instead, the Wiltshire monuments. A very similar layout to the one I have just outlined can be seen using Stonehenge and Avebury; it was this that I saw initially. It has already been demonstrated that the sites of Avebury and Stonehenge are intimately linked, but why locate them so far apart? The answer is simple and this was the link that made me see the correlation with the Giza planisphere.

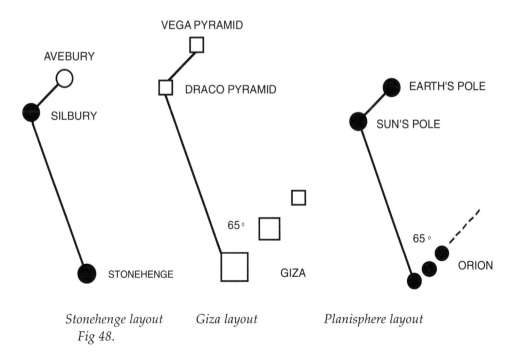

Stonehenge layout Giza layout   Planisphere layout
  Fig 48.

8. *Royal Planisphere*

Just like at Giza, where the Dahshur pyramids were ignored because of their remoteness, the Stonehenge site has always been divorced from Avebury. Now we know that the sites are intimately linked, we can join up the dots and see that the resulting layout is exactly the same at Avebury as it is at Dahshur. The angles between the monuments are the same at both sites. So we have another direct link between Avebury and Giza; again, it would appear that the same designer was at work on both sites.

The representation at Stonehenge is not quite the same as at Giza, though, for there is only one Stonehenge, not three. But should there have been three henges on Salisbury Plain? It may be considered to be stretching things, to make the theory fit a little better, by saying that the other Stonehenges were not built. Nevertheless, there is some evidence in favour of this theory.

We have already noted that the designer was being economical with the work on the Wessex sites, where only the most important stones were fully dressed and shaped. We can say with some confidence that time was at a premium on the Stonehenge site and work was not being wasted on fully dressing the less important items, like the Sarsen ring and the Heelstone. Again, over at Avebury, it can be seen that all these stones were left in the rough because it was not the form of the stones that was important here, it was their number and spacing, so why waste time in trimming them?

Could the designer have run out of time? Could invading tribes have coveted the prosperity of the Salisbury tribes and begun to invade the site, disrupting the work? Possibly, and there is another site that will confirm this idea; the site at Teotihuacan, in Mexico. Teotihuacan, we can speculate, is another site created by the same architect and, as I shall attempt to demonstrate in chapter IX, it was also never completed. Just as we see at Stonehenge, at least one of the Mexican pyramids was never finished in the complex that we see today. If we can see this happening at Teotihuacan – a site that mimics the Giza plateau so closely that it has to have had the same intended layout – then why can we not postulate that Stonehenge was abandoned in just the same fashion?

There are two more pieces of evidence that could tip the balance in favour of there being more Stonehenges in the original design. One of those pieces of evidence involves the bluestone mystery. The bluestones on the Stonehenge site form an untidy arrangement of stones that seem to be an addition to the site, and not part of the intended layout. Could these stones be from the extra Stonehenges; smaller, easier and quicker-to-build henges that could have mimicked the other stars in the Orion constellation? I am not alone in part of this speculation; classical archaeology is in agreement. One source says of these stones:

8. Royal Planisphere

There are further areas of uncertainty concerning the bluestones. The full description ... of their final arrangement at Stonehenge contains a suggestion that they may have stood, though not necessarily at Stonehenge, in an arrangement which included Trilithons (like the inner horseshoe at Stonehenge). They may have stood instead as a circle or other arrangement of shaped stones in Wales, an arrangement which may have included the novel idea of uprights and horizontal lintels in stone. It is, perhaps, an entire stone circle, which was uprooted and brought to Stonehenge, a suggestion which, if accepted, may help to explain the variety of stones within the all encompassing term bluestone. [9]

So, the bluestones could have formed another henge similar to Stonehenge. It only takes a quick look at the number of bluestones involved in this little mystery to see that, not only were these stones from another henge, but they seem to be from another 'Stonehenge', a copy of the original. There were originally 60 bluestones inside the Sarsen circle and some of these Bluestones were shaped as lintels. There are 60 Sarsen uprights and lintels in the Sarsen circle. There are thought to have been 19 bluestones inside the Trilithon horseshoe and, in turn, the Sarsen Trilithons themselves number 15, plus there were four Sarsens that were freestanding outside the Trilithon horseshoe – the Heel and Slaughter stones and their missing partners: that makes another four to make 19 in total.

So there is good evidence that the bluestones once represented an entire Stonehenge replica in miniature. This would not be a circle taken from Wales, but one taken from a place just to the north-east of Stonehenge, in the direction of the stars that form the belt of Orion. On second thoughts, perhaps this circle was never built. Would ancient man have really desecrated a sacred twin of Stonehenge, and dragged the stones to the real Stonehenge to be re-erected in such a haphazard manner, in an age when Stonehenge was still in use as a sacred site? Perhaps not.

An alternative to this theory is that the bluestones were trimmed and shaped where they were found, in the Preseli Mountains in Wales, then brought across to Salisbury in preparation for the construction of another circle; one that was never built. So, generations later there was still a pile of stones lying on the plains of Salisbury; a Stonehenge Lego set made to one-third scale, scattered on the ground. Not knowing the exact plans or the intended location for the stones, the following generations pulled them instead to their most sacred site and stood them inside the great Sarsen circle at Stonehenge.

Stonehenge could then have originally been designed as a row of three monuments, something like the geometric layout of the three barrows at the Cursus arrangement, or even the Winterbourne Stoke barrows. This design is a common theme in Neolithic sites and, amongst others, the Clava Cairns near Inverness also mimic exactly this 'Orion's belt' layout. In this northern interpretation of the belt, at Inverness, we even find that the compass orientation of these barrows, and the position of the third offset barrow, is exactly the same as at Giza. This copying of the layout of the belt stars of Orion is by no means unique to Giza and so the intention at Stonehenge could have been to build a similar arrangement. Clearly, the constellation of Orion was important in these times.

In the Wessex layout of these belt stars, though, the pyramids of Dahshur are now represented by the pyramid of Silbury and the Avebury ring. Dahshur lies to the south of Giza, while the equivalent of Dahshur in Wessex, Avebury, lies to the north of Stonehenge. At Giza, this layout of the stars on the ground could be confirmed by the presence of the Sphinx, sitting just out to the east of the site, in the same position as the constellation of Leo is on a real planisphere of the stars. It is a pity that there is no Sphinx equivalent at Stonehenge to further confirm the layout of these monuments as being the same as at Giza. But there again, were there any lions in Britain thousands of years ago? Why, then, confirm the layout of the planisphere with a lion?

Fig 49.   Zodiac of Dendra

8. *Royal Planisphere*

Even if there were a Sphinx at Stonehenge, one might well question the validity of using these 'modern' stellar constellations as pictorial markers for constructions dating from the dawn of man's history. Nevertheless, this is quite a valid proposal, because these 'modern' constellation pictures are themselves very old indeed. No-one knows quite how old, but they can be traced back at least as far as Mesopotamia and Egypt. This can be confirmed in many ways, with the most famous being the Zodiac of Dendra, which was discovered in the temple at the site of the capital of the sixth Upper-Egyptian county. Inside the temple, which is dedicated to Hathor, the Bovine god of Egypt, was a Zodiac of the constellations. It is now in the Louvre, in Paris. What may be surprising to some people, however, is that it is identical to the modern Zodiac, with the ring of twelve astrological constellations being exactly the same as in the horoscope section of the local newspaper.

On this ancient Zodiac then, we do not need to choose a lion for our confirmation of the planisphere, for there are many pictograms to choose from. We could choose something a little more appropriate to the culture in which the monument resides. We could choose a horse, for instance, from the constellation of Pegasus; although on the Zodiac of Dendra, this constellation seems to have been depicted as being headless.

Just out to the north-east of Avebury and Silbury, at a point that is exactly the same distance from Silbury as is Stonehenge, stands the white horse of Uffington. Uffington is a delightful caricature of a horse; one that seems to have been simply cut through the upper grass layer on the Wiltshire downs to expose the white chalk below. Such a simple method, and yet such a beautiful and enigmatic monument. It is so enigmatic that man has tended the site through the millennia, trimming the encroaching grass and whitening the outline of the horse with fresh chalk, for such monuments can be lost within a generation if they are not cared for. It is quite amazing how the 'sacredness' of a particular site can be transmitted through the generations, without one rebellious generation getting bored with this idea and leaving the site to the elements. Yet all this effort was not for the tourists, for there were none, so there was no financial gain to the community. They just knew it had to be done, perhaps because the 'gods' ordained it long, long ago.

Every seven years, the local squire and the village population would turn out at Uffington for the 'scouring',[10] to clean the monument and hold some sports and entertainments in the nearby Uffington Castle, an ancient hilltop fort. This must rank as one of Britain's oldest traditions, for Uffington is not a recent construction. It has long been thought that Uffington dates from at least the Iron Age, because some Iron Age iconography has a similar style. Therein lies another problem for classical chronology, as this comparison of styles is the only method of dating this monument; but what came first, the Iron Age iconography or the horse? If the Uffington horse had been on this site for many thousands of years, it would have surely been copied onto contemporary stoneware every now and then. As an alternative, it could be quite reasonably proposed that Uffington is actually a contemporary of the Stonehenge and Avebury sites, and there are many reasons for thinking this. In fact, I could find no fewer than five reasons for thinking that the Uffington horse is linked to Avebury and Stonehenge.

1.   Firstly, the real, solid geophysical evidence is that the construction of Uffington is exactly the same as the construction of the Aubrey holes at Stonehenge. The chalk has not just been exposed to reveal the horse; instead, deep trenches were dug and then immediately refilled with loose chalk. Just like at Stonehenge, this disturbance would have lain in the ground for eternity and any modern geophysical survey, or even a long drought colouring the grass, would have uncovered the horse. [11]

2.   Uffington and Avebury are linked together by the ancient Bronze Age road, known as the Ridgeway. Additionally, it was immediately obvious to me that the distance from Avebury to Uffington was the same as the distance from Avebury to Stonehenge. There was a definite geometric link here that was difficult to explain in any way other than a planned design.

3.   The horse itself measures 110 Zil yards in length,[12] or in terms of the units commonly used at Avebury, 10 double Zil rods in length; ten times the normal stone spacing used at Avebury.

4.   Then there is the astronomical evidence. Take a look at a real planisphere of the stars and draw a line from Orion to the northern poles. Just out to the upper right-hand side of this line, in just the same location as the white horse itself (relative to Stonehenge and Avebury), there is the constellation of Pegasus, the flying horse. In the Zodiac of Dendra it was a headless quadruped, more akin to a deer, while in the old kingdom of Wessex it was a stylistic horse.

5.   The usage of Pegasus in this fashion is quite significant. At Giza, the reference constellation for the pyramid planisphere is Leo, the Sphinx. It has been proposed that this constellation was chosen

8. Royal Planisphere

because of its alignment with the sunrise at the time of the pyramid's construction – a feature of Giza that was explained in the book *Keeper of Genesis* and something we shall review shortly. If this is the case, it is interesting to note that Pegasus is an opposing constellation to Leo in the night sky. This means that, whatever the date that is finally chosen for this 'rising constellation' theory, Pegasus will be doing exactly the same six months later. The one theory is balanced by the other.

Following in this novel logic, there is one further important observation to be made, for perhaps we also have a possible explanation for the peculiar stylistic layout of the Uffington horse. That strange square head on the horse can, in this context, be thought of as a copy of the 'Square of Pegasus', the physical layout of the constellation of Pegasus itself. If the pyramids of Giza are a copy of the belt of Orion, is it too much to see in the Uffington horse a copy of the square of Pegasus?

So, the story in this chapter is coming full circle. I started in Giza, where the layout of the pyramids seemed to mimic a planisphere of the stars. From there, the comparison was made with the Wessex monuments, which seem to copy the layout of the pyramids. Finally, there was the Uffington horse, which confirms the planisphere layout in the same way as the Sphinx does at Giza. The stellar layout of the henges is nearly complete. Stonehenge does, indeed, seem to mimic Giza in its role as the constellation of Orion.

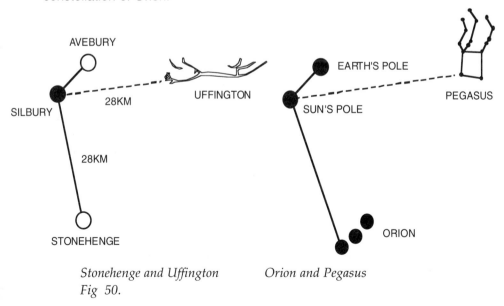

Stonehenge and Uffington　　　*Orion and Pegasus*
Fig 50.

8. Royal Planisphere

Perhaps Stonehenge *was* supposed to look like Giza, with a series of similar monuments all on one site. If so, we now have at least two representations of the stars that have been left for posterity on the Earth by the master architect and, at first glance, the two layouts look to be extremely similar. Having demonstrated this likeness, I believe that there can be little doubt now that the plan I have outlined was deliberately put there for us, left carved in the sands and chalklands for millennia, waiting for someone to come along and say 'why?'.

For centuries, dogma has insisted that the pyramids and henges dated from about 2,500 BC. This was because these monuments were difficult to date; it is not possible to date stone and historians were grasping at straws. Hence, the entire edifice of Old Kingdom chronology rests on a few king lists of uncertain origins. At Giza, a stele was found bearing Khafre's cartouche upon it, so the Second Pyramid became Khafre's Pyramid. Once a senior historian has agreed, then watch out for your career if you have an alternative opinion!

Never mind that there were no inscriptions, no grave goods, and no bodies – these pyramids were tombs, despite the evidence. Never mind that later Egyptian pyramids have crumbled into dust, whereas the earlier Giza pyramids, had they not been so close to Cairo and therefore been plundered for their stone, would have still been in perfect condition. Historians had spoken. In the far future, no doubt, we shall have a validated date for Westminster Abbey as the late sixteenth century, because King Henry VIII was found to be buried there.

Star date

If these layouts are indeed representations of the stellar constellations, they will have within their design an image of the stars and the celestial poles, frozen in time. It is by measuring the angles of these Earthly 'celestial pole' positions that we can unlock the dates for these monuments and compare them with our current era and time. Only then shall we find the true date of these sites. The layouts of Egypt and Wessex look very similar, but the question is: how similar? And therefore, how close to the date of Avebury is the date of Giza? The calculation required is very simple and easy to follow:

    a.   The angle we are most interested in for dating the pyramids and henges, is the obtuse angle formed when looking from Orion to the Sun's pole and then on to the Earth's pole. In the Giza layout, this

8. Royal Planisphere

would be measured from the Giza pyramids to the Draco Pyramid, and on to the Vega Pyramid. This angle gives us a measure of how far the Earth's pole was from the position of Orion, back in the era of the pyramid's construction. This angle measures 194°.

b.   We can make the same measurement at Stonehenge. The angle from Stonehenge up to Silbury Hill and on to Avebury (Avebury is obviously a representation of the Earth's pole, hence the Avebury 'Earth') provides us with exactly the same information. This angle measures very much the same as at Giza; 195° to be exact.

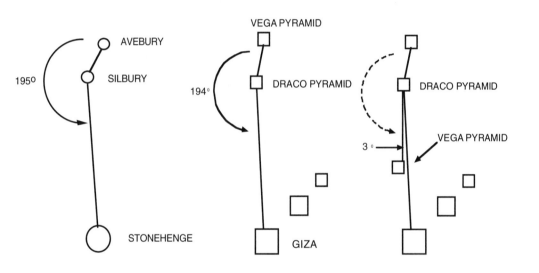

Monument layouts

Equivalent if built today

Fig 51.

c.   The next thing that is needed is the current position of the Earth's pole, so that we can compare the two layouts and see how far the Earth's pole has moved. Take a current star chart and measure the angle from Orion, through the Sun's pole, and on to the present day Earth's pole. The result is that this angle is just 3°; a very small angle indeed. If the monuments of Thoth were to be rebuilt to portray the present location of the Earth's pole, the Vega Pyramid would be the other side of the Draco Pyramid, and Avebury would be the other side of the Silbury Pyramid. It is obvious that the Earth's pole has

187

8. Royal Planisphere

drifted a long way in the intervening time since the construction of these monuments, and so many years must have passed. But how many?

d.   At last, here is all the information that we require to find out how far the pole has drifted. The differences between the position of our current Earth's pole and the position of the Earth's pole as indicated by the Vega Pyramid and the Avebury henge, are:

$$194° - 3° = 191° \quad \text{for Giza.}$$
$$195° - 3° = 192° \quad \text{for Avebury.}$$

What we are saying here is that the Earth's pole has wandered some 191° and 192° respectively, since the plans for Giza and Avebury were drawn up by their designer

e.   The precession rate – the speed at which the Earth's pole moves around the Sun's pole – is fixed at a very sedate 71.57 years per degree of rotation.

f.   The number of years that have elapsed between the construction of these monuments and the current era is therefore:

$$191 \times 71.57 = 13,670 \text{ years for Giza.}$$
$$192 \times 71.57 = 13,740 \text{ years for Avebury.}$$

This date can be given quite precisely because of the nature of these diagrams. Even if we have made an error in our measurements of these maps of half a degree, we still only get an error of +/– 35 years on the age of the monuments. One could take more accurate bearings from the sites to improve this, but one would imagine that the designer had already rounded to the nearest degree; so, there in an inherent error of +/– 35 years, and 13,670 - 13,740 years is the nearest value that we can obtain.

```
The date of the Avebury, Stonehenge and Silbury sites   is
                    11,740 BC +/– 35 years.
The date of the Giza plateau and the pyramids of Dahshur  is
                    11,670 BC +/– 35 years.
```

Perhaps it is now apparent why the Avebury site has always been held by a faithful few to be something special. It is not only from the drawing boards of the same designer as Giza, but it was possibly the first site to be constructed. Such a hypothesis is truly amazing. Yet, at the same time as all this, we also have a date for both sites that is more than double the previous best estimates of the experts. The dawn of man has just departed into the distant past and the history of civilization on this planet has more than doubled to 13,000-odd years. Historians will need to readjust their chronology by a huge margin to encompass this theory and there will be more proofs to come that indicate that this is not an idea born in a vacuum. There will be more evidence that the monument builders were far in advance of what we currently give them credit for.

There used to be a large sign just outside the monument of Stonehenge. It displayed a picture of the stones and the title above read, 'Who built it?'. It was a sign that betrayed the lack of knowledge that we had of all these sites; a sign of desperation. Now we have a much clearer understanding of the capabilities of the designer and later I shall attempt to explain more about this amazing individual.

Carbon dates

This theory that I have developed, of these monuments being both technical and ancient, is looking quite convincing in some respects. However, there is a major snag in this hypothesis: many artifacts around Giza and Avebury have been radiocarbon dated and none has shown up dates of this magnitude: or have they? Radiocarbon dating is a valuable tool in archaeology and it is not the purpose of this book to criticize all the advances made in this field over the last 50 years or so; but while this dating method can be quite a valuable technique for obtaining archaeological dates in some circumstances, there are other occasions when it can give some very misleading results. The tendency nowadays to rely on radiocarbon dates as though they are always accurate to within +/–10 years is misguided; there are too many variables involved to say that a particular sample is of this age.

For instance, the Lindow Bog man was dated, in 1985, using two different radiocarbon techniques, and the two methods gave a 400-year difference on a body that was only some 1,800 years old; a 22% discrepancy. This error was generated through the dating apparatus alone; it did not include any of the other errors that can be present in this technique.

There was also a big dispute over the remains of a woman who was also found in the Lindow Bog. Scientists dated this skull (with tissues remaining) to AD 500, or some 1,500 years ago. However, the police maintained that it was the skull of a Ms Bird, who was murdered in the 1970s. Not only was the skull very similar in its shape to the unusual appearance of the late Ms Bird, but also the police secured a conviction in the case. The courts had effectively declared that they did not believe the radiocarbon dates, which is not too surprising as the late Ms Bird was an immigrant and had distinctive Far Eastern features. Finding a Filipino deposited in the Lindow Bog some 1,500 years ago is pushing the bounds of credibility.

Radiocarbon dating is not always the precise tool we expect it to be; there are too many variables that can influence the results. In the case of the skull of Ms Bird, it has been suggested that the very old biological material of the bog had contaminated the much younger biological material in the skull, and had therefore made it appear to be older that it was.

Why are there so many possible errors present in this technique? Well, the fundamental principles of radiocarbon dating are relatively simple; it is all the variables that give the problems. Nature consists of three isotopes (three types) of carbon, and these are denoted as being C_{12}, C_{13}, and C_{14}. C_{12} is the basic stuff of life and is stable. C_{13} is present in the environment, but only in small quantities. C_{14}, however, is very different; it is detectable in only the minutest quantities and it is radioactive. Every now and then, a C_{14} atom will go 'ping' and turn itself into nitrogen, and in the process it emits a beta particle; this is the radioactive component used in the name of the technique.

In any given sample of C_{14}, half the sample will go 'ping' over a time span of 5,730 years. When a living organism dies, it will stop respiring (breathing), and so it will stop taking in any more C_{14}. Over the years after its death, the amount of C_{14} in the remains of that organism will decrease, and it is the amount of C_{14} that is left in the organism that is the basis of the radiocarbon dating technique. The less C_{14} in the sample, the older the specimen, but the amounts we are talking about are minute. In the LSC type of machinery, [13] there are only about 1,000 atoms to be counted in each sample, which is not a great number.

What are the errors that can be involved in radiocarbon dating? The first problem with the technique is that it does not come up with a known date; there are so many variables involved that can influence the amount of C_{14} in a sample, that the results have to be compared with a known sample. The usual reference samples are taken from tree rings, as it is possible to date the wood from the core of a tree through the simple technique of counting the number of rings. The Bristlecone pine of California was used for most of these dates because it grows so slowly, but this means counting rings only 0.25 mm apart, back through some 8,000 rings. This still only takes us back through 8,000 years and there are not many reference sources that can give reliable dates before this, so the dating of older samples is done through extrapolation of the more recent samples.

Some of the errors that can influence the sample to be dated include the ice ages, which can change the concentrations of C_{14} in the atmosphere by locking up, and then releasing, large amounts of C_{14} in the ice sheets. It is said of this that:

> The effect of these (glacial) factors on radiocarbon dates has not yet been established. [14]

And yet, the era of 13,700 years ago is the era of the re-advancement of the Scottish ice sheets during the WII ice age. [15] Other errors can be introduced by chalkland environments, which is pertinent to the Avebury site, of which it is said:

> The hard-water effect is not quantifiable, since it is dependent on local factors; there can not even be a general geographical guide to the likely age offset ... The approach taken is to assume no change with time, and evaluate the age offset using recent specimens of the same species from the same locality. [16]

But there are larger effects to be taken into account than these. The majority of the testing of Avebury and the associated sites was carried out in the 1950s and 1960s; this was coincident and the major atmospheric nuclear tests, with the first hydrogen bomb being detonated at Enewetak Atoll in 1952. The atmospheric test-ban treaty did not come into force until 1963. The result was that the amount of C_{14} in the atmosphere rose 100%. That was not the only source of possible contamination; many other radioactive elements were thrown into the atmosphere that could affect the results. As the early dating machinery was counting radioactive decay, not C_{14} directly as can be done nowadays, these alternate sources of radioactive decays could easily have affected the results. Put all this together, plus the fact that many of the machines themselves were based within the boundaries of atomic testing sites, and there are many possible sources of contamination.

This is not all. One of the major hazards in radiocarbon dating is establishing that the artifact is contemporary to the site that is being excavated, and not a more recent implantation. This is relatively easy if the site has layer upon layer of occupation, as this stratigraphy can positively separate each artifact into a known sequence and thus into a rough chronology. Any rogue C_{14} dates would then be easy to spot as they appear out of sequence within the deposited layers, and the wealth of data coming back from the lab builds up a consistent and verifiable chronology of the occupation layers.

Stonehenge is not that sort of archaeological site; there is no stratigraphy. Indeed, it would almost appear as if these monuments were designed so that nothing would directly give away the date of construction or the identity of the architect. At both Wessex and Giza, the sites were devoid of inscriptions and cleared of all evidence of their construction methods. We have no direct way of establishing how meticulous the builders were in this, but it would certainly not be in keeping with the general evidence on the sites to allow workers to bury some of their bone picks and shovels on the Avebury site, for instance. Most likely, these were later inclusions from renovation projects on the site; artifacts from a later era when such things were no longer deemed to be so important.

The archaeology of these sites shows this argument to be demonstrably so. Even at less important sites, the sacred nature of these ancient temples decreed that the sites should be kept meticulously clean; this was particularly noticeable at the recent excavations at the very large wood henge in Radnor, Wales:

> Detailed examination has revealed that the enclosed area was kept clear for almost 3,000 years. Outside the oval, archaeologists have found a normal level of flint and other prehistoric finds. Inside there have been almost no finds at all.
> "They must have kept it extraordinarily clean," said Dr Alex Gibson, an archaeologist who has spent much of the past six years investigating the site for Clwyd-Powys Archaeological Trust. "It remained untouched by normal 'secular' human activity from its construction in 2700 BC, through the late Neolithic and the whole of both the Bronze Age and the Iron Age, which ended after the Roman invasion of AD 43." [17]

It is much more difficult to build up a coherent chronology within sites that only have a few scattered remains from many differing eras in them and therefore, it is more difficult to verify both the competency of the lab and also to verify that the artifact is contemporary to the site's construction.

Unfortunately for the orthodox Stonehenge chronology, the vast majority of dated remains come from demonstrably intrusive burials. Yet, it says in the Bible that if someone touches a grave, they are unclean for seven days. [18] No self-respecting priesthood would have a burial that is 'unclean' occupying a prime site inside its sacred temple. It is quite obvious from the mass of burials around, but not on, the Stonehenge site that the priesthood here maintained similar standards and taboos to those detailed in the Bible. Burials took place in tumuli well away from the main temple precincts of Stonehenge and Avebury; thus, the burials discovered at Stonehenge mark its abandonment as a functioning religious site, not its construction.

Other datable artifacts were found in the primary layer of silt inside the henge ditches of Avebury and Stonehenge. The archaeologists excavating the site have simply assumed that the ditch started silting up as soon as it was constructed, thus the artifacts within this silt layer mark a point in time immediately after the site's construction. Unfortunately, this is rather convenient and presumptuous.

The Radnor site in Wales, as we have seen, was kept scrupulously clean. The Uffington horse has been tended and cleaned by the local inhabitants for perhaps 5,000 years. The walls of the Newgrange henge, just north of Dublin, collapsed one day onto bare earth. The archaeologists were rather mystified by this as any bare earth in Ireland is thick with plant growth inside a few weeks, so how did the walls of the henge fall onto bare earth? The obvious answer is that, like Radnor and Uffington, the site was meticulously groomed and maintained.

The clear inference is that these Neolithic sites were meticulously looked after by their ancient custodians. Thus, it is a perfectly reasonable suggestion to say that the layers of silt at the bottom of the Stonehenge and Avebury ditches do not mark the henge's construction era, but instead they mark the era of the site's abandonment. If this is so, then the C_{14} dates that have been so meticulously derived for Stonehenge, mark not the site's beginnings, but instead its eventual demise. This is not only a radical reassessment of the archaeologist's work, but it also infers that these sites are possibly much older than originally thought. The Radnor site in Wales was apparently maintained in a pristine state for some 3,000 years, until the Romans began interfering with the site. How long would a prime site like Stonehenge have been maintained as a functioning temple, before its ditches were eventually allowed to silt up?

The lab

Even if some of these artifacts were contemporary with the site, there are still two further factors that could explain the results that were obtained. Firstly, the laboratory always asks the archaeologists what the expected age of the sample is; as one scientist points out:

> This is not cheating! There are two reasons for asking. The primary reason is to ... avoid cross-contamination ... in particular, samples of substantial age (greater than 10,000 years) must not follow modern ones. [19]

So, by the laboratories' own admission, some of the older Avebury samples, for instance, could have been contaminated by more recent samples because of a lack of understanding about the ages of the artifacts that were being processed. Finally, the scientists hit back at the archaeologists because, at the end of this long process of trying to reduce and allow for the known errors that can occur in this complicated process, they derive a date for the sample they have been sent. Then the wrangling starts:

> Comments like 'archaeologically acceptable', while not very informative, are less frustrating than the bald 'archaeologically unacceptable' statements. Often there is no discussion of these 'archaeologically unacceptable' results, they are simply rejected by the archaeologist when evaluating the chronology of the site. Such unexpected or anomalous results can, however, be of great value. For example, they can alert the user to a problem with the laboratory [or alert the archaeologist to a problem with his chronology!]. These unacceptable results, perhaps more than others, need careful consideration; they may provide the greatest information. [20]

This is a prophetic plea, direct from the heart of a scientist involved in the field. It boils down to 'we may not get it right all the time, but do not reject us just because the dates do not agree with your theories'. We can just imagine the reaction of the archaeologists on site to a few bone samples from Avebury coming back from the laboratory labelled '11,500 BC'; they would be dismissed out of hand. We have a good illustration of this process at work, which can be seen from the results of a survey of Stonehenge, conducted in 1988 by Wessex Archaeology for the custodians of the site, English Heritage. Some of the previous radiocarbon dating had long been considered to be unreliable and, as one reference manual says:

> only a relatively small number of radiocarbon determinations had been obtained ... because of the perceived importance of

Stonehenge, great weight has been placed on these dates and they have become enshrined in the literature. The contextual integrity of some of these samples, however, is not necessarily secure, and most were obtained early in the history of radiometric dating ... [21]

A review was therefore begun into the radiometric data, including the three lonely samples from inside the Sarsen ring. Without much fanfare, the results of these modern radiocarbon dating tests were released. They also included some wood samples, which were found in some massive post holes, that lie underneath what is now the Stonehenge car park. These post holes were dated from 7,730 to 8,820 BC [22] (approaching 11,000 years ago).

These results are given but, despite the immediate conjunction of these post-holes to the Stonehenge site and their undoubted similarity to the Aubrey holes, they are immediately interpreted as being something totally alien. They are somehow thought to be the remains of large 'totem poles' that must have been erected long before Stonehenge was even dreamt of. The convenient separation of these two adjacent sites keeps these anomalous results neatly separate from the Stonehenge site, so that no major theories have to be reworked. Yet these dates are within 2,500 years of my proposed planisphere date. The gap between what was once considered to be fantasy and what tomorrow will be considered as established fact is closing very rapidly indeed.

Keeper of Genesis

Radiocarbon dating aside, it would appear that this may be a reliable date for the construction of Giza and Stonehenge, but is there any possibility of verifying this date? Is there a crosscheck for the Giza site in particular? Actually, there is another way of looking at this same problem. It has been pointed out in other works that the pyramid causeways at Giza mark the cross-quarter sunrises; that is, they mark the sunrise on the azimuth angles that lie exactly between the equinoxes and the solstices. That may sound a little complicated, so it may need further explanation.

At the equinox, the Sun will rise in the morning exactly due east of the observer. On the solstices at the latitude of Giza, the Sun will rise some 28° either side of due east; 28° north during the summer solstice and 28° south during the winter solstice. The Great and Second Pyramid causeways, however, are angled at 14° either side of due east – this is exactly half the Sun's full annual extent and so these angles are known as 'cross-quarters'. [23] But because the azimuth angle of the sunrise does not change in a linear fashion during the year, the cross-quarter dates do not lie exactly in between the equinoxes and solstices.

The equinox dates of March 22nd and September 22nd are probably well known, and the solstice dates of December 21st and June 21st are probably equally familiar. But the cross-quarter dates, when the Sun rises along the line of the Great and Second Pyramids' causeways, are probably something completely new. The Sphinx causeway, running out from the Second Pyramid, marks the winter cross-quarter sunrise positions, which are either October 22nd or February 19th. The Great Pyramid causeway marks the summer cross-quarter sunrise positions, which occur on either August 22nd or April 21st.

In fact, these cross-quarter dates are actually marking segments on a planisphere that are each exactly 30° displaced from the equinox dates. Astronomers mark out the sky in degrees of azimuth and the spring equinox is given (by convention) the 0° position, while the autumn equinox is therefore the 180° position. The cross-quarter dates occur at the positions of 30°, 150°, 210° and 330° around the night sky.

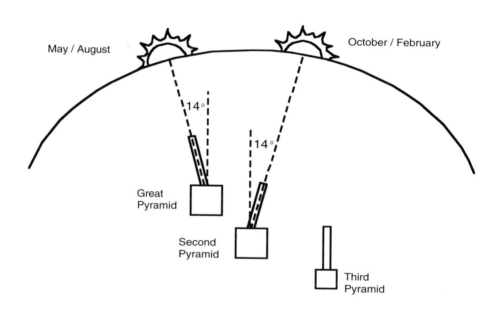

August/April and October/February cross-quarter sunrises
Fig 52.

8. *Royal Planisphere*

As can be seen, the Sun will rise along these cross-quarter positions twice for each causeway, during each year. This gives us a problem: can we sort out which of these dates could be linked to the constellation of Leo and used to date the construction of the Giza pyramids?

Central to the plan of the Giza plateau is the Sphinx, that megalithic leonine statue, resting to the east of the pyramids; the statue that the pharaoh Khafre carved his face upon and called his own. But this statue was of the era of the pyramids, not Khafre, and that is why the Sphinx has been weathered so much, despite the relatively benign climate of Egypt. We have already seen one use of the Sphinx in the planisphere layout of Giza and Dahshur, but it looks as though the architect may have squeezed in another puzzle for the Sphinx.

The Sphinx, of course, marks the position of the constellation of Leo and, as Graham Hancock has pointed out in his two books on Giza, the constellation of Leo appears to be sunken just below the horizon during the equinox sunrise in what was known as the Sep Tepi, or the 'first time'. Sep Tepi seems to be a nebulous concept; a time of the gods. In reality, Sep Tepi was an Egyptian expression for the founding of their nation and, quite possibly, this was the era during which the pyramids were built. Hancock's explanation for the date of Sep Tepi, based upon the pioneering work of Giorgio Santillana and Hertha von Dechend, led the way in this identification of the era of Sep Tepi and helped considerably in identifying the construction era of the pyramids.

The era in which we are living can be defined by the star constellation that is rising above the eastern horizon with the Sun, each morning, during the spring equinox. Currently we are in the twilight zone, between the end of the era of Pisces and the dawn of the age of Aquarius. Pisces, which will have been dominant from AD 00 to AD 2600, is the era that has been clearly identified with the relatively recent Christian religion; Jesus often being identified with the sign of the fish. Before this, the Egyptians had cults of the ram (Aries), which was the rising sign from 1850 BC to AD 00, and also an era of the sacred Apis bulls (Taurus), which was the rising sign from about 4500 BC to 1850 BC. [24]

But this dating system for the rising constellations must have a reference date for the observations, and that reference point is currently regarded as being the spring equinox, or March 22nd. This was the date originally used in many of the alternative books on this subject, including *Fingerprints of the Gods*. If the spring equinox was used as the reference date for these observations, then the constellation of Leo will have been rising with the Sun on March 22nd in about 8,800 BC. This date does not remotely match the date that has already been found by using the Giza

197

planisphere layout, so are there any alternative dates that will give a slightly better agreement?

Possibly, because that reference date for observing the sunrise may well have been corrupted down the years, and we can confidently propose this because the major pyramids on the Giza site actually point at the cross-quarter sunrises, not the equinox. In fact, if any causeway should be pointing at the constellation of Leo, it ought to be the Sphinx causeway itself, and this points not towards the equinox but towards the winter/spring cross-quarter sunrise – the sunrise on February 19th. There is a more satisfactory solution to this problem, but it is only to be found when using this spring cross-quarter date as a reference point. When using this new date, the position of the Sun against the background constellations is effectively changed by 30°, which equates to about 2,000 years of precessional motion. Thus, when using the Second Pyramid's causeway for the astronomical observations, the constellation of Leo will rise with the Sun on February 19th in the era of 10,800 BC.

This date is, of course, a favourite amongst alternative researchers for some reason; nevertheless, the logic for its adoption, as just given, is reasonably sound. This date is about 1000 years after the date derived from the Giza planisphere and there seems to be no mitigating circumstances that can lessen this difference. This difference in unlikely to be a reference to the start and finish dates for the Giza site, as 1,000 years is not only an inordinately large time span, but also a later chapter will show that the construction actually took about 100 years.

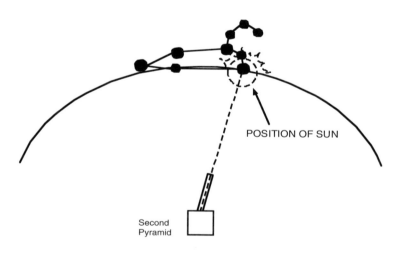

POSITION OF SUN

Second
Pyramid

Fig 53. Cross-quarter sunrise for February 19th 10,800 BC

8. Royal Planisphere

On the winter/spring cross-quarter sunrise – February 19th 10,800 BC – Leo will be seen to be sitting just on the horizon and rising with the Sun. In fact, the brightest star in the constellation, Regulus, appears to be aligned exactly with the Sun. Therefore, a good argument for the era of Sep Tepi may well be this 10,800 BC date; but if this were case then the changing of the constellations should actually take place at the winter/spring cross-quarter sunrise, as indicated by the Sphinx causeway, and not at the equinox. [25]

This new reference date for observing the phenomenon of precession would place us as currently being in the constellation of Capricorn, not at the dawn of Aquarius, and therefore this realignment of the observation dates would fly in the face of all the historical evidence gained from the theology of Egypt. If this were really the case, we would have to surmise that the true reference date for making these observations was forgotten many thousands of years ago, and that the equinox date was adopted instead. This is a possibility but, on balance, I think it unlikely.

Another alternative may center on what the ancient astronomers were actually looking for. Perhaps the stars of the constellation had to be visible in the pre-dawn glow, before the Sun actually rose above the horizon. If the Sun were 15° below the horizon as the observations were being made along the Second Pyramid's causeway, i.e. one hour before sunrise, then the two dates for Sep Tepi would match perfectly. But unfortunately, this change would once more put out all the historical dates derived from the theology of Egypt by 1,000 years. These historical eras for Taurus, Aries and Pisces in Egyptian theology seem to be based upon quite secure foundations, so once more there appears to be an unresolvable dichotomy.

Personally, I think that the Giza planisphere date is the more reliable method and so I shall use this date in any later calculations, but this is an area of the Giza design that needs revisiting and given more thought.

Legends of mirrors

The *Book of the Dead* is a compilation of the sacred funerary texts for the deceased pharaohs and it was inscribed inside many of the fifth and sixth dynasty pyramids. It detailed the priests' knowledge of the Universe and the cosmic journey that the departed pharaoh would have to take. What do these ancient texts have to say about this theory of Earthly planispheres?

> Sothis (the star, Sirius) is swallowed up by the Djuat, pure and living in the Horizon. [26]

8. Royal Planisphere

> The reed floats of the sky are brought down to me ... that I may go up on them to Horakhti at the Horizon. I go up on the Eastern side of the sky where the gods are born, and I am born as Horus, as 'Him of the Horizon', Sothis is my companion...[27]

Sothis is positively swallowed up by the horizon. In fact, even at its zenith, it is below the southern horizon as seen from Giza. An observer would have to travel south as far as Aswan to get a view of Sirius. One must be careful with these texts, however. The pattern of the stars would have been changing century by century and, although ancient Egypt was more traditionalist than any other nation, one can imagine that the stories of Sothis and Orion evolved somewhat to suit the star pattern of that particular millennum. However, some things do not change: Orion has always been close to the Milky Way, Sirius has always been Orion's companion, and the texts are emphatic that this was the area of the night sky that was most important to them.

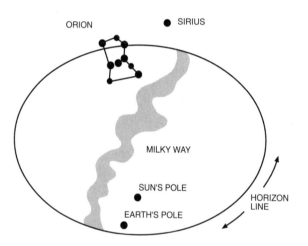

Fig 54. Planisphere chart for 11,670 BC

The texts continue and we are told in the *Shat Ent Am Djuat* (the book of what is in the Djuat), the ancient Egyptian funerary texts, to build on the ground a replica of a special part of the sky, called the Djuat. The Djuat has been identified by Sir E A Wallis Budge as:

> ... a material Heaven ... on the banks of the Heavenly Nile, whereon they built cities. [28]

8. Royal Planisphere

The book continues, and says that:

> Whosoever shall make an exact copy of these forms ... and shall know it, shall be a spirit and well equipped in heaven and earth, unfailingly, and eternally. [29]

> the hidden circle in the Djuat ... in the body of Nut (the Sky) ... Whosoever shall make a copy thereof ... it shall act as a magical protector for him both in Heaven and upon Earth. [30]

Certainly, we have been making some 'hidden circles' in the plans of Stonehenge, Avebury and the Giza plateau. If dualism is of any interest, there is plenty to be found here. In addition, it is a massive understatement to say that the copying and understanding of the megalithic planisphere is important.

Information saturation

This new history of these monuments implies that Stonehenge and Avebury may have been built first and that, after this site was completed, the designer went to Egypt to start the same kind of project there. But why? Why would our master architect want to embark on the same enterprise all over again? If one were to be very bold, it might be surmised that if the message the designer wished to leave was so important, he might want to create another site, just in case the first site was destroyed. He may have also been disappointed with the quality of the first effort and so moved to a better location, where the benign climate gave a longer building season; and a defensive shield of surrounding deserts to give a measure of protection from invading outsider tribes that, perhaps, disrupted work on the Wessex sites. A site where the resulting society could live and prosper in the millennia to come. It is an interesting thought.

Whatever the case, it has to be said that we now have rather too much in the way of information and technology for classical history to cope with. It was once thought that the first person to discover the precession of the equinoxes was Hipparchus, the Greek astronomer, in about 140 BC. Now it can be seen not only that the ancient monuments were set out with both the Earth's pole and the Sun's pole – indicating a thorough knowledge of the precessional effects – but also that the ancients must have known the form, shape and size of the Earth. On top of this, there is the knowledge of Pi, Pythagoras' theorems and the building technology to create these massive megalithic structures. Is all this not getting beyond the realms of the capabilities of the ancients and, at the same time, are the conventional explanations for all this incredible knowledge becoming totally inadequate? Are we not digging for ourselves a shaft that dives further and further down into the dark world of esoteric explanations for the dawn of the civilization of man?

Chapter IX

Teotihuacan

There were some dark days following the publication of the 'other book'; miserable days when I thought that I was all alone in this dispute with a multinational publisher and that all the years of hard work had been lost in an instant, taken from my grasp by a literary pickpocket. The loss was palpable, like losing a faithful dog or a family heirloom. The deepest of gloom lasted for just three days, however, when suddenly, on June 5th, things changed for the better. Quite unexpectedly, a very short letter arrived in the post from the publisher. It simply said:

> I am writing to confirm that we have ceased distribution of *Hall of the Gods* and are now in the process of withdrawing the book from sale. [1]

This was a bolt out of the blue. All it took was a simple letter from the smallest publisher in the world to the largest, and this happens! I had expected a long legal battle, an injunction to be in place at least, before any real action would be taken. Yet here they were, one of the largest publishers in the world, rolling over and capitulating with barely a shot. Something dramatic had happened and the format of the letter gave a small clue. Brief one-liners like this are often quite revealing because they are likely to be no more than a cover for the huge turmoil that is going on within the company itself. No publisher would voluntarily withdraw a book from public circulation, and announce in the publishing trade magazine that there was 'clear evidence of plagiarism', without some very high-level talks beforehand; talks that had identified a big legal problem. My second letter had hit another very raw nerve within their organization; two direct hits in a row; not a bad score given the scale of the problem. Whatever was really happening behind the scenes, it was a brief and unexpected victory in what was to become an escalating war.

Although the book had been withdrawn, there were two other major concerns that dominated almost every waking hour. Firstly, the offending book had already sold some 5,000 copies during its brief debut; a figure that would satisfy some of the smaller publishers in the lifetime of a book. In this respect, there would need to be some redress for the damage this had caused to my small enterprise. Secondly, it was quite apparent that the sole intention of both the author and publisher was to get the book back out on the shelves as soon as possible. To this end, I was bombarded daily by calls and faxes from a high-powered lawyer in London, who was always musing over 'alternative strategies' if I did not agree to a shotgun wedding with a known plagiarist. The inference was clear. I was to forget the attempted wrong because here was a possible source of financial support; the dangling carrot on offer being, once more, a percentage of the royalties on the new book. Oh, and by the way, if I did not agree they would find some other way of getting around the situation.

On the face of it, there were not many options open to me, and it is true that the royalties being offered would have plugged a glaring shortfall in my budgets. But a wrong is still a wrong and besides, the other book seemed to be no more than a compendium of other authors' works. Having ploughed my way through this new work, the only original sections, as far as I could tell, bordered on the outer fringes of fringe science. How could I be involved with such a book and such an author? Some may consider the book *Thoth* to be 'fringe' in its interpretations of these ancient monuments, but at least the underlying science in the book is indisputable. If an author is to make exceptional claims in his work, it has to start from very secure foundations: those of known science. I hope this work has achieved that balance and that it can be read and judged as a serious work, even if the conclusions it contains are highly speculative.

My answer to the impatient lawyer was a firm no, but I still needed to buy some time. The author's lawyer was still on the phone daily and there was a real possibility of some kind of republishing deal being developed behind the scenes. I needed to get a solicitor to threaten legal action if they did not stop. The wheels of justice, as anyone who has been involved can testify, turn at an exceedingly leisurely pace. In addition, my solicitor in London was proving to be very reluctant to take any action against the publisher.

Since all my previous contacts with solicitors had been simply to draw up the documentation for a house sale, I had naively assumed that all the practitioners in the trade were equally competent. Of course, since the dispute was a rather specialised subject, I had endeavoured to get a specialist in the field, one based in London. I was rather shocked to discover that my specialist was not all that special and the legal professional merely asked me what I wanted to do, without so much as even giving a list of options. Time was moving on, precious weeks were being wasted and not even a single legal letter had been written. It was time for a change; a chance to exit the cosy legal club of London and to seek independent advice from a much smaller market town solicitor.

It was only at that point that the legal effort changed up a gear and I discovered that the actions of this publisher were potentially a criminal offence. How a London firm of solicitors that deals in copyright cases on a daily basis – through its contacts with the agency that prosecutes video piracy offences – can 'forget' that copyright crime can be a criminal offence, is quite beyond understanding. Here was a major firm of solicitors telling a client that there was very little that could be done, when, in effect, the massive resources of the Metropolitan Police could be brought to bear on the case. It was tempting to think that the cosy London club was conspiring to keep this little problem under wraps.

Support

Despite the setbacks, things were improving, and they improved rapidly a week later as a result of a search on the Internet. Various correspondence, that seemed to display an ignorance of the facts, were being posted on a particular web-site, so I sent a stinging rebuke to the site, detailing my grievances in the situation. The result was remarkable. I had not realized until then that no fewer than eleven other authors had made formal complaints to the publisher; I was no longer alone. Suddenly my e-mail box started to come alive; other well-known authors started popping up with messages of support.

> Ralph,
> I got caught by him as well, I hadn't read your book previously but I am in the process of reading it now. Good luck in your action.
> Regards
> xxxxxx

> Ralph,
> I have read your latest note on the *BBS*, and I agree with every word

of it. I am the co-author of *The Hiram Key* with Robert Lomas which has been plundered in the same way as your book on Thoth. Two entire chapters have been lifted complete with many diagrams scanned directly from our book.

We would like to contact you again when we have read your work.

Best wishes

Chris Knight

The psychological boost of not being alone in this mess was invaluable. More importantly, the other authors also made it clear that they, too, were threatening unspecified legal moves if the publisher took no action. The situation had changed overnight. Then, a day or so later, another cryptic e-mail arrived.

Dear Ralph Ellis

28 June 1998.

Could you please call me. There are certain matters I would like to talk to you.

Many thanks

Robert Bauval

The letter was intriguing and I rang that evening. It transpired that Robert Bauval had also written in strong terms to the publisher about this new book, demanding its withdrawal. The letter back to him from Heinemann, almost by return of post, was that the new book had been withdrawn already because of a 'complaint from a different source'. This was perplexing, for he had no idea of my position and, like the other authors, he had never even seen my book. By this time there was also a rumour doing the rounds that I had settled with the publisher, so that the offending book, *Hall of the Gods,* could be reprinted. Needless to say, this concerned some of the authors considerably and they were greatly relieved to find out that this was not the case.

The tables had turned. Things were not just evenly balanced now; they had positively turned in our favour. Surely the other side would capitulate in the face of such solid opposition from a posse of no less than twelve authors? Surely we could end this quickly and relatively amicably and get back to the real job in hand, investigating the true history of the ancient past? Sadly not. Although Heinemann (Random House) admitted 'clear evidence of plagiarism' in the Bookseller magazine, the plagiarist, it seemed, did not recognize that he had done anything wrong. Not one syllable of apology left the tip of his quill, not one e-mail of contrition; all I received were veiled threats as to the power, influence and royal connections of his legal team. This was a seeker of ma'at, a seeker for the historical truth, but one who would not know what the truth was even if it camped on his doorstep. As is often the way, the petty politics of mankind was to drag on and on.

Outsiders often look in on these situations and say things like 'just settle your differences and get on with your jobs', or 'It does not matter where the truth comes from, as long as it is out in the open'. Admittedly, this legal squabbling probably does look petty from the outside. It may simply appear that one group of authors is ganging up on another, just because the content of a particular book is the same as previously written works. It may look petty, but in reality it is not. Theft is theft, no matter what the product. In many businesses, it is a quick method by which a rogue manufacturer climbs up on the back of solid research by a genuine company, and takes their ideas and concepts for free. The result in science and manufacturing could ultimately be that it may no longer be profitable to do basic research. If this were the case, innovation would die and new products would cease to be made. This is the reason why the patent laws were established and why they are rigorously maintained worldwide. Copyright crime is a serious threat to the technical improvement in products and processes, it is a threat to our standards of living.

Authorship is no different. A decent historical study, with some investigative reporting thrown in, takes years of research and plenty of investment. If the result of all that work is taken from the author, further research and further original thought will die with it. There was a precedent to set here; authors who wish to play this game, and the publishers who wish to back them, must be made to see the error of their ways. To that end, a legal battle erupted, spearheaded by Robert Bauval, who tirelessly fought for two long months, seven days a week, to prevent the plagiarist from re-releasing his book. It was a long and confusing saga, with many twists and turns, and it is a battle that simmers on even as this edition goes to the press. But without this legal conflict, the new titles of *Jesus, Last of the Pharaohs; Tempest & Exodus; and K2, Quest of the Gods* – advertised in the first few pages of this book – would not have been written. Yet these works may ultimately become more important than *Thoth*, so it would have been a great loss to those who are interested in this new history of mankind if the plagiarist had succeeded with his plans.

It is an ill wind that blows nobody any good, as the saying goes, and there was at last a possibility of some benefit accruing from this dark episode. The literary and legal maelstrom that had engulfed the copycat book had, at the same time, drawn in many of the established and well-known authors in the field. Not only was I now able to meet with all the other authors, but also, as the storm gathered pace, I found myself at the very center of the dispute; for in the eyes of the publisher and the plagiarist, it was only my work that had caused the withdrawal of their book.

The immediate outcome of all this sudden attention was that my book was instantly scrutinized by everyone in the field and many suggestions were made to improve its rather untidy format. It was strange to go from struggling solo author to being coached by the established professionals in this field, but such was the intensity of this storm and the scale of its fallout, that such things became commonplace. Where there had been independent authors scattered across the country, there was now contact and meetings. Things had probably changed for the better in many respects and the ugly duckling of a book by the name of *Thoth* had grown up at last; the result being this new improved edition.

Betrayal

We were on the home straight by now, the chequered flag in sight, *Hall of the Gods* was dead in the water, with no possibility of a resurrection. The other authors in this dispute had all distanced themselves publicly from the plagiarist and declared that they would never have any associations with him in the future. Sufficient pressure had been applied that a settlement was about to be signed that provided for a full public apology by the plagiarist, and which also prevented the republication of any future book that was in any way similar to *Hall of the Gods* and its proposed search for the 'Hall of Records'.

Then early one Saturday morning, Robert Bauval – who had been negotiating this deal with Random House executives all week – rang to say that Random House had just offered me a commercial publishing contract for my book *Thoth*. I was overjoyed; here at last was some recognition for all my hard work and, in my eyes, it showed a welcome degree of contrition on their part. What were the terms and conditions, I enquired? It transpired that I was to get a £5,000 advance on royalties, but only on condition that I sign the 'peace agreement' that we had been discussing with the plagiarist's lawyers earlier in the week. This initially sounded quite promising but unfortunately, the amended 'peace agreement', which was duly faxed to me, appeared to be much watered down from the original version for some reason. The original agreement had stated that:

> (The author) undertakes that (*Hall of the Gods*) will not be republished in part or in full in any means whatsoever ... [2]

But, in a unilateral fit of leniency, Robert Bauval had altered the text and the new wording declared:

> (The author) undertakes that he will not republish the (*Hall of the Gods*) in its originally published form. However, should (*Hall of the Gods*) be republished in a different form, then (the author) undertakes not to use the title *Hall of the Gods* .... [3]

This was backed up by a letter from the plagiarist, faxed to me by Robert Bauval, which stated:

> I have no intention of republishing my book *Hall of the Gods* using the same title or front cover, ever! [4]

The new form of words was about as watertight as the Titanic; sufficiently so to make me feel decidedly uncomfortable with this entire proposal by Random House. What were they up to here? I said that I would call the publishers on the Monday and sort out the details with them. But this was not good enough for Robert Bauval; I was to sign this 'peace agreement' immediately, very early on a Saturday morning – without even having seen the publishing contract from Random House and without having any confirmation from the publishers whatsoever. If I did not do so, then Robert would withdraw all his assistance in fighting this dispute and I would be marginalized by all his other author friends. I put the phone down with a resounding crash.

This was all very distressing, hurtful and extremely confusing. We had been on the brink of an amicable settlement and suddenly everything had changed – so just what was going on? A further layer of this convoluted intrigue descended upon us a week later, when an unexpected full-page spread was published in the British magazine *Quest*, advertising a tour of Egypt hosted by none other than Robert Bauval and the plagiarist author. In many eyes, this new association and cordial relations was rather akin to the Pope going on tour with Lenin.

Further confirmation of the scale of the intrigue came hot on the heels of the tour announcement. It now transpired that Robert Bauval was to write a book entitled *Secret Chamber: the Search for the Hall of Records*. This was a lucrative commission from Random House, the very publisher that Robert Bauval and Graham Hancock had left only two years before, and the very publisher we were fighting against to prevent the republication of the copycat book *Hall of the Gods* and its search for the mythical 'Hall of Records'. Thus, this new tour of Egypt was to be a strange union of bedfellows indeed, and in some eyes it seemed to be nothing short of a shotgun wedding conceived, organized and consummated in capitalism; and, whatever had happened during those lengthy negotiations by Robert Bauval down at Random House, I was now *persona non grata* at all levels.

True to his word, Robert now ensured that I was both marginalized and demonized, in the eyes of the public, as the vindictive rebel who could not even make a magnanimous gesture towards this poor plagiarist who had simply made a mistake while under great pressure. The ease with which the plagiarist had made this remarkable transition, from 'something sinister' to 'hapless victim', is indicative of the effectiveness of propaganda; the transformation was as simple and as sudden as the news media's 'terrorist' becoming a 'freedom fighter'. The simple solution to this perplexing situation, which was threatening to rapidly outflank my own position, was to do what Robert Bauval had already proposed: to go to the police and make a copyright complaint under section 107 of the Copyright Act. The repercussions of this sudden intervention by the forces of law and order, and the subsequent media attention that it produced, was all rather comical. Suddenly, the grand tour of Egypt by Bauval and the plagiarist was cancelled and the subject was never discussed again; it was a small and rare success in this escalating battle of wits.

But there were other repercussions to this police involvement and, needless to say, one of those was that my alleged publishing deal with Random House sank without trace. Robert Bauval has insisted in e-mails to myself, and in a public forum on the *Daily Grail* website,[5] that such a deal did exist and was offered; but several telephone calls and letters to Random House's executives produced nothing more than a steely silence – they simply refused to speak to me, either to confirm or to deny the presence of a publishing contract. Are we to believe that a professional international publishing house sends out publishing contracts to authors via a third party, and then refuses to answer the calls and correspondence from that same author? But if they do not engage in these kind of tactics, then why did they not deny all knowledge of the affair? The whole situation did seem a little bizarre and so the exact details and reasons behind this strange offer of a publishing deal, and its associated colander of a 'peace deal' with the plagiarist, remain an absolute mystery.

9. Teotihuacan

Atlantis

One of the things that surprised me most about this entire situation, though, was that the only major section that was not plagiarized from my book was the research on the Great Pyramid. Paradoxically, I thought that this was one of the best sections in the original book. The subject of the pyramids was actually the first thing I had been looking into in this tour of these ancient sites, and I had written a four-chapter manuscript on the topic. To be honest, apart from the measurement system theory, I had drawn a blank on much of the subject. The manuscript was far too speculative and it was dropped in favour of a study of the Wessex henges. Now that the henge sections were complete, it was time to look further afield and to dust off the old manuscripts that were lying under my desk, to see what I had written before on the subject. One of the first things that I noticed was a small section on Atlantis; this was another section in the original manuscript that had come to nothing.

The manuscript started with the observation that while all this frenetic building activity was going on in Europe and Africa, the rest of the world was doing very much the same sort of thing: building pyramids. While there was only one lonely pyramid in Europe – the Silbury 'pyramid' in Britain – there were plenty of similar monuments in Central America and China. Little serious research seems to have been done on the Chinese pyramids, which is partly a result of the political climate, but it also has to be due to a lack of interest. Travel has been possible in these parts of the world for some time, but the region is off the beaten track and not very popular. Nevertheless, the Chinese monuments seem to be quite splendid and pristine pyramids, in much the same design as Silbury but much larger, with the main group containing seven closely spaced pyramids. It would be interesting to see the start of some real archaeological work on this site, in particular. In contrast though, a great deal of work has been already been done on the Central American pyramids and in my manuscript I wondered if it was partly because of these monuments that a famous and cautionary tale was written.

Plato's *Atlantis* is a relatively short story of some 18 pages, which has caused commentary and speculation out of all proportion to its length or style. In modern literature, it tends to be the introduction to obscure and bizarre theories, and the death knell of any popular book, which seemed a good reason for giving the subject a wide berth. However, there was reason to look further into the tale, for the Avebury 'Earth' theory seemed to state, in no uncertain terms, that some small islands down in the South Atlantic, islands that lay beyond the Pillars of Hercules, were very important. They

9. Teotihuacan

were important enough to have been conspicuously picked out in an ancient megalithic map of the world – Avebury.

But the shadow of Atlantis still hung over my deliberations. Should I stay off such a topic, just because it has a bad name in serious research? The quick answer to this was no; this book had already trespassed on so many taboos that one more was not going to do any harm. Anyway, there should be no reason why one cannot take a serious and critical look at the Atlantis story, for some of the other ancient Greek myths have turned out to have a real historical basis. Erastosthenes' and Eusebius' city of Petra, for instance, which was rediscovered in Jordan; Homer's Troy, which was recently found to be located in western Turkey. So, could there be a grain of truth to Atlantis? Possibly, but firstly we should take a short overview of the myth.

Where did the tale of Atlantis come from? Plato (427 – 347 BC) puts its origin firmly in Egypt. The story was told to Solon, one of the seven sages of Athens, while he was visiting Heliopolis in Egypt. Solon (639 – 559 BC) was of noble descent and sailed for Egypt in 571 BC, where he stayed at both Heliopolis and Sais. Following this, he lived in Cyprus as the guest of King Philocyprus, returning to Greece in 561 BC. Unfortunately, none of his works, including the commentary on Atlantis, has survived.[6] The story passed through Critias, who narrated the tale to Socrates, and Plato recorded it for posterity in the works known as *Timaeus* and *Critias*. Apparently another Greek, by the name of Crantor, also visited Sais some 300 years later and was shown a stone column with hieroglyphics that confirmed the story of Atlantis, as narrated by Plato. Needless to say, however, no such column has been found by archaeologists at Sais.

The Atlantis myth is of a girl, Cleito, being impregnated by the gods and founding the ideal, and the original, civilization of mankind. This civilization lived on an island created by Poseidon in the Atlantic, 'beyond the Pillars of Hercules' (Gibraltar). The society was founded by five pairs of twins born to Cleito and these offspring ruled not only Atlantis but also:

... over the Mediterranean peoples as far as Egypt and Tuscany.[7]

They became the richest, most noble race the world had seen and the story glories in the splendour of the island of Atlantis, from the fertile plains to the canal-encircled citadel; the world had never before seen such splendours. The temple of Poseidon, for instance, was typical of the lavish ornamentation:

All the exterior of the temple they coated with silver, save only the pinnacles, and these they coated with gold. As to the interior, they made the roof all of ivory in appearance, variegated with gold and silver and orichalcum, and all the rest of the walls and pillars and the floors they covered with orichalcum. And therein they placed golden statues, one being that of the god standing on a chariot and driving six winged-steeds, his own figure so tall as to touch the ridge of the roof.[8] (A rather pharaonic scene, one might think.)

Such was the manpower of Atlantis that the army comprised 10,000 chariots, each with two horses and two spares. In addition, there were 20,000 archers and slingers, plus 30,000 light infantry; the navy in their turn had no fewer than 1,200 ships, such was the power of this nation. The nation was well governed, with a respected legal system, and it would seem that the inherited 'nature of god' (bloodline of the gods) was still strong within the people so that:

> Consequently they thought scorn of everything save virtue and lightly esteemed their rich possessions, bearing with ease the burden, as it were, of the vast volume of their gold and other goods; and thus their wealth did not make them drunk with pride so that they lost control of themselves and went to ruin.[9]

But alas:

> the portion of divinity (blood of the gods) within them was now becoming faint and weak through being oftimes blended with a large measure of mortality (blood of man), whereas the human temper was becoming dominant ... for they had lost the fairest of their goods from the most precious of their parts; but in the eyes of those who have no gift of perceiving what is the truly happy life, it was then above all that they appeared to be superlatively fair and blessed, filled as they were with lawless ambition and power.
>
> And Zeus, the god of gods ... marked how this righteous race was in evil plight, and desired to inflict punishment upon them ... Wherefore he assembled together all the gods into that abode which they honour most, standing as it does at the center of all the Universe; and when he had assembled them; he spake thus...[10]

Plato ends rather enigmatically at this point, as though the tale was never finished, or perhaps we are to guess the fate of the Atlanteans.

* * *

9. Teotihuacan

Speculation

This short tale has drawn more than its fair share of explanations by authors. The island of Atlantis has been situated from North Africa to Santorini, from the Mid-Atlantic ridge to Antarctica, and there are any number of reasons why it can not be found in any of these locations today. Certainly, there are some arguments in favour of the myth:

    a.   There are common legends and words found in the ancient civilizations on both sides of the Atlantic. Even the Atlantean five pairs of twins are quite reminiscent of the four pairs of sister-wives that comprised the Egyptian Ogdoad.

    b.   There is the common urge to build vast pyramids on both sides of the Atlantic; pyramid complexes that resemble each other rather too closely for coincidence.

    c.   Then there is the great age of the founding of the civilization of Egypt. Plato tells of the relative youth of Greece by quoting the Egyptians:

> As to those genealogies of yours which you have recounted to us, Solon, they are no better than the tales of children; for, in the first place, you remember one deluge only, whereas there were many of them; and, in the next place, you do not know that there dwelt in your land the fairest and noblest race of men which ever lived, of whom you and your whole city are but a seed or remnant. And this was unknown to you because for many generations the survivors of that destruction died and made no sign ...
>
> She founded your city (old Athens) one thousand years before ours (Egypt), receiving from the Earth and Hephaestus the seed of your race, and then she founded ours, the constitution of which is set down in our sacred registers as 8,000 years old. [11]

Note that this was told to Solon in about 575 BC. If we subtract 8,000 years from 575 BC, the founding of Egypt – according to Solon and the Egyptian sages – works out at 10,575 years ago. The founding of old Athens was 1,000 years before that, or 11,575 years ago. Casting your mind back to the Giza planisphere that we have constructed, the planisphere date is 13,670 years ago. While not exact, we are most certainly talking about the same sort of era.

9. *Teotihuacan*

Many previous authors have tried to take the Atlantis myth rather too literally, trying to identify a real island; one as big as is reported in the myth and situated somewhere out in the Atlantic. It is quite impossible that such a place could have ever existed. An island the size of 'Libya and Asia Minor' cannot be hidden in the Gulf of Mexico, whether or not Atlantis sank beneath the sea. Myths are myths but, nevertheless, they can still hide small grains of truth. So possibly, by stripping the myth down to its bare essentials, we can identify a possible source for the tale of Atlantis.

Atlantis then, looks as though it is an amalgam of two myths that have been stored away since the dim and distant past of civilization. Over those centuries, these myths have gelled together into the tale we are familiar with today. The separate segments of the myth are:

a.   A civilization, created by the gods, that became the wealthiest and most advanced society on Earth at the time. But a civilization that fell into the most basic trap of human frailties: they became corrupt and greedy. The gods, in their despair after all their lectures and warnings, finally deserted them.

b.   A lost island in the Atlantic, not some vast continent and not even an island that sank beneath the sea. This island is just a small dot in the ocean, which has been lost from the memory of mankind; a small dot that perhaps holds the lost repository of Thoth, the fabled Hall of Records. Could such an island be one of the Sandwich Islands, as indicated by the Avebury henge? Could we have found the site of the lost island of Atlantis?

It was for this reason that, back in the spring of 1997, I found myself at RAF Brize Norton, bound for the South Atlantic. It was a speculative trip, but one worth the time and trouble. The Avebury henge was quite specific in its meaning and so a reconnaissance trip was essential before a book was published, if only to ascertain that there was nothing obvious to be found there. I had found that the Royal Air Force is the only operator to run a schedule down to the Falklands and, since this is the only practical method of travel to the region, it is used regularly by Falkland Islanders and St Helenans alike to travel to Britain.

So it was with relative ease that I managed to book a flight southbound and found myself on an active RAF base, waiting for departure. It is not quite the same as turning up at Heathrow, but nevertheless the formalities of passing the main gate were fast and efficient, and I soon found myself in the 1970s-looking terminal. It could have been a regional airport anywhere in the world but for two big exceptions: all the buildings at Brize were green and the person at the check-in desk was big and hairy, with a fine assortment of tattoos running up both arms.

At length, we boarded our Tristar for the flight. It was an old and slightly battered civil airliner that had changed little on becoming a RAF machine. The flight reminded my of my many trips on Aeroflot; there was a slightly quaint feeling to the aircraft and its furnishings, and a home-made air about the catering. Hand-held televisions were issued because there was no central TV system in the aircraft. The giveaway as to the operator, though, was the drab uniforms for the stewards and the size of their biceps.

After the tribulations of the long journey, the initial aerial recce of the island revealed only a couple of significant things to report and most of this will be left for a later work. However, it is worth noting that the volcanic terrain of the island was interesting in itself, as it left me with distinct images of Egypt. The island consisted mostly of volcanic cinder cones and these formed themselves into pyramidal shapes, both large and small. It is difficult to say if this was significant in any way, but it was interesting.

Teotihuacan

The initial recce had only been a minor diversion in the story up to this point, but what about the rest of the Atlantis myth? What about this lost civilization? Although some authors have speculated on the possibility of a real lost civilization on an Atlantic island, it was quite obvious that the lost civilization could not be directly associated with these tiny islands in the far south. So how does the lost civilization fit into this story? In the book *Tempest & Exodus*, a good argument is made that the lost civilization part of the story may have been influenced by the destruction of Santorini (Thera), as has been speculated by other authors. Although this argument has some merit, there is another location that may equally be involved in the myth of a lost civilization.

There are some ancient civilizations across the Atlantic Ocean that may well have been associated with these myths and the greatest of these is located in Central America – the abandoned city of Teotihuacan. This ancient Mexican city should really be one of the seven wonders of the ancient world; although the pyramids of Teotihuacan themselves are simpler than their Giza cousins in their method of construction, the entire site is nevertheless a vast and imposing complex, measuring some 2.3 km from end to end.

Classical chronology has the compound started in 800 BC (although this is widely disputed), and it was in its heyday some 2,000 years ago, when the surrounding city was populated with some 200,000 people, who were organized into a highly complex society. The population was housed in sprawling suburbs, geometrically laid out and arranged around the pyramid complex; a city that would not look out of place in the modern world. The city covered an area of about 25 square kilometers, but was most densely populated in a central six square kilometers, all of which was paved:

> ... with small stones, held together with mortar to a depth of ten to one hundred centimeters. [12]

Such a city is rather harder to date than most ancient sites, as a well-kept and paved city produces little in the way of accumulated litter, upon which most dating processes are based. No stratigraphy means no certainty to the site's chronology. Additionally, if the housing is well built and rarely requires rebuilding, the city could in theory remain relatively unchanged for millennia. Certainly it is true that, economically, the city must have been one of the largest pre-industrial cities in the world. There were tens of thousands of people involved in crafts and, on market days, perhaps as many as a hundred thousand milling around the great market place at the center of the town, opposite the Citadel. Professor Rene Milton inferred that different types of workshops were arranged in separate neighbourhoods in the city, with over 500 workshops just for working obsidian alone. (Obsidian is a dark, volcanic, glasslike rock.)

He also has argued from his plans of the city that the central avenue between the pyramids, 'Way of the Dead', must have been decided on very early in the history of the city, possibly before the construction of any permanent buildings other than the pyramids. [13] As the city grew, however, so did the technology needed to sustain the burgeoning population. Milton found that Teotihuacan had many carefully laid out canal systems of branching waterways, and artificially dredged and straightened portions of river, which formed a network within the city and ran all the way to the lake, some ten miles away.

With these lakes and waterways, the Teotihuacanos appear to have been able to feed a vast population, using their system of 'chinampas', or floating gardens, on which they could produce some three crops a year. This system of farming is still used in some parts of South America and the marsh regions of Iraq. Further excavations have uncovered public baths, theaters, and ball courts. Sigwald Linne found inner courts to houses, complete with finely polished stone plugs to plug the drains still in situ. Beneath the floors of the houses were graves, complete with domestic utensils, jewellery and obsidian artifacts.

9. Teotihuacan

Despite all this work, the mystery of exactly when the pyramids of Teotihuacan were built remains as deep as ever; 800 BC is still a favourite, but some historians put it back as far as 3000 BC. Yet with the pyramid-building eras of Egypt and Britain ascribed as being contemporary to each other, even under the classical dating system, why not Teotihuacan as well? This would place Teotihuacan back to about 2,600 BC under the classical system, and a massive 11,500 BC with my re-dating of Giza. This may seem a leap of faith suddenly to re-date a site back by 8,000-odd years just because of a similar construction elsewhere, but remember that under the scenario that has been developed, the town and the pyramids do not even have to be of the same era. Nothing remains of the cities that built the Giza plateau, so why should Teotihuacan be any different?

Whatever the age of the city that is associated with the Mexican pyramids, the overall picture is one of a wealthy, thriving civilization; one with a very long and illustrious past, and every hope for the future. But at some point in time:

> ... some great holocaust hit the city. Charred areas around all or most of the city's temples and public buildings suggest they were deliberately burned. [14]

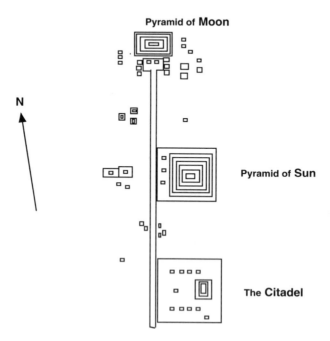

Fig 55. Layout of Teotihuacan

9. *Teotihuacan*

Whatever the cause, the end was dramatic. After AD 750, it would appear that Teotihuacan was a ghost town, with only the central one square kilometer being sparsely occupied. Leopoldo Batres was somewhat confused by the scene; he found communities that appeared to have burned to death in a conflagration, but other houses perfectly preserved, complete with roofs. The cause of the demise is unknown; climate change and ultimately civil strife were the most likely candidates, but this is unconfirmed.

The pyramid complex, as it was found in the nineteenth century, is another mystery altogether. Obviously, the city was deserted and has needed only a little clearing of the overlying debris to reveal the remains of roads and housing. The pyramid complex itself, however, was a little more enigmatic. The pyramids were originally constructed of a thick clay center, with a composite stone and mortar matrix shell as a casing to add stability to the inner clay core. All over this stone casing, the temples and pyramids had been covered with a thick layer of earth, up to 4 meters thick, and this layer appears to have been deliberately applied. The resulting monuments were not the neat pyramids we see today; they were like large man-made earth mounds and quite uninspiring. The largest of these pyramids were named the Sun and Moon, but these appellations are quite abstract and have no historical value.

In 1905, Leopoldo Batres began excavations. Initially, he probed the mound of earth on the pyramid of the Sun and found a layer of stone several meters under the earth. Using this as an excavation line, he began removing the earth at a rate of 80–100 tonnes per day; it soon became apparent that he had probed too far in some places and he nearly caused the collapse of one face of the pyramid. As Batres continued, and began to uncover the lines of a perfectly formed pyramid, he too mused that:

> The whole structure may have been ... covered with earth to cover it from human eyes. [15]

Prophetic words, indeed. Like the Silbury and the Chinese pyramids, the pyramids of Teotihuacan were covered in a deep layer of earth; a layer which could easily have protected the site for thousands of years, and so the pyramids themselves could have been constructed in any era. What is more, with the knowledge that we now have on the sites at Avebury and Giza, we can say with some confidence that this earth was most probably deliberately placed there by the designer for this purpose. The architect wanted a monument that would last for thousands of years, but monuments like Giza are difficult to build and, even if the finished pyramid could withstand the weather, the stones might still be stolen by future generations for other building projects.

9. Teotihuacan

The alternative to this strategy would be to build a vast monument, made of easier-to-handle clays, and give it a thin stone outer shell for stability. But such a structure would erode away in only a few generations, so in order to protect the site it would have to be buried under a vast heap of earth. This is just what we find at Silbury, Xian and Teotihuacan: vast monuments buried under a layer of earth. But since the all-important measurements of the site were contained in the stone structures that lay under the protective earth, it would seem obvious to me that this protective layer was deliberately applied so that a future technical civilization could finally uncover the stones and marvel at their mathematical symmetries. This is why the Silbury Pyramid should be stripped of its covering layer of earth and displayed to the world in all its intended glory.

But is this just my guesswork? Not at all; it was an idea that was originally proposed by the ancient historian, Josephus, in about AD 70, and he based his ideas on Biblical accounts:

> The children of Seth were the inventors of that peculiar sort of wisdom, which is concerned with the heavenly bodies, and their order; and that their inventions might not be lost before they were sufficiently known, upon Adam's prediction, that the world was at one time to be destroyed by the forces of fire and water, they made two pillars, one of brick and the other of stone. They described their discoveries on them both, that in case the pillar of brick should be destroyed by flood, the pillar of stone should remain, and exhibit those discoveries to mankind. [And in case the pillar of stone be destroyed by fire, the pillar of brick should remain.] Now this remains in the land of Syria to this day. [16]

The Biblical account is talking about the family of Noah, but the similarity here with Seth from the family of the Egyptian gods is undeniable. The passage is based on the Biblical story of the sons of Noah who built the tower of brick – the tower of Babel. [17] It may not be immediately obvious what the passage is trying to say to us, because of the confusing word 'pillar' in the text. The Bible calls this pillar a 'tower' instead, one 'whose top may reach unto heaven', and that is getting a little closer to the truth in this matter. For the real answer to this riddle, substitute the word 'pyramid' for the word 'pillar' and read the passage again.

Here we see a tradition of an ancient people recording technical details for posterity and inscribing these details into, or onto, the pyramids. Also we have an ancient tradition of two pyramids being made of two different materials, so that in case one was destroyed for whatever reason, the other might remain. This was quite a sensible precaution because the pyramid of brick to which the text refers is one of the brick ziggurats of Sumer, the tower of Babel. All of these brick pyramids have been nearly totally destroyed.

Here we have the reason for the different types of pyramidal monument that are to be found: not only was each made of a material that was suited to the capabilities of the local population, but also it was understood that the different structures had different life expectancies, depending on what the future held for that region. It would appear that the low-technology route of a mud and rubble pyramid, covered in earth, was the most successful of all the materials used; all of these pyramids have survived completely intact into the modern era. Only our technical civilization was sufficiently motivated to divert valuable resources into the otherwise unrewarding task of uncovering the earth-covered pyramids. The reason for all this activity would never have occurred in the distant past, as the driving force for this huge task was nothing less than national pride and tourism.

Batres was much criticized for his excavation work at Teotihuacan, but nevertheless his successor, Manuel Gamio, had much the same problems in his excavations of 1917. He soon realized that each structure would need reinforcing with new mortar as soon as it was uncovered, because the stone cladding of the pyramids had disintegrated, despite being covered with earth. Such was the scale of the task of digging out the temples that he was obliged to uncover only one face of each and leave the other sides under the mountains of earth. After many years, all of this earth was eventually removed from the site.

But the work was rewarding in places. The pyramids of the Sun and Moon are vast, but quite plain in their construction; just a simple statement of mass and presence, like the Giza pyramids. In contrast, on the empty site known as the Citadel, there was discovered:

> a quite small pyramid in six stages to a height of 22 meters, each stage consisting of heavy stone cornices with a sculpture of huge undulating serpents carved in relief, with heads protruding from petalled collars to represent Quetzlcoatl. Each snake body bore in the center a large humanoid head with a fanged jawbone, moustache and circular orbs over its eyes. [18]

Clearly, this pyramid belongs to a different era from that of the Sun and Moon Pyramids and, considering the size of the site prepared for the pyramid, it is quite obvious that the original intention was to build a much bigger version of the Sun Pyramid on this site. On excavating the vast mounds of earth covering the pyramid of the Moon, nearly 500 original stones of the stairway were found, including the original cornerstone. When the stairway was reconstructed, it was found that it had been:

Ingeniously designed with interlocking stones, to prevent slippage. [19]

This is a system not unlike the roof of the Grand Gallery at Giza, which had a similar system of interlocking roof lintels.

Giza correlations

The Sun and Moon Pyramids have been identified as being the first monuments on the site, and they are simple, plain architectural statements in clay and stone. Only the later temples introduced the ornamental gargoyles to the structure. So, the pyramids of Teotihuacan have many similarities with Giza and Silbury, and could it really be just coincidence that the shape of the pyramid complex at Teotihuacan so closely mimics that of Giza?

One of the legacies of the Conquistadors, however, is that the scripts and hieroglyphs of South America remain largely undeciphered, as the task of deciphering the complex language is rather difficult without a Mexican version of the Rosetta stone. One possible method of finding out if there were any deeper correlations with the other megalithic monuments around the world, would be to find a unit of measure in the complex and compare it to Egypt and Avebury to see if there were any mathematical correlations. This is by no means easy, as the site is not made to the same exacting standards as the Giza site, and so measurements are more likely to be to the nearest tens of centimeters rather than the nearest tens of millimeters. Milton started the process by taking long-distance measurements so that the errors in the disturbed buildings would be minimized, and he came up with a common multiple of 57 meters.

The baton was taken on by Hugh Harleston Jr in 1972. Harleston was an American engineer who had lived a quarter of a century in Mexico and had become somewhat obsessed with the challenge of Teotihuacan. His strategy was to measure vast numbers of relative proportions, initially taken over large distances, and refined where possible when original, undisturbed masonry was identifiable. The first number to emerge was again 57 m, swiftly followed by one-third of this or 19 m. Further investigation revealed one-third of this was also a multiple; this unit was 6.333 m.

9. Teotihuacan

Harleston thought that this unit was significantly close to the polar radius of the Earth to warrant mention; the polar radius being some 6,356 km. What he would not have known at the time was that the polar radius of the Egyptian Earth, as measured from scaling up the great Pyramid by the factor 43,200, was 6,333 km. This is an exact multiple of the Teotihuacan unit, which we could name the Quetzl rod after the god that was regarded as the architect of these pyramids, Quetzlcoatl. Parts of the complex which use the units of 6.333 m include the Sun and Moon Pyramids, the most central constructions on the site.

Harleston never did find a satisfactory smaller unit than the one above, his best guess being one-sixth of the 6.333 length, and there is probably a good reason for this: he never thought of dividing his new unit by 5.5 to derive a Pi-based unit. A new survey of the site may prove this one way or another; unfortunately, many of the reference books publish Harleston's data and the metric data in these surveys is derived from his new smaller unit, not the other way around, so there appears to be a certain amount of rounding involved in the measurements.

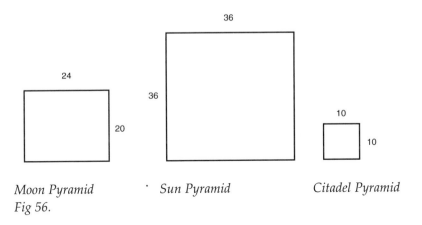

Moon Pyramid   · Sun Pyramid   Citadel Pyramid

Fig 56.

Decline

The complex society of Teotihuacan eventually came to a sudden end, either relatively recently or, perhaps, a long time ago. So what finally happened at Teotihuacan? Why did such a thriving society falter and die out completely? Well, it is only myth and guesswork from here on.

On the (admittedly speculative) assumption that the same designer was present during the construction of the Teotihuacan pyramids, the largest pyramid on the site should have been dedicated to the star Alnitak in the constellation of Orion and it should, like the Great Pyramid, have been the most prestigious of the three pyramids. But it was never built. The pyramids of the Sun and Moon were massive plain affairs with no adornments, just like the pyramids at Giza, but the small 'pyramid' that appears in the middle of the much larger foundations of the Citadel at Teotihuacan is of a different construction era altogether; it is heavily embossed with serpents and gargoyles.

Why was the expected, much larger, and plainer pyramid of Alnitak not built? The speculation, if it is not too wild, may well involve a return to the myths of Atlantis here. The great and mythical architect designed and built another pyramid complex at Teotihuacan, but the Atlantis myth now takes over and the people of this new civilization grew to like their new-found wealth. But:

> In the eyes of those who have no gift of perceiving what is the truly happy life, it was then above all that they appeared to be superlatively fair and blessed, filled as they were with lawless ambition and power. [The Great Architect] desired to inflict punishment upon them ... Wherefore he assembled together all the gods ... and when he assembled them, he spake thus ... (Plato).

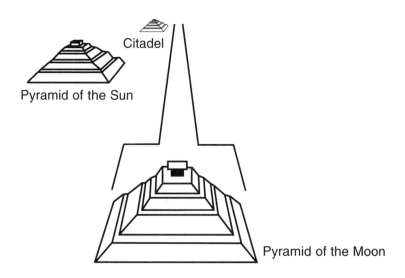

Fig 57. Layout of the Teotihuacan pyramids

9. Teotihuacan

Angle of the cosmos

Another enduring mystery at Teotihuacan is the peculiar angle of the 'Way of the Dead', the main processional road that runs through the pyramid complex – parallel to the sites of the Citadel and the pyramid of the Sun – and up to the pyramid of the Moon.

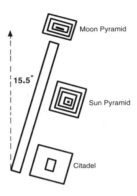

Fig 58. Angle of the 'Way of the Dead'

This main avenue runs up to the pyramid of the Moon at an angle of 15.5° east of north and it has always defied explanation because this angle cannot be identified with a normal astronomical event in our calendar. Yet this angle of the 'Way of the Dead', being so central to the site, should be important. In the eyes of Milton, it was constructed:

> ... possibly before the construction of any permanent buildings other than the pyramids. [20]

It could have been an angle just chosen at random, but would any designer constructing such a massive project really stand out on a grassy plain, point, and say 'Ok chaps, we shall go in this direction'? One would think not, especially as all the megalithic monuments we have looked at so far have contained so many mathematical and cosmological connotations. If this were the case at all these sites then there should be a mathematical or stellar explanation to this particular angle. Moreover, in our previous explanations of the Stonehenge and Giza sites, we are no longer talking about the site angles marking a simple sunrise or a moonrise; we are implicating a full planisphere layout.

9. Teotihuacan

So was Teotihuacan really a monument designed by the same architect, that was not fully completed, just like the Stonehenge site appears to be? If this was the case, then we can say with some confidence that the layout of the 'Way of the Dead' marks the belt of Orion, in which case there should be two further pyramids, some distance from the actual Teotihuacan site, that mark the positions of the Earth's and the Sun's poles. Even if they do not exist, we can always calculate the position in which they should have stood, just like we did at Stonehenge.

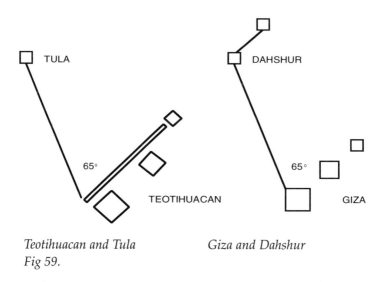

Teotihuacan and Tula   *Giza and Dahshur*

Fig 59.

The angle between a line through the belt of Orion and a line from Orion to the Sun's pole is about 65°; the same angle that we found on the Giza site. If the angle of the Way of the Dead is about 15° east of north, the angle to the location of the two expected pyramids would be 65° minus 15°, or 50° to the west of north. If we travel up an angle of 50° west of north from Teotihuacan, we find the pyramid complex of Tula. In fact, the complex lies some 63 km from Teotihuacan, or an exact 10,000 multiple of the rod length that is used so often on this pyramid site.

Tula contains only one pyramid that has been fully excavated, so until further work is completed on the site to uncover the predicted second pyramid out to the north-west of the Tula Pyramid, the jury must still be out on this one. But it is still a very large coincidence that a pyramid can be found that mimics so precisely the layout of the Dahshur pyramids in relation to Giza.

Chapter X

Great Continents

The answer to one of the greatest riddles of the pyramids had been pinned up on the wall of my office for months. It is funny how a sheet of paper can sit there for week after week without one really noticing it and then suddenly one day, for no particular reason, it jumps off the wall and demands your full attention. This is exactly what happened to the Great Pyramid diagram in my office. I had been convinced that the Avebury Earth concept must be related in some way to the layout of the internal chambers of the Great Pyramid, as I was convinced that these galleries and chambers were part of an ancient blueprint or drawing that explained something technical or mathematical.

Because of this rather radical belief, I had been looking into the possibility that the angles of the small shafts that run out of the main chambers were latitude pointers for the Sandwich Islands, so that a link could perhaps be established with Avebury. As the Sandwich Islands are in the Southern Hemisphere, I had hung the diagram upside down to make the shafts point downward; the diagram seemed to make more sense that way, the latitudes pointed south instead of north. It was to be a full two months after doing this that I suddenly spotted the link between the Great Pyramid and Avebury.

However, the details of that discovery would be jumping ahead of time; conversely, the majority of the research into the pyramids had been much more methodical and tedious, but revealing nevertheless. The task I had set myself was to take a new and radical look at the Great Pyramid, in just the same way as I had done for Avebury. Just as at Avebury, I was not going to underestimate the capabilities of the pyramid's designer; if the small and relatively crude constructions of Avebury and Stonehenge could have held so many mysteries as they apparently do, in comparison, anything and everything should be possible in such a magnificent edifice as the Great Pyramid of Giza.

We have previously looked at some of the internals of the Great Pyramid and the subtle mathematics contained in the metrology of the King's Chamber. But the primary item of interest inside this pyramid is often not the King's Chamber, but the Grand Gallery (G Gallery). The G Gallery is quite a marvel of engineering; a vast corbeled vault that rises up through the pyramid at an angle of 26° 02´, with a length of exactly 88 tc (46 m) from the bottom of the gallery to the Great Step at the top. The dimensions of this vault are immense, not only in length, but also in the soaring 16.46 tc (8.6 m) height. For such a vast construction, the problems of structural integrity in carrying the millions of tonnes of stone above are equally immense. So much so that the roof was constructed of individually locking slabs of limestone, forming a saw-tooth roof-line: a design that prevents any shear forces in the roof building up and causing slippage down the length of the Gallery.

The obvious question that has to be asked, however, is what was all this for? The other passages in this pyramid are minute: only about 1 m high and barely enough to crawl through. If the small passages were good enough for the purpose of access to and from the chambers, why suddenly expand out into an awesome 8.6 m high passage? The expense, in terms of engineering complexity and construction delays, dictates that there was an overriding reason for making the G Gallery the way it is. It *is* important.

A similar comparison could justifiably be made for the 'relieving' chambers that reside above the King's Chamber. What was the purpose of these? No-one has come up with a very satisfactory answer to this design either. The normal explanation is that the ceiling of the King's Chamber required some stress relief from the massive weight of the pile of stones that lies above it. This is a reasonable attempt at an explanation, except it does not explain why each set of beams should have a smooth and polished underside. It also remains a fact that no other chamber on the Giza plateau needs such a device, including the Queen's Chamber, which resides below the King's and therefore has even more weight pressing upon it. If the Queen's Chamber does not need 'relieving chambers', then why does the King's?

A recent book on Egypt took these 'stress relief' claims one step further and claimed that the roof beams in the 'relieving chambers' were under so much stress that they had cracked. But in truth, the only weight upon these beams is the few grams of stale air in each of the small chambers above, and even that weight is balanced by the air pressure from below. It is a statement of fact that the 'relieving chambers' do not relieve any stress and do not perform any function in regard to the weight of the pyramid above the chamber: their only architectural function could possibly be to keep the walls of the King's Chamber's attic from collapsing inwards. The term 'relieving chamber' is therefore a misnomer, and 'attic chamber' would be more appropriate.

It is also quite apparent from all the other examples of pyramid chambers that we have, that attic chambers are not normally required for a room in a pyramid. There are only two real differences with the King's Chamber which differentiate this chamber from others:

a.   The King's Chamber has a flat ceiling which does need some stress relief.

This is true, but a flat ceiling could have easily been added under some pitched roof beams. For the integrity of such a construction, take a look at the top attic chamber; has this first set of roof beams suffered unduly just because it is the first flat ceiling underneath the pitched roof? No, of course not.

b.   The added rigidity (stiffness) of the granite used in the chamber, in comparison with the softer limestone in the core of the pyramid. The Queen's Chamber, in comparison, is constructed entirely from limestone.

Again true, but the designer overcame this problem by making the walls of the King's Chamber separate from the floor and the core stones of the pyramid. In this case, if there were excess pressure from above, the granite walls would just sink into softer limestone below the chamber, and the floor of the chamber would effectively rise up the walls slightly. In fact, this appears to have happened just as planned.

In this case, why did the designer go to the vast expense and bother of constructing the attic chambers above the King's Chamber? This question, as I crawled down the descending passage of the Great Pyramid, struck me as being central to the whole conundrum of the pyramid saga. Each of the descending passages in the pyramids, angle downwards at about 26° from the horizontal. On paper, this does not really mean much, but as I crawled down the shaft backwards, with my head bumping the ceiling at every other step of my cramped legs, it began to mean much more; this was hard work. These passageways were ludicrous, either as entrances to secret passages, as walkways for a funerary procession or as access-ways for the workmen that built them in the first place.

10. Great Continents

Blueprint

The tombs in the Valley of the Kings show us what a sensible tomb should look like; the shafts in these tombs are wide, tall and angled downwards at a sedate 10 - 15°. The access to and from the tombs within is easy and dignified for the assembled priests and royalty. The difference between the valley chambers and the one I was in was all too obvious. Most of the time I was reduced to crawling on hands and knees: my back ached, my head was bruised and, if it were not for the duck-boards fitted to the shaft, I would not even have been able to climb out. If anyone had visited any of these Giza or Dahshur pyramids in ancient times, they would have needed a very long set of ladders to get up to the entrance of the pyramid and a very long rope with which to climb up the shaft again. Once more, it was obvious that these great monuments were *not* tombs; the physical reality of these shafts was proof enough.

Coming back to the original question of what the G Gallery really meant to the designer, the answer to this has to lie in our interpretation of what these pyramids were for. The G Gallery and the King's Chamber's attic roof system make no sense in terms of a tomb, but they make every sense in terms of a drawing board, a vast limestone blueprint. In a blueprint, there are the construction lines for the drawing – mere aids for the draughtsman to draw his picture – and then there are the real outlines of the drawing itself. If the structure of the Great Pyramid was designed as a 'blueprint', there must be some way of differentiating between the 'construction lines' and the drawing itself.

The obvious answer is that the small passageways are the construction lines; mere access ways that are only necessary for the construction workers to complete their job, and for us to discover and measure their work. The real drawings on this megalithic blueprint are any component in the pyramid with a height of 2 tc (1 m) or more, plus the much smaller 'air shafts', which are obviously not access shafts for the workers. Both the G Gallery and the attic chambers are, therefore, part of the blueprint and so they ought to have dimensions containing meaningful numbers. They do.

I was not able to get access to the attic chambers and so I have used the data gathered by Sir Flinders Petrie. He reported that the distance from the top of one attic chamber to the top of the next one turns out to be half the height of the King's Chamber, or just over 5.5 tc. Not only are the attic chambers themselves, therefore, intimately related to the King's Chamber dimensions, but they are also evenly spaced, one to the next.

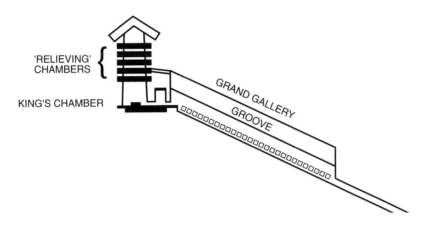

Fig 60. The Grand Gallery and attic chambers

Looking at the measurements of the G Gallery, there are more meaningful dimensions to be found here. The gallery is exactly 88 tc long, or one-fifth of the length of the base of the pyramid; therefore the G Gallery is again related to other dimensions within the pyramid's design. But is this enough proof that this particular section of G Gallery is the section we need to measure? The full length of the gallery from wall to wall is 91.36 tc, what I am doing here is taking the section of the G Gallery from the vertical face of the Great Step.

One reason for taking a measurement from the G Step is that the upper end wall of the G Gallery slopes inwards, but the G Step, being vertical, provides a much more useful reference point. When building a structure like the G Gallery, it is not very easy to make vertical walls and still take the lateral stresses of the surrounding rock; witness the size of the roof blocks required to take the stresses in the King's and Queen's Chambers. It is much easier to angle the walls inwards, which is what we find at the top of the gallery and in all the simpler chambers in the pyramids at Dahshur. To construct vertical walls is very difficult and there must have been a good reason for it in the case of the King's Chamber.

The architect was well aware of this and aware also of the confusion the sloping walls of the G Gallery might cause when decoding the pyramid. Which length does one choose? Happily, the designer has helped us out here, not only by making the length between the vertical faces exactly 88 tc – which is a convenient fraction of the pyramid's external dimensions – but also by placing a number of notches in the low shelf that runs the length of the G Gallery. These notches have caused, like most things in the Great Pyramid, a great deal of speculation. There have been theories as diverse as joist holes for a wooden floor; holes for timbers to support the blocks of stone used to plug the ascending passage; and even in one book:

preparation of ascending mortals on way to millennium [sic].[1]

Although each idea has its own merits, they are conjecture without any real proof and are mostly based on the theory of the pyramid being a tomb. But this pyramid is not a tomb and so the significance of each item it contains should be either for practical engineering purposes, or for something mathematical or perhaps astronomical. The small notches are no exception to this. The designer has arranged the notches so that there are 27 notches between the Great Step and the bottom of the gallery,[2] which means that there are 28 sections of gallery in between the 27 notches. If the distance down to the bottom of the gallery is 88 tc, then the distance between the center-line of each notch becomes:

88 divided by 28 equals 3.14286 tc, or the number Pi.

The distance between each notch becomes Pi tc, so the function of the notches is just a neat little cross-check of the intended dimensions of the G Gallery; that's all.

The same technique was used at the henge at Newgrange in Ireland. The access corridor here is composed of 22 upright stones on the left-hand side of the passageway, with 21 stones and a deliberate space on the right. The number 22 was most probably derived from the Π ratio once more, so perhaps passageways containing Pi ratios were thought to be important in these monuments.

It is apparent that each item in the pyramid has some mathematical significance, and the next item is no exception. For this we come back to the Great Step itself, and this item has another function in this design. It has been sited in this exact position by the designer, because it allows the floor of the Queen's Chamber to be equidistant between the floor of the King's Chamber and the base of the pyramid. To allow this to occur, the King's Chamber has had a slight lift up using the Great Step and the Queen's Chamber a slight let down via the Queen's Step in the Queen's Chamber corridor. Actually the floor of the Queen's Chamber is not quite equidistant between the base of the pyramid and the King's Chamber floor-line; it is a few centimeters out.

As it is likely that the chambers were supposed to be equidistant, there appears to be a small error in the actual construction; yet this error may actually give us a valuable insight into how the internal structures of the pyramid were laid out by the surveyor on the site. This brings us the physical problem of turning the plans for the pyramid into a real stone edifice; just how did the designer lay out the angle of the G Gallery and the descending passage, for instance?

Surveyor's approximation

The internal passageways of these pyramids seem to have descending and ascending angles of about 26°, but how were these angles surveyed? One simple way of surveying the angles would have been to use a Pythagorean triangle of 89-80-39, which not only gives a right-angled triangle but also gives an acute angle of 25.989° (25° 59.4′), which is quite accurate enough to the angle of 26° for normal construction purposes. Laying out measuring rods or ropes equal to these three Pythagorean lengths would give the builders the required angle of 26°. It is more than possible that construction of the G Gallery used this method, as the hypotenuse of this Pythagorean triangle is 89 units in length; while the G Gallery roof-line, which represents this Pythagorean hypotenuse, is conveniently 89 tc long. A gentle hint by the designer as to the construction method used?

It is difficult to tell if this is so, but as I heaved myself up the steep incline of the G Gallery – again only possible because of the recent wooden duck-boards put in place – one thing seemed certain. This edifice had been designed with great care and an eye to detail. As I brushed my hands across the almost undetectable joints between the blocks, and observed building lines that went off into the far distance without a single wiggle in sight, I could feel the skills and pride of the artisans. I could sense the power and brilliance of the designer. There was a plan in all this.

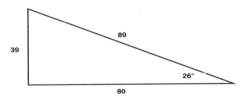

Fig 61.   The 89-80-39 triangle

It is quite possible that the ascending passage and the Grand Gallery could have been surveyed using the Pythagorean triangle method, as proposed above. The angle of the ascending passage, which climbs at 26° 02′, does conform more closely to the Pythagorean angle 25° 59′, than does the descending passage which measures 26° 26′. [3]

But, while the Pythagorean method is quite a valuable surveying tool, it is not the only method that could have been used by this enterprising designer. Another solution to the problem would be to use star sights, as proposed by Richard Anthony Proctor (1837-1888). If a suitable star was chosen that lay a short distance from the Earth's pole of that era, this could be used for star sights down the descending passage. The latitude of Giza is 30° N, so the horizon lies at an angle of 30° displaced from the Earth's pole. In order to survey an angle of 26°, a star that is displaced exactly 4° from the Earth's pole is required (30 - 4 = 26°); a star that was visible at its lowest culmination at night during the building season (i.e. the sighting must be taken at the lowest point in the star's rotation each night). The surveyor on site could then take a star shot and exactly calculate the markers for the next day's work.

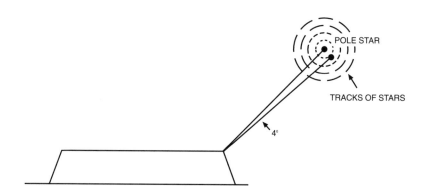

Fig 62.   Taking sightings for the next day's work

Unfortunately, the possibility of finding a star in exactly the right location in any particular era is quite slim. Undoubtedly, a star in an approximate position would have to be used instead; one close to but not quite 4° from the pole. Despite the Pythagorean triangle surveying method being theoretically more accurate than this 'approximate' star sight, it may either be more difficult in practice or, more importantly for the designer, it may not leave a 'record' inscribed in the building that betrays the construction date of the pyramid.

10. Great Continents

Bearing in mind the latter theory, it is reasonable to assume that star sights were used for the descending passages, as the angle of each descending passage in each pyramid varies slightly. Yet the builders were quite fastidious in getting other angles, such as the slope of the exterior face, accurate to within a few seconds of arc. The builders were quite capable, therefore, of defining an accurate angle with which to construct a shaft or casing block.

But if star shots were used for the survey, the angle of the descending passage in each pyramid *would* vary in much the same fashion as we see, because the position of the star being used would move slightly over the years, due to precession. In fact, this could well be the main reason for using star sights when surveying the descending passages, as this change in angle therefore dates each pyramid relative to the next. If the pyramids were built consecutively, then this would also give us a construction time for each pyramid.

It is difficult to say which star was used, as it depends on the era of the construction and the exact position of the Earth's pole; but, if the sightings were taken at the spring equinox, there is a suitable star that could have been used in the era of 11,670 BC. It is a faint fifth magnitude star that lies on the boarders of Lyre and Hercules.

Construction time

At the equinox in this era, there was a convenient star that would have been visible at night, passing the due north meridian at its lowest point in the sky. The interesting thing about this rather insignificant star, apart from it being a useful 4° from the Earth's pole of that era, is that it lies very close to the path of this wandering Celestial Pole. In fact, the Earth's pole would be closing in on this star as the years went by, lessening the angle between the pole and the star from 4.5° to 4.0° to 3.5° etc, in successive generations.

As I have said, over a normal lifetime the change in position of the Celestial Pole is very difficult to observe, but if accurate measurements are being taken for surveying a building, that small change in the angle of the reference star could easily make itself apparent in the building. If this particular star was the one that was used, it would have been seen to be ascending slowly in the night sky, up and away from the horizon as the years passed by. Any structures using this star's position and angle in their construction would have this 'signature' built into its fabric. In the case of the pyramids, it would have the effect of increasing the descending shaft angles from 25.5° to 26.0° to 26.5° etc, as the years rolled on.

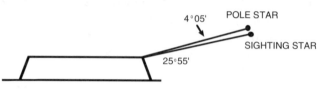

Construction of the Second Pyramid

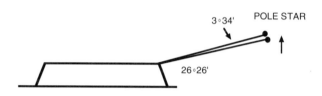

Construction of the Great Pyramid
Fig 63.

Not only can we see and measure this signature in the pyramids, but we can actually calculate how fast that rate of change would have been. In other words, it may be possible to calculate the number of years between one pyramid and the next. Now that is a small revelation and I am surprised it has not been written about before, but it is perfectly true. If this was the method of laying out the descending passages, we can now calculate the building time for each pyramid. The descending shaft angle of the Second Pyramid is 25° 55′, the Third Pyramid is at 26° 02′, and the Great Pyramid is 26° 26′. So, there is a slow increase in the angle of the shafts from the Second to the Third and through to the Great Pyramid, just as predicted.

There is also another shaft on the Giza site that we can use, in addition to those in the pyramids. This is the little-known 'trial' shaft to the east of the Great Pyramid, which was discovered by Flinders Petrie. [4] Petrie called this shaft a 'trial' shaft because he thought it might have been a practice for the real thing inside the Great Pyramid. In the light of these new theories, however, there may be a different interpretation for it. Petrie's reasoning was simple; these shafts have the same dimensions as the actual descending passage inside the Great Pyramid and they are complete with foreshortened versions of the ascending passage, the Queen's passage and the beginning of the G Gallery. It was quite sensible to envisage these shafts as being practice areas for the surveyors and workers.

10. Great Continents

Mathematically, however, there is a problem with this. The shaft angle on the 'trial' passage is 26° 33′, which would place the construction of these shafts as being later than the Great Pyramid, not earlier than it.

As an alternative scenario, perhaps these were not practice passages but, instead, a hint to future archaeologists that the similarly shaped descending passage inside the Great Pyramid may contain a similar layout, if one looked closely. If this were the case, then they should not be called 'trial' shafts but 'guide' shafts. Remember that the ascending passage inside the Great Pyramid was originally totally concealed; there was only a descending shaft visible. But as the descending passage in the 'guide' system looks very much the same as the Great Pyramid's passage, it may well set someone thinking... If this 'guide' passageway has an ascending passage, then what about the Great Pyramid?

The other reason for the 'guide' system of passages is that, without another pyramid or shaft to consecutively follow that of the Great Pyramid, it is not possible to get a construction time for either the Great Pyramid or the whole site. Quite conveniently, there is suddenly another shaft to measure and this feature allows us to estimate the construction time of the Great Pyramid itself. When calculating these construction times, bear in mind that the precession rate of the sighting star is not quite the same as has been calculated previously in chapter VII. The fact that this star does not lie on the Ecliptic has to be taken into account, so its apparent rate of drift due to precession will be less than the normal one degree in 72 years. For this star, the number of years that will pass, in one degree of its movement, will be about 180.[5]

If we use the shaft angles on all the shafts at our disposal, including the Vega Pyramid at Dahshur, the construction timetable for the pyramids designed by the great architect would look like the following:

Pyramid	Passage angle	Difference	Construction time in years
Second	25° 55′	7′	21
Third	26° 02′	18′	53
Vega	26° 20′	6′	18
Great	26° 26′	7′	21
Guide passage	26° 33′		
Total for all pyramids	38′	113	

One would suspect that the extra length of time, indicated for the Third Pyramid, would include time spent on the pyramid causeways and Sphinx. There are some further thoughts on the validity of this data:

a   The exact number of years between each pyramid is approximate (+/– 10%) until an exact angle of inclination for the Earth, and so in turn the exact position of the Earth's pole can be ascertained. The proportions between the measurements will stay the same, however.

b.   The order in which the pyramids have been constructed, mimics the order that has been postulated for the pyramids at Teotihuacan in Mexico, with the largest pyramid on the site, the Great Pyramid (which represents the star Alnitak), being the last to be built.

Secret shafts

The next task was to investigate the enigmatic 'air shafts' inside the Great Pyramid. Unfortunately, the Queen's Chamber was not open during my visit; it had not been open for some time and so these shafts were not viewable. However, the King's Chamber includes another pair of these peculiar shafts; although at first glance they do not seem that remarkable. It is yet more desk work that improves on this position, and there is no better illustration of the shafts than those designed by Rudolf Gantenbrink on the *Cheops* website. The diagrams there clearly illustrate the complexity of the engineering involved in making these peculiar little shafts. This complexity can only mean one thing: they may be little but, to the designer, they were far from being insignificant. The engineering solution required to fabricate these shafts was immense, so their purpose should be equally significant.

This logic dictates that these shafts were vitally important to the design of the pyramid, so it should be possible to derive a solution and a purpose to their peculiar form. The complexity of these shafts can be seen, for instance, in the two King's shafts which exit the pyramid at the same level, despite the different angles involved. The northern shafts also encounter the G Gallery, so they are forced to bend around the gallery while keeping a more-or-less straight profile when viewed from the east or west. The snakelike paths of the northern shafts were so complex that Rudolf Gantenbrink, the German engineer (who designed and sent a miniature robot up each shaft), thought that they were:

> therefore the most important construction in the pyramid. The designer could have moved the shafts a few meters to the west and avoided all this trouble, but no, he instead made four complex bends in both of the northern shafts. [6]

In addition to all this, it is a matter of established fact that the Queen's Chamber shafts are even more mysterious than those in the King's Chamber. The Queen's Chamber shafts were left completely sealed, with the last few centimeters of the shaft not cut through the stone into the Queen's Chamber. Why should this be? It is obvious that this arrangement was deliberate; there can be no way in which the master mason on the site 'forgot' to cut through the last few centimeters of stone. So what was the designer playing at? One can only be led to think that this is another of these little games. It has long been rumoured that the solution to the pyramids was to be found by a true searcher for the secrets of Thoth, not by some tomb-robber blundering around inside the pyramid.

Having found some hidden meanings in the King's shafts, the investigator is then subconsciously tasked to look further into the pyramid to see if the Queen's Chamber holds more secrets. The architect is expecting someone to go and search for these shafts in the Queen's Chamber. If this is true, it can be speculated further that the full solution to the Great Pyramid cannot be found without using the Queen's Chamber shafts, and this is so.

This plan was partially foiled by Waynman Dixon in 1872, who was thinking along these lines anyway, despite the prevailing thoughts of the time that suggested the King's Chamber shafts were only air vents. Mr Dixon tapped along the Queen's Chamber walls and, upon hearing hollow sounds, he was surprised to find that a piece of wire could be inserted into the stone joints at this point for more than a meter. The Queen's shafts had been found.

At first, the small (in cross-section) shafts were probed with metal rods in an attempt to find out their lengths. To their surprise, a few artifacts contemporary to the pyramid fell out: a plumb weight, the top of a surveyor's pole and a small section of measuring rod; all of which had presumably tumbled down the shaft in antiquity when the pyramid was being built. Because the shafts were sealed at the bottom, these artifacts could not be retrieved by the original builders. They are now in the British Museum, London; although it would seem that the measuring rod, which is the only artifact that could have been carbon dated, is now missing. [7]

These enigmatic shafts were then left until quite recently, when they were further investigated in 1993 by Rudolf Gantenbrink and his small robotic vehicle, Upuaut II. The little machine crawled its way up the southern shaft and discovered a 'door' at the far end. An attempt at surveying the north shaft was not so successful because of its design. The designer had to snake this shaft in a complicated way around the G Gallery; again, this is a most extraordinary feat of engineering for such a seemingly unimportant shaft. Unfortunately, the bends in the shaft to the left and right were rather tight. In addition, it would seem that the architect had made a mistake in surveying the northern shaft. One of the blocks started off at too shallow an angle; to compensate, a new angle had been forged in the next block to get back onto the correct profile. It was only a slight correction, but enough to stop the little robot in its tracks. [8]

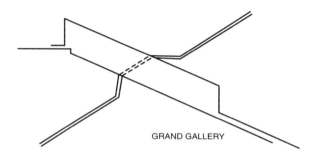

Fig 64.   The G Gallery and the shafts

The angle of elevation of these shafts and the length of the Queen's shaft, up to the enigmatic 'door', were measured with great accuracy. The preliminary results of this investigation were:

Shaft	Angle	Length
King's south	45°	
King's north	32° 36´	
Queen's south	39° 36´	113.8 tc
Queen's north	Approx. 39°	[9]

As I explained previously, the star sighting theory cannot be taken too literally, as there are so many stars to choose from. The facts could be made to fit almost any era, depending on the date in the year and time of night that was thought to be correct for the observations. But having found the relevant star and era of construction, there will still not be any form of verification that the results from the theory are correct. This dichotomy is abundantly clear in the book *Keeper of Genesis*, where the star shaft theory contradicts the evidence of weathering on the Sphinx and the relevance of the sunrise in the era of Leo; which, in turn, both indicate a much greater age for the monuments on the Giza plateau.

Subsequent data from Rudolf Gantenbrink has disclosed more

bends than previously thought in the lower sections of these shafts. The details of these bends and their significance in the Great Pyramid's design are covered in some detail in the book *K2, Quest of the Gods.*

If these shafts are not air vents and if they are not star pointers, what then is their function? What do they mean? Are they important? Yes, these shafts *are* important, but the answer to this riddle is not very complicated at all, just as I stated at the beginning of the book. In fact, the real answer to all these problems is so simple that many people will probably laugh at its childishness. The architect of Giza was certainly doing his level best to help us decipher the pyramids but we, in our desire to show our technological superiority, have been looking at possible solutions that were far too complex; this is child's play in comparison.

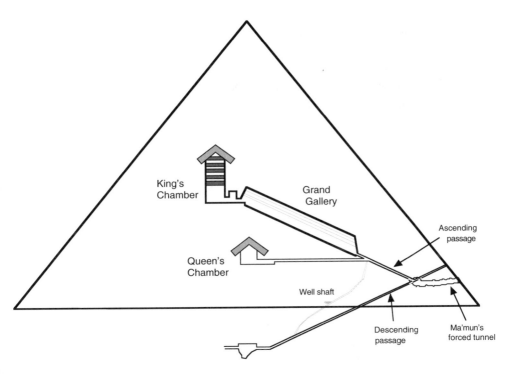

Fig 65. Great Pyramid's internal galleries

To find the complete answer to the great mystery of the Great Pyramid, we firstly need to go back to Avebury in England, and the secrets that we uncovered in chapter V, with the rings of Avebury and Stonehenge being representations of the Earth floating in space. Not only are Avebury and Stonehenge representations of the Earth, but Avebury in particular is also a map of the Earth. Avebury has that picture of Stonehenge sitting on the 52° parallel of latitude north and just below it are the Sandwich Islands, which are represented as being in the southern hemisphere, on the 58° parallel south. Avebury, in reality, is just a child's drawing of some of the features on the surface of the Earth – no more, no less.

Looking at some of the most ancient myths of the gods, particularly the gods of Sumer, we also find an abiding interest in the form of the Earth. After the great flood, the gods divided up the continents of the Earth between themselves. The continent of Africa came under the jurisdiction of the god Enkiite, and Asia was commanded by Enlilite; between them came Arabia, which was given to the mother goddess Ninhursaga.[10] And so we have the divisions of all the major continents that would appear on one side of the globe as seen from a distant vantage point in space, the divisions of the lands that were made by the gods themselves. Perhaps this is a small hint as to what one may expect to find.

Armed with this new information, if we look again at the Great Pyramid and its internal galleries, we may see the answer to the greatest mystery of all time; an answer that was hanging on my office wall for months; an answer that is as plain as it can possibly be.

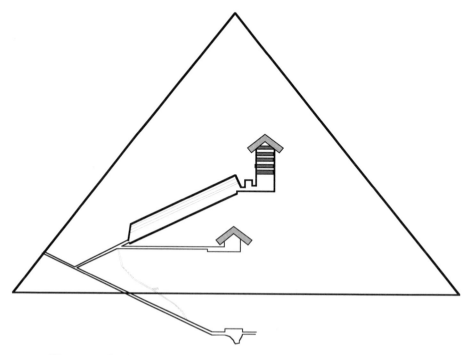

Fig 66.   The Great Pyramid, mirror image, west to east

It was so simple; the design of the Great Pyramid is exactly the same as Avebury's; it is merely a child's drawing of the Earth! That may be easy to say, but obviously it must be harder to see, otherwise this solution would have been solved long ago. So if the Great Pyramid's map of the Earth is not making itself apparent yet, try hanging the diagram correctly – for Khufu's continents cannot be easily seen until the picture is in its proper orientation. Unfortunately for us, all the standard diagrams of the internals of this pyramid are taken looking from east to west. This is just a convention; there is nothing special about this perspective, except that it happens to be wrong. To see the 'Earth map', a mirror image of these standard diagrams is required; a section through the pyramid, looking from west to east, as shown on the previous page.

This change in perspective should have done the trick, but still the orientation is not quite right. If it is still difficult to see anything remotely looking like the Earth, then turn the book upside down. The simple and lateral answer to this whole conundrum is that the classical diagrams of the Great Pyramid and its internal galleries, that we are used to seeing, are all the wrong way up! It is no wonder that the internal galleries of the Great Pyramid have not previously been seen for what they are, for the diagrams in every book in the world have been so confusing. If we look at the diagram again, in its proper orientation with the book upside down, the continents should be readily apparent. The great mystery of the Great Pyramid, the great secret of the world that has passed through some 500 human generations, is nothing more than another child's map of the continents of our Earth.

a. The King's Chamber to the left of the diagram (when upside down), and the attic roof system below it, are simply a representation of the continent of Africa.

b. Likewise, the anti-chamber next to the King's Chamber is Arabia.

c. In this case, the low entrance passages on either side of the anti-chamber become representations of the Red Sea and the Persian Gulf, which protrude into the land mass either side of Arabia in the real world.

d. The Grand Gallery, that imposing edifice that has defied any explanation so far, is a stylized representation of Asia; especially the line of the south-east coast of Asia, up through China. If we take a look at the world map, we see Asia soaring upwards at an angle of just about 26°, the same as the Grand Gallery. In this case, the part of the

G Gallery adjacent to the anti-chamber represents the subcontinent of India.

e. The Great Step is possibly the line of the east coast of the Caspian Sea.

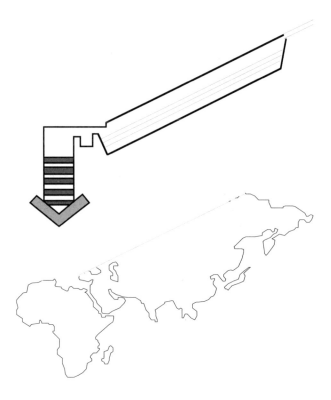

Fig 67.   The Great Pyramid's chambers, inverted

The simplest answers are always the best and, as simplicity goes, this explanation beats them all. The form of the continents matches the shape of the Great Pyramid's galleries and chambers exactly. The theory even explains those mysterious attic chambers that lie above the King's Chamber; the outline of the attic chambers simply mark the outline of southern Africa. The chambers have been designed in this fashion because constructing a completely empty room to the full height of this stylized 'Africa', with vertical walls rising all the way up to the gable beams at the very top, would be architecturally impossible; the walls would instantly cave in. Hence, the designer saw the requirement for bracing beams going across the width of the King's Chamber. Besides, just like the Queen's air shafts, someone has to go and look for the attic chambers, so this solution is more of a challenge.

The continents

But the architect always uses these opportunities to the full and this is no exception to the rule. The architectural requirement here demands some lateral reinforcement to the walls of the King's Chamber, so why not add a double function to these support beams? As expected, the attic chambers not only provide physical structural reinforcement to the chamber itself, but they also provide the absolutely vital tangible reinforcement that the 'Africa' theory requires. There *is* a positive cross-check to this theory.

All five attic ceilings above the King's Chamber are of equal spacing, and this spacing is half the height of the King's Chamber itself. So we could, in theory, place another support beam halfway up the King's Chamber, to make the whole construction more symmetrical. But this would make the King's Chamber look as though it was designed by troglodytes; it would be much less impressive than the present tall ceiling. It would seem then, that the decision was taken to miss out the first set of support beams and make the King's Chamber more imposing, with the remainder of the support beams stacked, one upon the other, up as far as the massive gabled roof beams at the very top of the roof system.

The giveaway that the attic chambers are not just functional supports to the walls of the chamber is that, on each set of support beams in each of the attic chambers, the underside (the ceiling) has been cut with great care until it is perfectly smooth; while, in complete contrast, the upper sides of each monolith (the floor of each chamber) have been left in the rough. If these support beams were merely structural devices, why bother to spend all that time and energy in cutting the undersides smooth? If there is one thing we can positively say about these monuments, it is that nothing was done without a purpose; there was no effort wasted in cutting rocks that did not need cutting. So why was so much time and energy spent on polishing the very tough granite of the support beams that were hidden away from view above the King's Chamber?

Simple; in the new theory of the megalithic Earth map, the support beams are placed running perpendicular across 'the continent of Africa' and so the flat, smooth bottom of each set of support beams (the ceiling) marks a distinctive line across this drawing of Africa. This is a cognitive marking that is made all the more plain by the knowledge of the thousands of man-hours that each of these lines took to manufacture, and so to draw. If we include all the beams in this diagram, including the symmetrical beam that could have been placed across the middle of the King's Chamber, there would have been six beams in all. If anyone has already come to the conclusion that we can now trust these new explanations of these monuments, they will not be too surprised to learn that, from Egypt southwards, the continent of Africa crosses 60° of latitude on the real Earth. There is exactly 10° of latitude down the length of Africa for each beam in the chamber and so the underside of each beam marks the precise line of each 10° of latitude in this megalithic depiction of Africa.

    If the floor of the King's Chamber lies at the latitude of Giza, at 30° N, then the ceiling of the chamber would be 20° above this and so the ceiling of the King's Chamber marks the 10° north parallel. The equator is marked by the support beam above this, the first support beam in the attic chambers. Each and every 10° of latitude down through the continent of Africa is clearly marked by its own support beam, all the way to the bottom of Africa at 30° south. Below this last support beam, the little remaining point of southern Africa is denoted in this pyramid's design by the chevron shape of the huge final, inclined roof beams, the beams that crown the King's Chamber:

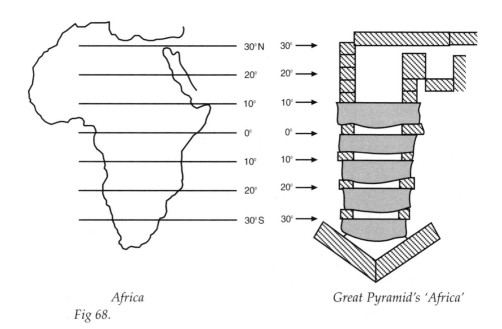

Africa   *Great Pyramid's 'Africa'*

Fig 68.

This is a rather neat solution to the galleries and chambers that comprise the Great Pyramid. It is a very simple theory, yet one that can explain every room, gallery and chamber within the entire edifice, including all those perplexing items like the G Gallery and the attic chambers. How many other theories can do that? Once more, the principle of Occam's razor dictates that the simplest answer is most often the right one; is this not the simplest of all the theories expounded for this monument?

To be self-critical once more, it may be pertinent to ask that if this is really the case, then why is Iran seemingly the center of this map and not Egypt? Wouldn't the architect have placed his own country at the center? There are two reasons for this offset of Egypt on the Great Pyramid 'Earth map'.

Firstly, it may simply be because, if we look at a globe of the Earth and try to arrange Asia and Africa to be in view on one side of the globe at the same time, the resulting picture will naturally center the globe on Iran. It all makes perfect sense: we are looking at nothing more than another child's map of our world.

Secondly, it finally transpired that the architect did place the most important of items on the map's center-line, only it was not the Great Pyramid and Egypt that were the most important items to be displayed. It will be shown in *K2, Quest of the Gods*, that the prime monument of interest that was being shown on this map actually lay in the Himalayas, directly on the center-line.

This solution to the Great Pyramid is so simple and sweet and if it is taken together with the 'Earth' diagrams of Avebury and Stonehenge, it must be becoming quite plain to the vast majority of people that this has not all happened by accident. This is the ma'at (the truth) that the Egyptians knew existed, but did not know the answer to: the ma'at that has spawned the many varied, and sometimes bizarre, attempts at understanding the pyramids. Imagine the frustration that has percolated the generations of intelligent, sensible and logical people. Eminent people, like Sir Isaac Newton, who knew that there was something special about the Great Pyramid, but who did not have all the information at their fingertips to allow a full understanding. Imagine the collective sigh that would emanate, if they could only know that the answer to the mighty Great Pyramid is that it is a map of our world. Imagine their puzzlement at that solution, as indeed, we can recognize our own, that the ancient designers of these enigmatic monuments not only knew the outline of the Earth's continents, but that they would want to preserve it in stone for us to witness.

So we have a map of Africa and Asia sitting in the desert. Why? This is not just a geographical and cartographical lesson for us by the architect;

quite the opposite. The Great Pyramid was purposely sealed, perhaps in the hope that only a technological generation in the distant future would find the answers to this mystery. In addition, this mystery can only be solved if the form of the continents of the Earth are known in the first place; so this would be a pointless lesson in the extreme. So what was the designer doing? Well, if the monument of Avebury was perhaps pointing at some southern islands in the Atlantic, then surely the pyramids must do something similar, and indeed they do.

The next great secret of the Great Pyramid involves those enigmatic 'air shafts' once more. They were most certainly not designed as air shafts, and neither were they star pointers; they are much closer to home than pointers to the stars. Just like at Avebury, these enigmatic little shafts are nothing more than 'latitude and longitude' markers. But before the angles on these shafts confuse everyone entirely, remember that the mighty Great Pyramid is more of a mathematical enigma than is little Avebury, so it is unlikely that these shaft angles will be found to be pointing directly at one particular spot. No, to find the co-ordinates that are given by Giza, it will be necessary to look deeper into the problem than that. The answer to this ultimate conundrum lies in the book *K2, Quest of the Gods*. It is a long story that will eventually lead us on an epic trek halfway around the world and to the 'throne of the gods', nestling among the highest peaks on Earth.

Hall of Records

Having found two maps and their respective markers in different monuments, it is clear by now that the architect must have been pointing at something quite important. If a designer decides to go to the trouble of creating the biggest stone constructions in the world – buildings that were completed many thousands of years ago – the reason for their construction must be quite important. If we also recall the legends of Thoth from chapter III, we can now see these myths in a different light. We now know that there is much more to these ancient traditions than many people would have ever given credence to before. Thoth, as we saw at the beginning of the book, was reputed to have buried two or three caches of knowledge around the world: hidden repositories of learning that may hold the secrets of his civilization; manuscripts that will at last tell us where the lost technological civilization of Thoth came from. If these massive monuments have any secret purpose, it has to be this: they point at these legendary repositories, the mythical Hall of Records.

This is a speculative conclusion, but I think we have travelled well beyond the realms of traditional history to worry about such trivialities. If the arguments outlined previously – of all these ancient monuments being technical diagrams of the Earth – are in any way acceptable to people, then a little further speculation is not going to do much harm. The ancient myths said that there was something special and technical in the design of these monuments and we now see that this is correct. The myths also said that Thoth left repositories of knowledge somewhere on the Earth, so why should there not be a grain of truth in this as well? Why not indeed, for the maps that we have uncovered seem to be pointing at precise locations on the surface of the Earth, and for what other reason should this be so?

If such a repository of knowledge actually existed, just imagine if we could uncover these ancient manuscripts and documents and discover a library that could expose the secrets of how these pyramids were built; and perhaps more importantly, indicate to us just how far in advance of our primitive technology these people really were. This must represent the ultimate treasure hunt, one far beyond anything that has been attempted in the past; a hunt for a technical 'Holy Grail', a quest to find the secrets of a 'god'.

Chapter XI

The Final Frontier

The deductions in this radical new look at our ancient heritage have been deliberately kept to a minimum so far, to allow the individual reader to form his or her own conclusions about the evidence that has been uncovered in these monuments. However, I would suggest that, in the light of these revelations, there is a glaring problem here. If one is in any way to believe these new interpretations for the design of these ancient monuments, an explanation is required as to how this was done. Just fobbing the designs off onto a mythical demigod called Thoth or Zil, as I have been doing occasionally in the text, is by no means an explanation for these events. How did this ancient architect come by all this technical information? How was the construction of these great monuments achieved? If the problem is looked at logically, there are only two or three solutions that are available to anyone who has been persuaded by the explanations for these megalithic monuments. These are as follows.

a.   The designer could have received information and assistance directly from the gods. Many people in this modern environment will have difficulty with this idea; the concept of direct intervention by the gods has rather gone out of fashion in recent decades. But survey after survey on the subject still indicate that the majority of people in Europe either believe in the concept of a god or are agnostic about the situation. A common response to a direct question might be, 'I think there must be something out there, but I don't know what'.

But the possibility remains that if an individual believes that 'there may be something out there', then that 'something' may have given the designer some divine insights. This is not a comprehensive answer to the problem, but it is worth considering.

On balance though, I think it is the least likely of the three suggested answers.

b.   There could have been an ancient and more technical civilization than classical history will currently admit to. This is an often-cited possibility, but a difficult one nevertheless. Undoubtedly, there are some very ancient and very technical artifacts out there in the wider world and most of us will have read all about some of these anomalous artifacts in past works of this nature; but one or two artifacts do not make a civilization. How did such a hypothetical civilization make such tremendous advances in technology and science, yet leave no traces of their cities, transport network, industry or trade?

The concept of very small pockets of ancient technical kingdoms in a wider sea of ignorance seems to be at odds with what we generally understand to be true in this world. Even within the small pockets of ancient and advanced civilization that we are fully aware of, there is precious little evidence of how this advanced technology and architecture was achieved. How could Egypt, for example, develop such advanced stone-cutting concepts as diamond-tipped drills without leaving any trace of how these tools were made? The concept of an advanced ancient civilization is a valid one, but it is currently lacking in evidence.

c.   There could have been assistance from elsewhere in our vast galaxy, intervention by a civilization from another world. Now this is another thorny issue that tends to cause much derision in both scientific and religious communities. But let us not pass over this option too quickly.

Once more, if we take a straw pole of the European population, asking the question, 'Is life possible elsewhere in the Universe?', the answer is most likely to be a resounding – Yes. The second question to ask the public would be, 'Do you think any of this life in the Universe is intelligent?', and again the result is likely to be a resounding – Yes. The third question in this trilogy would have to be, 'Do you think that any of this life has visited the Earth at any time in the past?'; a question which would probably produce a very mixed bag of results. Uncomfortable as it may seem to many people, however, this concept of alien intervention remains a quite valid (if previously unproven) hypothesis and it is one that is worth closer study.

So what sort of simpleton would seriously believe in beings arriving on the Earth from another world? Well, the question is probably a little ambiguous: what does one mean by beings from another world? Taken at its most equivocal level, the term 'alien' could cover all the major gods that are central to the major faiths of this world. In which case, almost every person in the world believes in some sort of alien visiting the Earth; one that manifests itself in some form or other.

The concept of 'god' in this context could be considered as being just an entity or an individual that does not come originally from our Earth. So we have the standard paradox of the modern world, in which the very people who will happily pour such derision on an alien visitation theory are probably quite content to believe in 'god' conversing with Moses on Mount Sinai. But at the end of the day, what is the difference?

If the majority of people are happy with the concept of an alien visitation, an alien called 'god', it may be valuable to look further into the question of what sort of gods have visited our Earth in the distant past. Are they, perhaps, the Christian ideal of a being that has infinite powers and an intangible countenance? Are they gods that are capable of both creating the vast spirals of stars in our Universe, known as galaxies, and at the same time content enough to dabble in the intimate and trivial affairs of man? Or are these gods something more tangible and humanoid, with impressive, but nevertheless finite, powers?

If one's version of a god is more comparable to the second type of deity, then such a god is but one step away from a flesh and blood being from another world. At the same time, this concept is not very far from the Christian ideal either. The bodily composition and appearance of the Christian version of god is quite specific. It states quite clearly in Genesis that man was made in the image of this god. In return, this means that this god must look like man. The Bible is quite specific, therefore, in saying that the Christian god resembles a humanoid being; one that does not originate from this Earth. [1]

This humanoid form of god is further confirmed in the Bible, for instance, in the paragraphs detailing the destruction of Sodom and Gomorrah. In this passage, Abraham wishes to plead with god for the release of his family before the destruction of the town and so the 'god' appears to Abraham in the form of three men. Abraham, being the host, fetches some water and washes the feet of god and then he has his wife Sarah bake some cakes for god. [2] This is not quite the intangible being that many people imagine this god to be and the explanations for this strange dichotomy are taken much further in the books *Jesus, Last of the Pharaohs* and *Tempest & Exodus*.

11. The Final Frontier

Masons

Having challenged one of the key issues in the Christian faith, who else, in this varied and uncertain theological environment that is being uncovered, would be most likely to be receptive to the idea of an alien visitation to the Earth in the distant past; receptive to the idea of a visitation by a humanoid god with finite powers? One other source, surprisingly enough to some people, may be Masonic. The Freemasons (brother masons), according to most literature, are split into two denominations: one decidedly secular and the other more inclined to be theological.

The secular Masons appear to know nothing of the true nature of the craft and have merely used the craft as a gentlemen's club. In many instances, it is nothing more than a method of career and business advancement in the secular world, which is a rather contemptible side to an organization with such an ancient history.

This fragmentation of Masonry into non-theological sects has always been a problem for the craft, for there is a central conundrum that is very difficult to solve here. Masonry has long been secretive, which is partly due to the persecution that has been suffered in both ancient and recent history, and partly a result of the secrecy that surrounded the ancient Egyptian priesthood and their customs. But how does one evangelize and expand the organization when the core tenets are supposed to be secret? The result has often been a proliferation of Masonic sects, which do not always represent the true form of the craft. Bearing this in mind, there is one particular Masonic sect that may possibly give the clue to the core beliefs of the theological side of Masonry, the 'Order of the Eastern Star'.

This order was born of a group of Masons in France, who believed that Masonry had strayed from its basic roots, and that much of the standard initiation ceremonies were irrelevant or badly taught. In particular, the ban on female members was thought to be erroneous because the fundamentals of Masonic theology are supposed to have come to us directly from the pharaohs of Egypt, and the Egyptians clearly encouraged the role of the priestess. It was only Saul, the founder of Christianity, who was a rabid misogynist:

> But I suffer not a woman to teach, nor to usurp authority over the man, but to be in silence. [3]

The Order of the Eastern Star, therefore, moved from France to America and, finally, to the more remote regions of Australia, where its doors have always been open to new recruits of both genders. However, the aspect of this sect that is of more interest to this book is its literature, which spells out the basic tenets of the craft. The literature of this sect indicates that the craft believes that real flesh and blood gods landed on Earth some 12,000 years ago, and then educated and civilized mankind – flesh and blood gods that are the basis for the legends of Thoth.

It is difficult to know if this belief is representative of main line theological Masonry, because the upper circles of Masonry represent a closed society and they hold their cards exceedingly close to their chests. What we do know, however, is that even mainstream Masonry declares quite openly its ancient Egyptian heritage, and one glimpse of a Masonic lodge will instantly confirm this. The basic rituals of the craft also require an apron, a darkened chamber, a sarcophagus of some kind and a female skull. These seemingly bizarre requirements are needed to role-play a symbolic death and resurrection and, of course, the pyramids and the rituals of ancient Egypt supplied all of these items. The Masonic apron was worn by all the pharaohs, while the pyramid chambers provide a dramatic theatre for the action, complete with frightening reverberating echoes for the oratory. Each chamber also contains an empty sarcophagus; custom-made for an initiation rite.

This is quite a coincidence, which could be explained by later generations simply re-using the pyramids for these rituals and thus developing a need for these items. Equally, however, these rituals could be very ancient indeed and the pyramids could have been designed with subterranean chambers for just this purpose, as is clearly demonstrated in the book *Tempest & Exodus*. Such a theory neatly sidesteps the 'tomb' theory for pyramid construction and the pyramids, with their open chambers, become no more than ritual centers for passing on the traditions of the priesthood and for perpetuating the history of mankind. If this is so, a few proposals can be put forward that may take us quite close to the real truth that lies behind the craft.

Firstly, if these Egyptian origins are entirely true, then the Masons will have been playing at 'Chinese whispers' for the last 13,000 years or so. With the best will in the world, the messages and instructions that were first delivered when the pyramids were constructed are bound to have become diluted with time. Quite possibly, some of the teachings are nothing like the originals.

Secondly, as I have indicated previously, the instructions to the priesthood are likely to have been deliberately incomplete. There would be absolutely no point in manufacturing all these secrets in stone, in all the continents of the world, and then telling everyone exactly what it all meant. In this case, the Masonic hierarchy will definitely *not* have known the true functions of the Great Pyramid and Avebury.

But these explanations for the ancient monuments would probably not have happened if the Masons had not kept up the general interest in Egyptian theology within our society. The history of Egypt has been continuously pushed forwards into the public arena over the years, even if we have not been directly aware of it. In addition, without the surveying and eventual protection of these ancient sites by prominent people with Masonic affiliations, much of this evidence in stone and earth that attracts the tourists today would just not exist. Not only would many of these monuments have disappeared, but much of our national heritage would have gone with them; we have much to be thankful for in this respect.

Likewise, without the promotion of the concept of alien beings visiting our planet, we would probably not be psychologically attuned into accepting the arrival of beings from other worlds quite so readily. Just think of the number of films and books on the subject, and the way in which they are promoted. In reality, it is only through this type of esoteric propaganda, like the sci-fi series *The X-Files*,[4] that the modern public is now quite willing to accept almost any evidence as being from an alien visitation. It has got to the stage where even an area of flattened cereal plants is nowadays considered by some to be 'proof' of a visitation. For these people at least, the Avebury and Great Pyramid 'Earths' should be more than enough evidence to say that alien feet did at some stage, in ancient times, 'walk upon our green and pleasant lands'.

Yet the *X-Files*-type propaganda has had a longer history than one might think; in fact, the basic concept has been used by the esoteric fraternity for the last thousand years at least. In the eleventh and twelfth centuries, when the major church-building era was in full swing throughout Europe, a peculiar character was carved into many of these fine Christian buildings. The outsider is actually the Green Man, that curiously 'pagan' face that either peeps out of the foliage or has the foliage creeping out of himself in the decorative stonework of the churches and cathedrals of England. Who might the Green Man have been? Some pagan forest deity perhaps? But if this were the case, the question remains as to how such a minor character forced his way into nearly every cathedral in Britain?

The more radical answer, that he was the Egyptian god Osiris, is the only way to make sense of the situation. Only Osiris would have had enough influence to force his way into our churches, because he was central to the theology of the major cathedral-building organization of the era, the Templars; from whom the craft eventually evolved. Osiris was the supreme god of Egypt, the ruler of the dead, and he was always depicted as having green skin. And while the fraternity had to be a little more subtle in those days with their *X-Files* depictions – with followers being continually faced with the terrifying prospect of meeting the Catholic inquisition – it was probably quite amusing and satisfying to some individuals to see the Egyptian god Osiris in every Christian cathedral.

In a similar vein, perhaps there is another piece of esoteric propaganda that has crept into more recent usage, that of the little green man from Mars. This may sound funny initially, until again it is remembered that Osiris was the green god from another world. The world is full of such allusions; one just needs to know the key that makes sense of them.

Scientific interest

Who else may be receptive to the idea of beings arriving from another world? Certainly science has nothing against it. Of all the members in a given population, the average scientist could easily be said to be most likely to believe in the *probability* of other civilizations in the Universe. Conversely, a scientist would perhaps be most likely to doubt the evidence that has been given in support of this concept so far.

So why should otherwise rational scientists believe in the probability of alien civilizations? Simply because of the enormity of the Universe. The Universe is huge and the number of stars within it immense. In fact, in the latest census of stars, it has been calculated that there are some 2×10^{23} stars in the Universe. That is the number 2, followed by no less than 23 zeros! This is rather too large a number to visualize easily, but perhaps the best description is the common comparison with grains of sand.

How many grains of sand do we need to equal the number of stars in the Universe? As many as there are grains of sand in a large shovel? Too small? How about the number of grains of sand in a dumper truck? Too big? Think again, there are as many stars in the Universe as there are grains of sand on every beach and in every desert on the whole Earth. That is why scientists can believe in probabilities.

The numbers can be whittled down as much as we like; throw out all the white dwarf stars, neutron stars, red giants, fiery blues; dismiss the opportunities of life on multiple stars (binaries), ones too close to the galactic centers with unstable orbits and any other oddities we care for. Forget about life on planets like Mercury, which are too hot and arid, or gas giants like Jupiter and Saturn that have no solid surface, or even the cold isolated moons like Triton or Europa. Discount any opportunities of life evolving through alternate chemistries, insist on water-based life only. Insist on finding an Earth-like planet, revolving in an Earth-like orbit, for an Earth-like historical period of stability around an Earth-like Sun. Whittle the numbers down by whatever means is desired and the answer will still end up indicating that there are thousands of millions of potentially habitable planets out there – planets much the same as Earth.

In this case, if life elsewhere in the Universe is so likely, why is there so little evidence for the presence of other civilizations? This again, is probably due to the enormity of the Universe. It is an enormous place to search, even if there are millions of civilizations out there. Put it this way, if there were 10,000,000 solar systems in the Universe inhabited by technical civilizations, we would need to look at 2×10^{15} stars (that is 2,000,000,000,000,000 stars), before finding one of them.

Of course, we don't need to go there ourselves; we could listen in to their radio transmissions, but in this respect we do not do much serious looking or listening. Space programmes like SETI – the Search for Extra-Terrestrial Intelligence – get very little funding and are probably not looking in the right locations in the first place. There is a big problem with such searches; in order to tune into transmissions from another world, you need to be on the right frequency, and yet there are billions and billions of frequencies to chose from. Initial SETI programmes looked for radio transmissions around 'the water hole'; the fundamental frequencies of the hydrogen molecule (21 cm wavelength), hydroxyl (18 cm) and water (3.5 mm). Collectively, these are known as the water hole, because hydrogen and hydroxyl make water.

There are problems with this idea, however; not only are these naturally very noisy frequencies through random molecular transmissions, but they are not frequencies we use ourselves for commercial transmissions, so why should any transmissions be found here? The latest SETI mission was much more comprehensive; it could scan a million frequencies, automatically looking for unnatural modulations, but again this survey is based on the normal radio spectrum of domestic and satellite transmissions, which are perhaps not the right frequency bands to look in. Even if these were the right bands, the number of frequencies that are monitored are still a drop in the ocean.

Would other civilizations be using these particular electromagnetic frequencies? If one thing is certain about our own usage of radio, it is that we have gone up the frequency spectrum quite rapidly in the space of one century of radio. Higher frequencies can not only carry more information, in this information-dependent world, but they are also more focused. We can target a particular location and use far less power in the transmission if a high frequency is used, especially if we utilize a coherent (laser) waveform. In this case, a more likely place to look for extra-terrestrial transmissions would be up in the X-ray band but, alas, we are not yet in a position to observe and decode such wave bands with our current technology.

For the ultimate in penetration of the interstellar medium for these hypothetical communications, perhaps a neutrino radio is what is required. We can detect neutrinos and it is not too great a jump in science to say that someone else has learned to control them. It may be science fiction at present, but let's put it another way. At present, our search for extra-terrestrial life using radio transmissions is rather like someone trying to detect signs of a civilization on Earth by using a flagman on a hill, looking at the City of London for signs of communications.

The voyage

The next question, bearing in mind the continual reports of UFOs buzzing the Earth, is would it be possible for another civilization to pay us a visit? Yes, but there are other problems here which may limit the number of visits that any one star gets from a particular alien civilization. The problems are energy and relativity. To illustrate the problem, let us look at what a traveller would have to endure if they wanted to travel through our Galaxy in *Star Trek* fashion; in search of new life forms, to boldly go where no alien has gone before.

To give us a baseline, so that our imagination does not run away with us, all of the following stays within the limits of conventional physics, including that of relativity. It may well be possible that there are ways around some of the present physical problems of space travel, but we could speculate endlessly on such fantastic technologies and not come to any sensible conclusion. It may be conservative, but realistic deductions can only be made by extrapolating the physics that we know really exists.

The nearest star to our Sun is Proxima Centauri, which lies at about 4.2 light years away. With our current technology, a fast space probe might be travelling at about 25 km a second or 90,000 km an hour, on its long journey towards Proxima. So how long would it take to get there at this enormous speed? Five years, perhaps? Too little? How about fifty years then? Too much? Again we must re-adjust our concepts of reality, for the answer is just a little over 50,000 years! Clearly then, we must improve our technology considerably, in order to make space travel anything other than an idle curiosity.

* * *

11. The Final Frontier

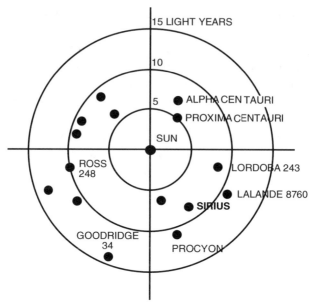

Fig 69.   The local stars

One method that could be used to speed up this hypothetical space probe, would be to replace the current chemical propulsion units with ion thrusters (rocket motors that spew out charged particles which are travelling at a speed close to that of light), with the energy supplied by a fusion reactor. All these technologies are technically just around the corner; with some more funding from our governments, these systems could be up and running in about ten years. But still the Galaxy would loom very large. The advantage of ion thrusters is that the amount of reaction fluid (fuel and reaction-mass to be thrown out the back of the rocket) needed in the spaceship is much smaller than with chemical rockets, so the acceleration of the ship can carry on much longer and attain much higher velocities. This would be a great advance over chemical boosters, but still the amount of fuel required would be enormous, which would slow the acceleration down. But at least the total time to Proxima would be down to reasonable levels.

The British Interplanetary Society proposed a mission of the ship *Daedalus* in a similar fashion, created out of technology available today. In this version, the motor was a simple system of mini-hydrogen bombs, which would pulse the ship up to cruise speed and back. In this simple mission to Proxima, a massive 50,000 tonnes of fuel would be required and the payload of the ship would still not be big enough to carry a full life-support system, so it would have to be an automatic probe. Even with this 'advanced' technology, 50 years would still pass before the interstellar cruiser would slip into an orbit around Proxima; and just think of the problems of getting that massive fuel-load into orbit. [5]

The next technological milestone would be to get a much more efficient fuel than a simple fusion reaction and thus shed a few more kilos of fuel from the rocket. A matter/antimatter generator would be nice. If this kind of motor could be engineered to convert, say, 90% of its mass into pure energy (according to the equation $E = mc^2$), instead of the fraction of 1% that is converted in fusion reactions, all of this vast amount of energy could then be pumped out the back of the spaceship in the form of high-energy light. Such a ship starting its journey would make quite a spectacle in the night sky above the Earth, although the 'light' would be too far up the spectrum to be seen directly. Where it hit the interplanetary medium, however, it would create a sheath of glowing particles: very pretty. If a rocket were constructed with 90% of its mass being fuel, it might just be able to accelerate the ship up to 90% the speed of light and back again to orbital speeds. [6]

A spaceship doing 90% the speed of light would reduce the flight time to some 4.7 years. But hold on a minute: this does not allow for the acceleration out of the Solar System and deceleration at the destination, and these would increase the time by a considerable factor. In fact, on such a short journey, and allowing for a comfortable acceleration of 2g, [7] the ship would have to start slowing down before it even got to a sensible cruise speed. Even at these huge speeds, approaching the speed of light, it would still take decades to get to the nearest stars, and nearly 50,000 years to reach the center of our galaxy. Travel to other galaxies would be virtually impossible, with journey times of 850,000 and 680,000 years to the nearby galaxies of Leo I and Fornax, both of which are a part of our 'local group'!

Colony

Another method of space travel that has been much talked about would be a space colony or even hibernation, methods that merely serve to lessen the boredom of the journey. But, in pursuing this line, the impossible journey-times loom large once more. A space colony would be a massive construction and even if it were possible to accelerate such a space 'ark' to a speed approaching ten times our current tiny probes (that is, about 900,000 km/h), it would take nearly 12 million years to cross the outer spiral arm of our galaxy. Clearly this is quite out of the question.

Within the normal laws of physics, there is only one way of making reasonable progress across the galaxy and that is by having either machines (androids) that do not mind high accelerations, or by having a gravity drive. Gravity drives are bordering on science fiction, but nevertheless it is a fact that gravity will accelerate a human body (or anything else) without that body being aware of the acceleration. It does this by acting invisibly on each atom throughout the whole body independently, and this could become the basis of an elegant method of accelerating a ship up to near-light speed. Whichever of these methods is used, one could hopefully accelerate up to, say, 99% the speed of light in a short time using high accelerations, and so arrive reasonably swiftly at the destination. It is by no means a perfect solution, but it is feasible.

Nevertheless, with conventional physics, the trip to Proxima can never be less than 4.2 years relative to an Earth observer, and the trip across the arm of our galaxy, some 10,000 years, so this still makes interstellar travel virtually impossible. Or does it? There is one advantage of these high relativistic speeds, which can help us in this respect. Because of relativity, time for the traveller on the spacecraft is running much slower, and so his or her perceived journey time can be much less than this. (Much less the closer you get to the speed of light, but anything over 99% and the fuel required to attain that speed becomes astronomic.) The penalty with relativistic travel, however, is that any personal contacts with one's home planet will be effectively severed. A fresh-faced traveller may return to the home planet after a trip of 30 years and find some 1,000 years have elapsed on the home planet since they departed. With such disparities in people's time frames, these interstellar travellers would have to be completely independent of their home planet.

So where does this leave the case for or against alien visitations? It is reasonable to assume that if the Earth has had an alien visitation in the past, using conventional physics, it is highly likely that this would have been a massive mission lasting years or even centuries. Millions of 'alien years' of work would have gone into the construction of the vast spaceship and it would have had a crew of the best available professionals or the best androids aboard. With such a grand project, we can be sure of one thing, on arriving in our Solar System and manoeuvring into orbit around the Earth, the mission of these seasoned space-travellers would not be to cut a few circles in a farmer's field.

The mission would be, by necessity, long and detailed and while it would be impossible to hide such an event from a technical civilization, it would not be so difficult to disguise it from a primitive one. Thoth, the 'god from the sky', would have been a catch-all phrase that would satisfy any Neolithic village. The gods would spend many years detailing the life forms, geology and topography of the planet and the Solar System. If some cultural engineering were deemed necessary, this might take several generations, a good 150 years' work? This would not be out of the question for a people who have mastered the art of near immortality.

Fictional gods?

If the concept of a home-grown and ancient technical civilization is rejected, could these monuments be the result of an ancient visitation instead? Could the incredibly clever designer, the mythical Zil/Thoth, have come from a local star like Sirius? Could this enigmatic individual have been responsible for human civilization as we know it? It is a radical notion and not one that is to be discussed lightly. Nevertheless, such a visitation *is* a possibility, however remote that possibility may be.

In fact, this is a possibility that has never been taken seriously before because there was simply no evidence in favour of it; no evidence whatsoever. Now, however, there *is* evidence. If these explanations for the design of these monuments is to be taken seriously, then there is now direct and positive evidence in favour of a visitation. The question is, can this subject become a topic that is discussed seriously and openly, without the usual direct links to the lunatic fringe? Can we sit down and discuss the results of such an event without the implied sarcasm? This is a serious topic.

While suggesting alien intervention as an explanation for the presence of these great monuments may be radical, it *is* a possible answer. It would not only explain the deep mysteries of the pyramids and henges, but also explain some of the other little mysteries of man's traditional history. This intervention scenario would certainly explain the sudden appearance of the major civilizations of the world. As we have seen, this still remains a thorn in the side of conventional historians, who often explain this in terms of 'invasions from other cultures', without explaining where those other cultures came from.

It would also explain other mysteries, such as the sudden appearance of the three major crops of the world. Just as the dawn of civilization was upon us, the three continents of Earth each suddenly produced a different grass that fed the emerging civilization on that continent: rice in Asia, corn in America and wheat in Europe. These were peculiar grasses in evolutionary terms, that put a disproportionate amount of effort into producing big, fat seeds. But this effort makes no sense in evolutionary terms. Big, fat fruits have evolved to induce animals to eat the fruits and disperse the seeds that are contained inside. With the grasses, the reproduction strategy is different, as the fruit body is a caryopsis, in essence a seed. Inducing an animal to eat this seed would succeed only in killing the seed, which in evolutionary terms is nonsensical. Hence, the usual strategy for the grasses is to produce many small, light seeds, for wind or rain dispersal.

So, were these fat, juicy grasses just out there on the plains waiting to be cultivated by mankind? Or were they created specifically for this task by visitors, to feed the new emerging civilizations? It is worth noting, in this context, that wheat in particular has a peculiar genetic make-up; it has more genes than humans. It would appear that, at some time in the distant past, the number of genes in wheat doubled up, perhaps through a process of poor mitosis. However, this situation could also have resulted from genetic engineering.

There is one other major question that the visitation hypothesis raises. If the Earth has been visited in the distant past by another civilization, why was it not published more openly? Why the subterfuge and secrecy? If there was a plan to the pyramids – a galactic message – why not inscribe it in huge letters into the walls of the chambers? $E = mc^2$ carved into a wall would be enough; we would understand. Why would a highly civilized and highly technical civilization want to play games instead; with hidden shafts, maps of the world, and precessional dates?

Isaac Asimov and Arthur C Clarke may have an answer to this conundrum. In the 1970s, the science fiction writer Asimov wrote some short stories based on the concept of alien beings visiting other worlds. Asimov proposed in these stories a law of non-intervention in the affairs of fledgling civilizations. An emerging society should be able to develop or die according to its own natural selection; the job of the visiting space-farers was to observe and record, not to interfere.

Arthur C Clarke came up with a slightly different scenario, which is more in keeping with recent human endeavours in the natural world here on Earth. Clarke's alien civilization had a further role, that of nurturing new civilizations. In his epic book and film from the late 1960s, *2001, a Space Odyssey*, Clarke's extra-terrestrial beings visited the Earth and saw that all was not well. A fledgling race had emerged on the Earth, but the climate was harsh and the vegetarian race of apemen was floundering simply for the lack of a good diet. The visitors saw that intelligent life on Earth would soon be extinguished if nothing was done to help them.

Accordingly, a monolith was placed on the Earth. This small monolith had the power to educate and it taught the fledgling civilization how to fend for itself, how to hunt for food. The result, in a dramatic jump in the film of some 100,000 years from apeman to spaceship, was mankind. As a calling card of their visit, Clarke's gods left another monolith on the Moon. When finally exposed to the light of day, by excavators, the Moon monolith 'telephoned' home to say that mankind had arrived in the galactic society.

As a story of our emergence from prehistoric times, one could speculate that, in the light of the revelations in this book, Arthur C Clarke was remarkable in his foresight, especially as his Moon monolith was originally conceived as being a small pyramid. A very logical scenario for the construction of the pyramids could run parallel to the script of *2001, a Space Odyssey*. As in Clarke's story, the modified non-interference policy would seem to have dictated that no evidence of the visit, except for the monuments, was left behind. No pictures, no texts, no equipment, no technology, nothing. That is why the monuments were of substantially human construction; they gave nothing directly away by their appearance. The pyramids and henges are a little too big and too precise for Bronze Age/Neolithic man, but at the same time they are not too obviously alien.

Following this logic, however, there is another glaring question that has to be asked. If everything had to be so secret, why build the monuments in the first place? Actually, there is even a good rational answer for this. In reality, the monuments were primarily devised as an educational work project, one that formed and moulded the emerging society. They were the projects that developed the skills of the artisans that a civilization requires: the architects, stonemasons, carpenters, rope-makers, foundry-men, metal workers, quarrymen, miners, transport workers, tool-makers, even jewellers for setting the stone-cutting tools. All of these trades were required for the construction of these monuments. In addition, since someone decided to bring some of the materials down a river at Newgrange, Stonehenge and Giza, we also need some shipbuilders and sailors. And by utilising such concentrated numbers of workers, a new method of food production would also be required; so efficient farmers, farm tools and machinery, and storage facilities would need to be put in place.

To control and govern this vast hoard of workers, a hierarchical system of government would be required: a group of people that could plan ahead; ensure that some food is stored for the winter; control the petty disputes of individuals; and control the collective demands of pressure groups. The society needs leadership. The way that this was achieved is interesting in itself, for the leadership imposed on this huge band of workers was represented by the Sarsen Trilithon stones at Stonehenge, and this still appears to be the Masonic view of society.

There are two upright stones in the Stonehenge Trilithon and, similarly, there were two central pillars in the Temple of Solomon. These pillars represent the king and the priesthood, which is why the upper echelons of society today are known as upright citizens or pillars of society. The lintel on the top of the uprights represents the government or civil service, and only if all three stones are present will the nation be stable and prosperous.

The reasoning here is, presumably, that if three distinct ruling classes were created, then no particular power base would have a monopoly of power. This would tend to stop the formation of dictators; individuals that may cause social chaos. If a king became too powerful, the independent priesthood could muster opinion against him and vice versa. Throughout history, and in virtually every kingdom, we can see evidence of this interplay in action. Some of the disputes between church and state were resolved amicably, some not. In whatever way the result was achieved, however, the outcome seems to have been a gentle oscillation of primary control between the two rival power bases, with neither side winning ultimate control.

The third limb of the Trilithon in this power structure is the government or civil service. This group is essential to provide a damper against excessive swings in civil and theological policy. An authority can make as many edicts and proclamations as it likes, but it is the civil service or government that implements the new policy and so provides a damper against radical regimes. The government also provides a source of continuity between successive kings and religious leaders. These changes in administration are always dangerous times, the state is often rudderless and open to rival power battles; the civil service at these times maintains the status quo until a new incumbent is found. In other words, the lintel maintains the upright stones at about the same height, otherwise the lintel may fall off.

As can be seen, the construction of a simple henge or pyramid can create an entire society and, once created, societies can become self-sustaining. No one limb of a society can easily break away and go off at a tangent, because the society as a whole is utterly dependent on all of its limbs functioning properly. If one splinter group does start creating problems, the rest of society will quickly gang up against it and urge it back into the fold because, at the end of the day, we know that we will all suffer the consequences. We all know that it is hard work being a member of society; long hours, thousands of petty little rules and often very little reward for our endeavours. However, we also know, deep down, that those outside society, or those within societies that are disintegrating, have an infinitely harder time of it. This, if nothing else, keeps us firmly in check.

11. The Final Frontier

Conclusion

It is time now to come out into the open and declare our allegiances. Has the evidence that has been displayed here been persuasive enough? I started this manuscript as the biggest skeptic that the world has seen; there were just a few mysteries that needed looking into, that was all. The journey has been longer and stranger than I could possibly have expected and it has persuaded me that the impossible may well be possible. Forget the recent UFO sightings – these are most likely there simply to keep this subject in the public eye – but the ancient visitation theory is now looking like a definite possibility. For the record, I will state now that I have been persuaded that a visitation *has* occurred in the distant past; another civilisation arrived and decided to give us a start in life and then went on their way to the next promising star on their list. We were given a leg-up on the slow climb to civilization. But even from this short visit, that occurred so long ago, we can conclude several things from the actions that appear to have been made on this planet.

a.   Their society was helpful rather than aggressive towards emerging civilizations. If the prime mission of these beings was one of colonization, there was at least, at the same time, a degree of respect towards other societies that were found along the way. This could result from two possible scenarios: firstly, the visitors may be altruistic by nature or, secondly, they may not be the most powerful entity in the galaxy – there may be a galactic police force to enforce this kind of regulation. One would be safe to presume that the former is the more likely.

b.   What can we deduce from the societies that were created on this planet? Well, certainly it would appear that the visitors were not interested in equality here. We have the creation of three elite power groups for each civilisation and then there is the huge body of the underclasses, which ranged from the highly educated to the simple artisans. Was this a model taken from the visitors' own experience? Are we to infer that highly developed societies still run regal and theological power bases?

c.   If the organization of the visitors' own society is open to question, we can nevertheless see with a degree of certainty that their race at least had a sense of fun. While the monuments were necessary to create society, they could have taken any shape or form.

The final design appears to have been chosen more as a jolly jape than for any technical reason; they probably caused great mirth among their fellow beings.

d.　　While the visitors were manifestly dictating the form of the monuments and the society, they were quite happy to let people experiment and work under their own rules and regulations; there was no evidence of the heavy hand of the dictator here. Each society that evolved was distinct from the others and each monument was tailored to the needs of that particular society. Even on one project, such as Avebury, it was apparent to the archaeologists on the site that there were distinct groups of work parties, and that each appeared to have its own standard of workmanship. This does not exactly sound like the activities of slaves being goaded by whips.

e.　　One last, and major, thing we can positively deduce from all these monuments that were scattered around our planet is that the visitors were not coming back to our Solar System for a very, very long time. There would be absolutely no point in creating these massive monuments, designed to stand for thousands of years, if one intended dropping in every couple of years to see how things were progressing.

It is a statement of fact then – a fact that is embodied in our historical monuments – that we are on our own in this world, uncomfortable as that may seem to some people. Just by the simple process of examining a henge or a pyramid, we can say that the 'gods' are not looking over our shoulders all the time; they are probably not even particularly concerned if we survive. A horse can be shown a lake of civilization, but it cannot be forced to drink; besides, there will be many more promising candidates for the visitors, in their search of this vast galaxy. This may be a revolutionary reinterpretation of world theology, but it is an interpretation that is supported by the Hermetic texts, the supposed teachings of Thoth.

While it is hard to quantify the veracity of these texts, these traditions do insist that when man was 'created' in the image of 'god' – however we wish to translate that phrase – we were made in the complete image. We are not just physical, but also the intellectual peers of god. We became fledgling gods ourselves, 'godlets' capable of our own independent thought and creation:

If then you do not make yourself equal to god, you cannot apprehend god; for like is known by like. Leap clear of all that is corporeal, and make yourself grow to a like expanse with that greatness which is beyond all measure; rise up above all time, and become eternal; then you will apprehend god.

Think that for you too nothing is impossible; deem that you too are immortal, and that you are able to grasp all things in your thought, to know every craft and every science; find yourself home in the haunts of every living creature ... but if you shut up your soul in your body, and abase yourself, and say 'I know nothing, I can do nothing, I am afraid of earth and sea, I cannot mount to heaven; I do not know what I was, nor what I shall be'; then, what have you to do with god? Your thoughts can grasp nothing beautiful and good, if you cleave to the body, and are evil. [8]

Thoth and his colleagues were not here to spoon-feed us all the way through this life with constant interference, as is proposed by most religions. It is for us as individuals, and collectively as nations, to decide our policies, societies, morality, technology and science. It is only by us rising above the biological nature of humanity that we shall approach the levels of 'godlets' ourselves and we have a long way to go in this respect. This, therefore, is the main reason why the ancient British, Mexican, Chinese and Egyptian cultures did not immediately flourish after 11,600 BC: it is all very well being shown what to do, but organizing it ourselves is quite a different matter. Take a look at post-colonial Africa to see what can happen to such societies.

Back in the ancient world; this same transition from Neolithic hunter-gatherer to technical nation super-state was obviously not an easy one, despite the initial guidance. In this particular competition, Egypt can rightly claim to have been at the forefront for longer than any other nation in the history of man. Despite this, it was little, isolated Britain that finally spawned the technological revolution of the world. In fact, the industrial revolution started in a little town called Ironbridge, located just 150 km to the north of Avebury.

Is this a coincidence? How much of this technical development was due to the guidance of the visitors? Even if the ancient technical skills were forgotten thousands of years ago, the re-emergence could still be due to the development of a society based on their original concepts. Is it any coincidence that science advanced fastest in a society that was relatively free, and that rejected the totalitarian habit of punishing individuals who dared to think of revolutionary concepts. The nations of the East once held the technological lead in this world; is it any coincidence that the West finally superseded them at the time of the Renaissance?

11. The Final Frontier

First contact

The introductory lessons in nationhood by the visitors resulted in the seemingly benevolent and open culture of Old Kingdom Egypt; one that was always welcoming towards its neighbours when they were in trouble, just as they welcomed Abraham. [9] However, like the peoples of Atlantis, even in the isolation of Egypt the new society gradually became infused with a more generous proportion of human greed. Upstart dictators in the provinces thought they could do a better job of government, especially if they based their economy on the stolen goods of a defeated city. Eventually, Egypt learned the lessons and retaliated in kind, and so the major empires of the world emerged; Britain's included. They waxed for a while and then, predictably, they waned as they finally ran out of resources to pilfer. The world had become the unstable place that we are so familiar with in the early twenty-first century: we are truly no more advanced than the ancient peoples of Avebury and Giza.

What is the next step in the history of man going to be? It is a reasonable question because we may have to make these choices fairly soon. This may well be the dawn of one of those major advances in our history that occur from time to time. If the lost repositories of Thoth, the ancient 'Halls of Records', are real and if they are ever found, we may be on the brink of another revolution. Not just a revolution in our understanding of history and theology, but a technical revolution as well. For the lost repositories were thought to hold the technical knowledge of Thoth and we can be assured that this technology was far in advance of our own.

Classical Egyptian Chronology

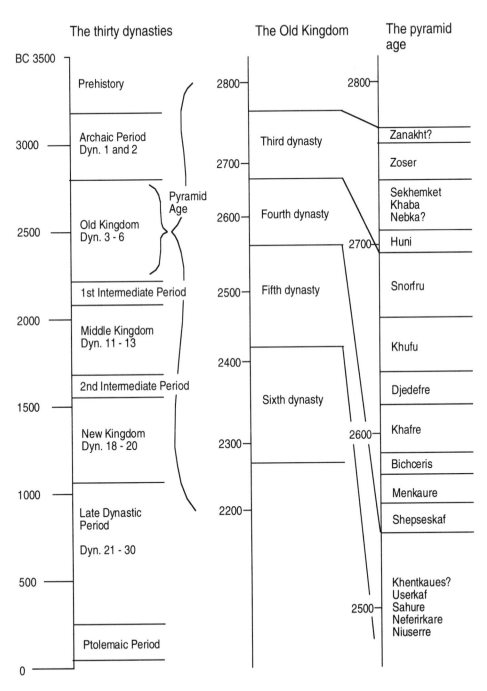

Notes & References

Chapter 1

1   Antiquities of the Jews, Josephus Flavius   LCL 2:238.
2   Bible, Mathew 13:55, Mark 6:3, Galatians 1:19.
3   Pyramid Odyssey, W Fix.
4   Pyramids and Temples of Gizeh, Sir Flinders Petrie.
     The traveller's key to Ancient Egypt   p 123,
     The pyramids of Egypt   I E Edwards p118,
     Determination of the Exact Size of the Great Pyramid, J H Cole.
5   An average of measurements from;
     Petrie (passageway entrance) 52° 53´,
     Edwards 52° 52´,
     Petrie (cladding stones) 52° 49´,
     Piazzi Smythe (core stones) 52° 49´.
6   The Pyramids of Egypt   I E Edwards p143,
7   Complete Pyramids, M Lehner p122.
     This has been a little known fact, because many text books give an angle of
     52° 20´ for the Second Pyramid slope angle. This error has been perpetuated
     around the world because this is the angle reported in 'Pyramids of Egypt'.
     However, Mr Edwards has made a mistake here. The angle of 52° 20´ is
     derived from the present height of the pyramid, which is 136.4 m. The *original*
     height, including the missing capstone as reported by Edwards himself, was
     143.5 m and this gives an angle of 53° 5´.
8   Manetho, Loeb Library.
9   Egyptian Pyramids, Lepre.
10   Pharaohs & Pyramids, G Hart.
11   Pyramids and Temples of Gizeh, Sir Flinders Petrie.
12   Pyramids of Egypt,   I E Edwards.
13   Ibid.
14   Mummies Myth and Magic, C El Mahdy.
15   Pyramids and Temples of Gizeh, Sir Flinders Petrie.
16   Pyramids of Egypt,   I E Edwards p156.
17   Ibid p158.
18   Pyramids and Temples of Gizeh, Sir Flinders Petrie.
19   Egyptian Pyramids, Lepre.
20   Egyptian Myths, G Hart.
21   Stonehenge, J Richards.
22   Professor Richard Atkinson, archaeologist on site 1940s.
23   Stonehenge in it's landscape, R Cleal, K Walker, R Montague.
24   Avebury, C Malone.
25   Newgrange, C O'Kelly.

Notes & References

Chapter 2

1   Egyptian Myths,   G Hart.
2   Ibid.
3   Encyclopaedia Britannica.
4   Egyptian Mythology, V Ions, p84.
5   Gods of the Egyptians, V Ions, p407.
6   Ibid p414.
7   The Egyptian Hermes, p33.
8   Dionysus, Nonus V-570, XIII-30, XIV-110.
9   The Gods of the Egyptians, W. Budge, p400.
10 Stonehenge (TV Film) A Thom, Third Eye Productions.
11 Avebury, Caroline Malone (English Heritage).
12 Avebury 1:500 topographical survey by English Heritage.
    The actual measurement is exactly 10 m short of the 1,082 m. But the south-eastern quadrant is some 10 m short of all the others, and the stones have been squeezed in tighter here to get the required number to fit in. This strongly suggests that this quadrant was made too small, and should be considered to have been designed as having the same dimensions as the other quadrants.

Chapter 3

1   Encyclopaedia Britannica.
2   Ibid.
3   Ibid.
4   Riddle of the Pyramids, Kurt Mendelssohn, p73.
5   Stonehenge, Neolithic man and the Cosmos, J North.
6   Bible, I Kings 7:15.
7   Ibid   7:19.
8   Ibid   7:17.
9   Ibid   7:18.
10 Colliers Encyclopaedia.
11 Ibid.
12 Fingerprints of the Gods, G Hancock.
13 Ibid p461.

Chapter 4

1   Encyclopaedia Britannica.
2   Bible, Ezekiel 43:13.
3   Ancient Egyptian Literature, Lichtheim.
4   Pyramids and Temples of Gizeh, Sir Flinders Petrie.
5   Weights and Measures of England, R Connor.
6   Statutes Vol 1 p206.
7   Ibid.

8   Law of weights, O'Keefe.

9   Statutes.

10   Weights and Measures of England, R Connor.

11   Ibid   p36.

12   Bible, Genesis 7:17.

13   Bible, Exodus 24:18.

14   Bible, Numbers 14:34.

15   Bible, Mathew 4:2.

16   Bloodline of the Holy Grail, Gardner.

17   Nuggets from King Solomon's Mines.

18   Dissertation upon the Sacred Cubit of the Jews, Sir Isaac Newton.

19   A description of the pyramids of Egypt, Greaves.

20   Dissertation upon the Sacred Cubit of the Jews, Sir Isaac Newton.

21   Ibid.

22   Bible, Genesis 41:43, Exodus 2:10
       Antiquities of the Jews, Josephus Flavius LCL 2:238.

23   Bible, Mathew 27:57, John 19:38.

24   The life of Joseph of Arimathea, printed by R Pynson AD 1520.

25   The Antiquities of Glastonbury, William Malmesbury AD 1130.

26   Encyclopaedia Britannica.

27   Ibid.

28   Joseph of Arimathea and the Grail, M Finlay.

29   Bible, Acts 8:1, 8:3.

30   Bible, Acts 9:21.

31   Habakkuk Commentary, Dead Sea Scrolls, X 9-10 (Vermes p288).

32   The Spear of Destiny, Trevor Ravenscroft.

33   Josephus Antiquities 4:64.

34   The Round Table, Professor M Biddle.

35   Professor J Flemming. Article in Hampshire Telegraph, 9th September 1976.

36   Winchester Castle and the Great Hall, John McIlwain.

37   Egyptian Pyramids, I E Edwards.

Chapter 5

1   Mars Mystery, G Hancock, R Bauval.

2   Stonehenge and Avebury, R Atkinson.

3   Avebury, Caroline Malone, English Heritage.

4   Ibid

5   Maps of the Ancient Sea Kings.

6   Jewish War, Josephus Flavius, LCL V, 220.

7   Bible, Mathew 13:11.

8   Nag Hammadi Scrolls, Gospel of Philip.

9   Bible, Mathew 15:26, Mark 7:27.

10   Moses and Monotheism, Sigmund Freud.

Notes & References

Chapter 6

1   Letter from the publishers.
2   Part of the Random House group.

Chapter 7

1   Stonehenge, Sir Flinders Petrie.
2   Stonehenge, in its landscape, R Cleal, K Walker, R Montague.
3   Hoyle gives a value of 49.8°, but this was taken from photographs; Petrie's data is from on-site observations.
      Stonehenge, Plans, Descriptions and Theories, Sir Flinders Petrie.
4   Comparison quoted in, Stonehenge, Neolithic man and the Cosmos, J North.
5   On Stonehenge, Sir Fred Hoyle.
6   Ibid.
7   Ibid.
8   Ibid.
9   Article "Deep Freeze", New Scientist Magazine, 14.2.98.
10

$$\psi = \text{Cos}^{-1}\left[\frac{\text{Sin }\Sigma}{\text{Cos }\Gamma}\right] + \frac{\text{hs x Sin }\Gamma}{\sqrt{(\text{Cos}^2\,\Gamma - \text{Sin}^2\,\Sigma)}}$$

where

    ψ = Position of sunrise, in degrees, measured from true north
    Γ = Latitude of Stonehenge
    Σ = Inclination of the Earth (23.5°)
    hs = Apparent declination of the Sun. (approx, minus 0° 46').

11   Secret Gospel, Smith.
12   The Library of History, Book II Ch 47, Diodorus Siculus.
13   Leob Classical Library, C Oldfather.

Chapter 8

1   Encyclopaedia Britannica.
2   Orion Mystery, Robert Bauval, Adrian Gilbert.
3   Ibid.
4   Ancient Egyptian Religion, R David.
5   The Sphinx, Selim Hassan p 76.
6   Ancient records, J Breasted p320.
7   Egyptian Pyramids, I E Edwards. &
      British Museum Dictionary of Ancient Egypt, I Shaw, P Nicholson.
      Edwards gives the Draco pyramid angle as 43° 36', and the Vega pyramid angle as 43° 22'. Shaw and Nicholson give the same angle for both pyramids, namely 43° 22'.
8   Ibid.
9   Stonehenge, Julian Richards.

10   Guide to ancient sites of Britain,   J Bard.
11   National Trust information notice on site.
12   Guide to ancient sites of Britain,   J Bard.
13   Liquid Scintillation Counting.
14   Radio carbon dating, S Bowman.
15   Principles of Physical Geology, A Holmes.
16   Radio carbon dating, S Bowman.
17   The Independent newspaper report 26.11.00.
18   Bible, Numbers 19.
19   Principles of Physical Geology, A Holmes.
20   Ibid.
21   Stonehenge; in its landscape, R Cleal, K Walker, R Montague,
      Stonehenge; Neolithic Man and the Cosmos,   Professor J North.
22   Ibid.
23   Keeper of Genesis, G Hancock.
24   MacStronomy on-line software,   Elton Software 2.0.3
      Redshift II, Maris Multimedia.
      The differences between these dates and other quoted dates may be due to
      the Gregorian calandar used in these programs. The date of the equinox drifts
      and this has to be allowed for. Even allowing for this, the two stellar packages
      quoted showed a 200-year difference between some of the dates (Redshift II,
      being the more comprehensive package, is probably the more accurate.)
25   Ibid.
26   Pyramid texts,   line 151.
27   Ibid   line 927.
28   The Egyptian Book of the Dead,   Wallis Budge.
29   The Bbook of the Duat, the Egyptian Heaven and Hell, Wallis Budge.
30   Ibid.

Chapter 9

1   Letter from Heinemann, the publisher, a division of Random House.
2   Letter drawn up by Pye-Smiths, solicitors for R. Ellis and R. Bauval, 23/07/98
3   Fax from Robert Bauval, 12/09/98.
4   Letter from plagiarist author to R. Bauval, 18/09/98. Forwarded to me by
      R. Bauval, by fax, the same day.
5   Letter from Robert Bauval, published on the *Daily Grail* on the 9th Jan 2000.
6   Atlantis Myth,   Bellamy.
7   Ibid.
8   Timaeus and Critias, Plato.
9   Ibid.
10   Ibid.
11   Ibid.
12   Teotihuacan, L Batres.
13   Mystery of the Mexican Pyramids, Tomkins.
14   Ibid.

15   Teotihuacan, L Batres.
16   The Antiquities of the Jews, Josephus Flavius   LCL p71.
     (Josephus ben Mattityahu, approx 38 - 100 AD).
17   Bible, Genesis,   11:4.
18   Teotihuacan, L Batres.
19   Ibid.
20   Mystery of the Mexican Pyramids, Tomkins.

Chapter 10

1   The Great Pyramid decoded,   Le Mesurer.
2   Pyramids of Egypt, I E Edwards   p 117.
3   Ibid.
4   Pyramids and Temples of Gizeh, Sir Flinders Petrie.
5   Redshift II Mutimedia Astronomy (Computer program), Maris Multimedia.
6   Telephone conversation Rudolf Gantenbrink.
7   Orion Mystery, R Bauval, A Gilbert.
8   Telephone conversation Rudolf Gantenbrink.
9   Fax memo from Rudolf Gantenbrink.
10   Miscellaneous Babylonian Texts, G Barton.

Chapter 11

1   Bible, Genesis 12:10.
2   Bible, Genesis 18:1-10.
3   Bible, Timothy I 2:12.
4   *The X-Files*, produced by the company called 1013, a code that denotes the
     date of the demise of the Templars on October 13; the date is in the American
     format. This term is also used in aviation meteorology as an atmospheric
     pressure setting, 1013.25 mb. The decimal places, in this case, define the time of
     the strike against the Templars of 0600 am (or 0.25 of a day).
5   Arthur C Clarke,
     The Daedalus Mission, British Interplanetry Society.
6   The speed of light is about 108×10^7 km/hr.
     One light year measures the distance travelled after one whole
     year at the speed above. This is about 9.3×10^{12} km.
     In addition our galaxy is thought to be 100,000 light years in
     diameter, and it is thought to contain about 2×10^{11} stars.
7   2g, twice the force of gravity that is normally felt on the surface
     of the Earth.
8   Corpus Hermeticum XI.2.
9   Bible, Genesis 12:10

List of Diagrams

List of Diagrams

Photo Credits

All plates are taken from the Author's own collection, with the exception of plates 11 and 20.

Plate 20. The seven-branched candelabra, courtesy of Mallorca Cathedral.

Index

Index

Index

Index

North Pole ~ 152, 156.
Northern hemisphere ~ 115.
Norton, Brize ~ 215.
Nu ~ 45.
Nut ~ 45, 201.

O

Obsidian ~ 217.
Occam's razor ~ 84.
Ogdoad ~ 46, 214.
Old Church ~ 96.
Old Sarum ~ 108.
Oliver Cromwell ~ 97.
Olympic foot ~ 91.
Orion ~ 22, 170, 173, 175, 178, 179, 182, 184, 185, 186, 187, 200. *See also* Sirius.
  Alnilam ~ 170.
  Alnitak ~ 170, 238.
  belt of ~ 172.
  Mintaka ~ 170.
Oronteus Finaeus ~ 124.
Osiris ~ 45, 129, 256, 257.
Oslo ~ 147.
Otradnye ~ 3.
Owen, Tobias ~ 105.

P

Palestine ~ 1, 69.
Patrick, St. ~ 96.
Pegasus ~ 185.
  constellation of ~ 183, 184, 185.
  square of ~ 185.
Persian Gulf ~ 243.
Persians ~ 2.
Petra ~ 212.
Petrie, Flinders ~ 9, 16, 28, 29, 41, 141, 236.
Philander ~ 91.
Philip, Gospel of ~ 128.
Philippe Buache ~ 124.
Philocyprus, King ~ 212.
Pi ~ 7, 57, 59, 60, 61, 62, 63, 65, 66, 68, 69, 84, 85, 86, 90, 102, 104, 132, 141, 155, 162, 201, 232.
  Archimedes ~ 60.
Piazzi-Smyth, Charles ~ 89.
Pillars of Hercules ~ 211.

Piri Reis ~ 124.
Pisces ~ 197, 199.
planisphere ~ 173, 178, 182, 183, 184, 195, 197, 200, 201, 214.
Plato ~ 46, 211, 212, 213, 214, 224.
Pleiades ~ 161.
Polaris ~ 152.
Poseidon ~ 212.
precession ~ 70, 153, 154, 163, 165, 171, 172, 188, 201, 235.
Preseli ~ 34, 181.
Proctor, R ~ 234.
Proxima Centauri ~ 259, 261, 262.
Ptolemaeus, Claudius ~ 170.
Ptolomy. *See* Ptolemaeus, Claudius.
Pynson ~ 94.
Pyramid Texts ~ 45.
Pythagoras ~ 103, 141, 142, 157, 165, 166, 167, 201, 233, 234.

Q

Queen's Chamber ~ 11, 26, 28, 83. *See also* Great Pyramid.
Quetzl rod ~ 48, 223.
Quetzlcoatl ~ 47, 221.

R

Ra ~ 173.
radiocarbon ~ 35, 189, 190, 191, 194. *See also* C14. Lindow bog.
  dating ~ 189, 190, 191, 195.
  laboratory ~ 194, 195.
Radnor ~ 192, 193.
Ramesses II ~ 18.
Random House ~ 138, 208, 209, 210.
Red Pyramid ~ 8, 17, 18, 19, 103, 175, 176, 177. *See also* Draco Pyramid.
  chambers ~ 173.
Red Sea ~ 243.
Renaissance ~ 71.
Resistivity anomalies ~ 117.
Rice ~ 263.
Richard I ~ 78.
Ridgeway, the ~ 184.
Rinaldi, C. ~ 29.
Robert Bauval ~ 210.
Rod of Argos ~ 47.
rods